Completing Distinctions

Completing Distinctions

DOUGLAS G. FLEMONS

Foreword by Bradford P. Keeney, Ph.D.

SHAMBHALA
Boston & London
1991

Shambhala Publications, Inc.
Horticultural Hall
300 Massachusetts Avenue
Boston, Massachusetts 02115

Shambhala Publications, Inc.
Random Century House
20 Vauxhall Bridge Road
London SW1V 2SA

9 8 7 6 5 4 3 2 1

First Edition

Printed in the United States of America on acid-free paper

Distributed in the United States by Random House,
in Canada by Random House of Canada Ltd., and
in the United Kingdom by the Random Century Group

Library of Congress Cataloging-in-Publication Data

Flemons, Douglas G.
    Completing distinctions / Douglas G. Flemons.—1st ed.
      p.   cm.
    Includes bibliographical references.
    ISBN 0-87773-545-X (alk. paper)
      1. Family psychotherapy. 2. Taoism. 3. Bateson,
Gregory. I. Title.
RC488.5.F58   1990   89-43611
616.89'156—dc20   CIP

Design by Melodie Wertelet

TO MY TEACHERS

Between what I see and what I say,
between what I say and what I keep silent,
between what I keep silent and what I dream,
between what I dream and what I forget:
poetry.
 It slips
between yes and no,
 says
what I keep silent,
 keeps silent
what I say,
 dreams
what I forget.
 It is not speech:
it is an act.
 It is an act
of speech.
 Poetry
speaks and listens:
 it is real.
And as soon as I say
 it is real,
it vanishes.
 Is it then more real?

—Octavio Paz
(translated by Eliot Weinberger)

CONTENTS

FOREWORD

Gregory Bateson once proposed that "it takes two to know one." His preference for doubleness provided us with a desire to emphasize *relationship* over things. What was too easily forgotten, however, was that double views, double hearings, double acts, and double takes only lead to the relational realization of "things." A distinction between two may be closed (or completed) to become one.

To know two, extending this logic of relationship, necessarily requires the presence of *three*. Whereas Bateson's double lens paradoxically takes us to "things," a triple somersault is necessary to see relationship. This next big jump moves us from tossing two balls to juggling at least three.

It is precisely at this point that the master juggler Douglas Flemons enters the scene. In his remarkable book, he advances the Batesonian tradition beyond the game of two. In one hand he releases the ancient tradition of Taoism. In the other hand we find the more contemporary insights of Batesonian cybernetic epistemology. Caught in midair between the other two is the ever-present question and discipline of how to therapeutically address human problems. In his juggle, we derive deeper understandings of each perspective through the dancing flight of all three.

Our juggling author, upon closer examination, can be seen in this text as actually juggling three parts of himself. Douglas Flemons is, in fact, a practicing Taoist, a systemic therapist, and a cybernetic epistemologist (not to mention that he is also an accomplished juggler!). What is recorded in this text is most fascinating: the juggler being juggled.

Three traditions of ideas and practices toss our author into a recursive flight of abstractions weaving in and out of one another. What is cooked, to borrow a metaphor from Stewart Brand, is a most satisfying slice of mental baklava.

Reader, think twice (make that thrice) about entering the spins of the following pages. It is not for the passive onlooker. This text invites the reader to participate in its movement. The rhetorical juggling of Douglas Flemons doesn't require that *you* catch anything. It sets up the possibility of your being caught in its dance of intertwined separations and connections, including the difference and relation between the reader, the read, and the ever-moving voice of the author. Three cheers for a magnificent performance.

BRADFORD P. KEENEY, PH.D.
College of St. Thomas
St. Paul, Minnesota

ACKNOWLEDGMENTS

It was my brother Tom, inveterate scout that he is, who first acquainted me with Eastern philosophy and introduced me to the sinologist and teacher Titus Yü. Titus patiently guided me into and through the eliptical world of Taoism and offered me the opportunity to collaborate with him on an etymologically grounded translation of an ancient Chinest text; the learnings gleaned from our years of working together in the late 1970s and early '80s are woven throughout the present book.

Anthony Wilden piqued my interest in, and contributed to my understanding of, the work of Gregory Bateson. I found Bateson's notions helpful as I puzzled over Taoist writings, and Taoist thought helpful as I mused over Bateson's essays. This circling juxtaposition of ideas has stayed with me as a method of inquiry, and I have incorporated it in this book as a method of explanation.

Through his teaching of the martial art T'ai Chi Ch'üan, Master Raymond Chung helped me, over the years, to appreciate and incorporate Taoist principles in ways that would have otherwise been impossible.

Anyone familiar with the scholarship of Brad Keeney will recognize my tremendous debt to his work, particularly to his *Aesthetics of Change* (1983), where many of the important voices that I drew on in the writing of this book—including Gregory Bateson, Francisco Varela, Wendell Berry, Gary Snyder, and Heinz von Foerster—were first brought together. As Brad's student, and later as his colleague, I deepened my understanding of Bateson and learned much about the practice of therapy and the discipline of improvisation.

The discerning comments and suggestions of my editor at Shambhala Publications, Jeremy Hayward, contributed greatly to the clarity of the final draft. Jeremy and the others at Shambhala—especially Peter Turner and Jonathan Green—created a most supportive ambiance for the completion of the manuscript.

Moyra Jones was an important source of inspiration and a perceptive critic. Larry Cochran was perhaps the first to suggest that my interests in Bateson, Taoism, and therapy could be successfully entwined. David and Kathee Todtman broke trail for my trek to Texas, where much of the idea development and part of the writing took place. They offered intellectual stimulation and warm friendship, along with great cappuccino.

My friends and colleagues at Nova University—Ron Chenail, Sharon Boesl, Anne and Bill Rambo, John Flynn, Wendel Ray, Loren Bryant, and Marguerite McCorkle—each contributed to the text in unique and important ways. Their comments, digging up of sources, reading of drafts, and many other kindnesses are deeply appreciated. Ron, with his thoughtful mind and expansive library, was particularly helpful. Connie Steele, at the University of Tennessee at Knoxville, closely read an earlier draft and made a number of pertinent suggestions.

The questions asked by my students have encouraged me to think and speak more clearly. The questions posed by my clients have challenged me to work and play more imaginatively.

Shelley Green, Jerry and Barbara Gale, and the Braudt family provided long-distant, but closely felt support.

My parents and my brothers stood behind me all the way. To them, and to everyone else, I offer my heartfelt thanks.

Completing Distinctions

1 | The Relation Between

l(a

le
af
fa

ll

s)

one
l

iness

—*e. e. cummings*

DAUGHTER I did an experiment once.
FATHER Yes?
DAUGHTER I wanted to find out if I could
think two thoughts at the same
time. So I thought "It's summer"
and I thought "It's winter." And
then I tried to think the two
thoughts together.
FATHER Yes?
DAUGHTER But I found I wasn't having two
thoughts. I was only having
one thought *about* having two
thoughts.
—*Gregory Bateson*

Any act of knowing, any knowing act, begins with the drawing of a distinction, with the noting of a difference. A boundary is created when a whole is distinguished from a part of itself—as in ecosystem/species, paragraph/sentence, family/child—or when a part of a whole is simply differentiated from another part—as in foreground/background, yesterday/tomorrow, husband/wife. The relationship formed by such acts of demarcation constitute the "stuff" of mind. Knowing is composed of boundaries imposed.

It is to the exploration of this fascinating, relational nature of mind—and its implications for the art of living and the practice of therapy—that much of this book is devoted.

The Taoists and Buddhists were perhaps the first to recognize that in the marking of a difference, the boundary that *separates* the two sides of the created distinction necessarily *connects* them. However, this relational insight also runs as an undercurrent through the work of Gregory Bateson, as well as of Francisco Varela, George Spencer-Brown, Wendell Berry, Gary Snyder, and others. A most interesting conceptual tool spirals into form if this instance of distinctive understanding is allowed to pivot on itself. The distinction *connection/separation* describes the doubleness of the relation between the two sides of a difference, and in so doing it comments on itself, as it connects and separates connection and separation.

It is thus that the introductory poem and conversation—and their juxtaposition—prefigure much of what is to follow. A leaf falls, parenthetical to the invocation of loneliness: "l (a/ le/af/fa/ ll/ s)/one/l/ iness." The syncopated symmetry of the leaf's descent is not described but inscribed by the shape and the time of the telling. Each line depicts part of the story, as the leaf dips first this way—"le"—then that—"af"—and then reverses back—"fa"—before pausing, fluttering—"ll"— pausing again, and continuing down.

Loneliness speaks of isolation, of separation. It begins and then completes the rhythm of the leaf's fall—"l . . . /one/ l/ iness"—and in so doing establishes a resonance: The insularity of loneliness and the singularity of the detached leaf are each metaphoric of the other. It is the connection between these two expressions of separateness that sparks meaning in the poem, that brings it poignantly to life.

William Carlos Williams says mind and poem "are all apiece." As the daughter in the quote from Bateson came to realize, mind, like a poem, always weaves. The act of thinking two disparate thoughts—such as "it's winter" and "it's summer"—necessarily ties the two of them together. The attempt to separate is itself a connection. The form in which this idea is presented mirrors what is said: There is one conversation between two "distinct" people about "having one thought about having two 'distinct' thoughts." The interchange between father and daughter is excerpted from one of Bateson's *metalogues*, a type of dialogue where "not only do the participants discuss [a] problem but the structure of the conversation as a whole is also relevant to the same subject."[1]

Form and content rhyme; connection and separation entwine. Such is the unique pattern of each of the quoted passages and of the connections between them. At still a more encompassing level, it is descriptive of the structure of this book as a whole. Like a poem or a metalogue, it will attend to the coincidence of meaning and the manner of its expression: The distinction *connection/separation* will be used as a relational map with which to explore the relationally mapped ideas of Bateson and of Taoist philosophers, and to chart a relational orientation to therapy. The path taken will not be direct, but will cycle, spinning and looping, turning and returning its way within and between these three domains of knowing and acting.

The company is not as strange as might first appear. In a sense Bateson plays host to the other two, despite the fact that he never wrote about Oriental philosophy and had serious reservations about the whole enterprise of therapy. Common to all three is an awareness of, and a sensitivity to, levels of context and meaning, and an understanding of how these levels interconnect in intricate and often paradoxical ways.

Although Bateson never wrote *about* Taoism and Zen Buddhism per se, ideas from both traditions are interspersed throughout his writings,[2] and, indeed, his systemic approach to mind has a distinct Oriental flavor. Bateson first started talking about Zen practice in the 1950s,[3] at a time when he was "picking the brains" of Alan Watts,[4] and although he remained peripheral to it, he maintained ties to the San Francisco Zen community up until his death in 1980: He spent his last few days and died, at the age of seventy-six, in the guest house of the San Francisco Zen Center.[5] Bateson respected the vision of the artist and the mystic; but he considered himself a scientist, and worked and wrote in that tradition. It is thus not surprising that he would begin a talk at The Naropa Institute in 1975 in the following way: "What I want to say, quite simply, is that what goes on inside is much the same as what goes on outside. And I say this not from anything like a Buddhist position, but just from the position of an ordinary working stiff engaged in Occidental sciences."[6]

Bateson was hardly "an ordinary working stiff," and his scientific focus was far from traditional. Devoting his rapt attention to "the pattern which connects," his varied excursions into the fields of anthropology, biology, communication theory, psychiatry, evolutionary theory, ecology, and aesthetics were in the service of the development of a new "epistemology," that is, "an indivisible, integrated meta-science whose subject matter is the world of evolution, thought, adaptation, embryology, and genetics—the science of mind in the widest sense of the word."[7] The metaphor of "mind" provided for him a means of characterizing the circuitous relations that obtain between the parts of a system and between systems.

The beginnings of this and many related ideas can be traced to his involvement in the cross-disciplinary Macy conferences, held in New York during the late 1940s and early 1950s. These meetings provided a unique forum where innovations from mathematics and engineering were rigorously applied to a variety of other fields.[8] Focusing on the nature of "circular causal and feedback mechanisms in biological and social systems," the talks marked the formal beginning of the science of cybernetics, the study of the organization of systems in terms of communicational pathways and self-corrective patterns of circular process.[9]

Considering cybernetics to be "the biggest bite out of the fruit of the Tree of Knowledge that mankind has taken in the last 2000 years,"[10] Bateson adopted and adapted many of its key notions, including Bertrand Russell's Theory of Logical Types, circular causality, entropy, negative and positive feedback, the distinction between analogical and digital processes, and between information and energy.[11] As important contributions to the development of his "science of mind," these cybernetic ideas warrant explanation; the definitions that follow can perhaps serve as cairns to help mark the direction of Bateson's trail.

1. Russell's *Theory of Logical Types* distinguishes between levels of abstraction. Originally invented as a way of eschewing paradox in the world of logic, the notion of logical types is used by Bateson as a way of charting the classification inherent in all perceiving, thinking, learning, and communicating. A class is a different logical type, a higher level of abstraction, than the members it classifies: The class of "all books" is itself not a book; the name of a thing is itself not a thing, but a classification of it. At a still more abstract level, the class of "classes of rectangular objects," which would include the class of books, the class of cereal boxes, the class of picture frames, and so on, is not itself a class of rectangular objects, but a way of classifying these classes, and as such is a higher logical type. The name of the name is not the name. This hierarchy of types—classes, classes of classes, classes of classes of classes, and so on—provides a convenient bridge to the critical notion of *context* and the interdependence of wholes and parts. The notion of levels makes clear that learning, for example, is a contextual affair; one not only learns, but simultaneously learns how to

learn. Similarly, according to Bateson, "the very process of perception is an act of logical typing. Every image is a complex of many-leveled coding and mapping." [12]

2. *Lineal causality,* where "A causes B," is but a partial arc of the circuitous relations that obtain in the world of ongoing interaction. *Circular causality* refers to the reciprocal nature of systemic process: A responds to B's response to A, to which B, in turn, responds, and so on.

3. In contradistinction to *pattern,* which is connected to notions of order, redundancy, and organization, *entropy* refers to disorder, randomness, and muddle.

4. The term *feedback* is descriptive of the loop structure of systems, whereby information from or about the system returns to it, thereby influencing the shape of the circuit. Whereas *positive feedback* changes the system's stability (as in the spiral of schizmogenic runaway), *negative feedback* stabilizes the system's changing (as in the circle of self-corrective homeostasis).

5. Each step in a communicational sequence is a transform of the previous step. In *digital* communication, such as written (and verbal) language, there is no formal connection between a sign and that of which it is a transform: The word *mountain* is no taller than the word *valley;* the word *sun* is no brighter or hotter than the word *shade;* and there is nothing particularly lionlike about the word *lion.* In *analogical* communication, such as kinesics and paralinguistics, magnitudes are used to code magnitudes, and there is thus a recognizable connection between the transform and that which it re-presents: A lowered voice, long pause, raised eyebrow, or expansive gesture will generally correspond (directly or inversely) to a magnitude in the relationship to which it refers.

6. *Energy* belongs to the world of substance, to quantities and things, impacts and forces; *information* belongs to the world of form, to relationship, pattern, and organization. Distinguishing between information and energy is itself an

informational act, in that it defines a *difference:* Information is, in Bateson's terms, a difference which makes a difference.

A cairn, like a pointed finger, takes on significance not when it captures one's attention, but when it directs it elsewhere. Similarly, an idea becomes most important not when it answers a previous question, but when it makes possible the asking of the next one. These cybernetic ideas allowed Bateson to ask fascinating questions about the nature of mind. From 1952 to 1962, he directed a series of research projects which investigated levels of abstraction and paradox in communication. He and collaborators John Weakland and Jay Haley, with William Fry and Don Jackson as consultants, studied everything from ventriloquism and the training of guide dogs for the blind, to humor, play, hypnosis, and schizophrenic communication. Of the many important theoretical ideas developed during the course of the project, the notion of the double bind was preeminent, and once it had been formulated, in 1954, it served to direct subsequent inquiry.

The double bind provides a contextual way of describing the complexity of conflicting demands across different levels of context. If solving a problem of learning or adaptation at one contextual level thereby creates a problem at a more encompassing contextual level (thus undermining the original solution), the tangled situation as a whole can be described as a double bind: "The organism is then faced with the dilemma either of being wrong in the primary context or of being right for the wrong reasons or in a wrong way." [13]

The matter can also be approached in terms of the way in which freedom is determined. As any good hypnotist, magician, or comedian knows, the offer or availability of freely choosing between alternatives at a given contextual level brings the particularities of choice into the foreground of conscious awareness. This necessarily relegates to the background (i.e., out of awareness and out of the realm of conscious choice) the higher-level *context* or *premise* determining the range and meaning of the offered alternatives. The presence of choice (between particularities) at one level masks—and in some sense precludes—choice (between premises) at a more encompassing level. The theory of the double bind found particular illustration in the paradoxical patterns and learning contexts of schizophrenic communication,[14] but Bateson considered its formal characteristics capable of handling the contextual complexity of a host of other relational phenomena, including play, learning, psychotherapy, humor, art, religion, hypnosis, dreams, creativity, addiction, adaptation, and the processes of evolution.[15]

Description embeds prescription—or as Bateson would say, all communication has a dual aspect: "Every message in transit has two sorts of 'meaning.' On the one hand, the message is a statement or report about events at a previous moment, and on the other hand it is a command—a cause or stimulus for events at a later moment."[16] Although the double bind was not advanced as a theory of therapy—it says nothing, for example, of how a therapist should conduct a session—the contextual view it proposed carried certain therapeutic implications. Over the ten-year course of the Bateson project, the researchers, as part of their interest in the communicational nature of psychiatry, regularly saw patients for therapy; however, there was a shift about midway through the project from working with individuals to treating whole families.[17] This significant move helped launch the field of family therapy. According to Bateson:

> Family therapy . . . denotes more than the introduction of a
> new method and more than a mere shift in the size of the social
> unit with which the therapist feels he must deal. Indeed, the
> very change in the size of the unit brings with it a new epis-

temology and ontology, i.e., a new way of thinking about what a *mind* is and a new concept of man's place in the world.[18]

Although Bateson saw patients from 1948 to 1963,[19] he did not consider himself a clinician. First and foremost a theorist, he was interested in such subjects as alcoholism, schizophrenia, and psychotherapy not as phenomena in and of themselves, but as "examples of formal relations, which will illustrate a theory."[20] As he put it: "I do not need schizophrenic patients or unhappy families to give my thinking empirical roots. I can use art, poetry or porpoises or the cultures of New Guinea and Manhattan, or my own dreams or the comparative anatomy of flowering plants."[21]

Bateson saw therapy as a species of applied science, and he was deeply wary of its instrumentality: "We social scientists would do well to hold back our eagerness to control that world which we so imperfectly understand."[22] Indeed, he was far from pleased with the ways his ideas were generally translated (he would probably have said "corrupted") into therapeutic theory and practice.[23] The spirit of, and reasons for, his rancor are nicely caught in a metalogue written by Mary Catherine Bateson; in it, her father is withering in his condemnation of the field.

> FATHER There's still . . . the problem of the misuse of ideas. The engineers get hold of them. Look at the whole god-awful business of family therapy, therapists making "paradoxical interventions" in order to change people or families, or counting "double binds." You can't count double binds.[24]

Attempting to enumerate double binds is rather like trying to count the humor in a comedian's monologue—there is no localizable "thing" to itemize. As with humor, double binds characterize the multilevel relationship within and between statements and between participants in an exchange.

The "paradoxing" of clients to which (Gregory) Bateson refers speaks of manipulation, a purposeful act which tears the contextual fabric of relationship:

> A screwdriver is not seriously affected when, in an emergency, we use it as a wedge; and a hammer's outlook on life is not affected because we sometimes use its handle as a simple lever. But in social manipulation our tools are people, and people learn, and they acquire habits which are more subtle and pervasive than the tricks which the blueprinter teaches them.[25]

A little later in her metalogue, Mary Catherine Bateson suggests how family therapy, a field that, after all, developed out of an appreciation of the importance of contextual integrity, might have gone awry:

> DAUGHTER   See, what I think is going on is the same process that produces the monstrous beetles with extra limbs,[26] the same thing is creating a monstrousness in the family-therapy industry, and other places too. Some of the information has been lost, an essential part of the idea.[27]

This suggestion introduces a number of pressing questions. What critical information is missing? And can the rent be repaired? It would be naive to assume that a particular lacuna could simply be localized, analyzed, and then appropriately sewn up. As in genetic coding, "a single *bit* of information—a single difference—may be the yes-or-no answer to a question of any degree of complexity, at any level of abstraction."[28] At what contextual level, then, has family therapy gone off track? Are some clinicians, some schools less "monstrous," less inclined to quantify patterns and chop up ecologies? Is all theory implicated, all practice tainted? Are there bits and pieces that are salvageable, or is the whole enterprise necessarily thrown into question? And even if we were able to identify particular problems, is there anything that can be done as a corrective?

The danger in addressing such questions and attempting to redress the problems they help identify is that one's actions may make the situation worse. One who attempts simply to "fix" a systemic situation, be it biological, societal, or familial, is poised from the outset to commit ecological blunders. When action is organized as a solution to a perceived or believed deficit, it necessarily becomes defined in opposition to that which is identified as a problem. The resulting mutual determination of problem and solution has the distinct potential of setting both in place. Gregory Bateson, in an interview with Stewart Brand, explains that any action stemming from the desire to do something—indeed, anything—as a corrective of "pathology" is fraught with difficulties. One is caught in a Taoist dilemma from the outset.

> The moment you want to ask the question, "What do you do about it?" that question itself chops the total ecology. I'm really talking Taoism, you know. The pathology is the breach of Taoism. And you say, "Well, now what's the cure for a breach of Taoism?" You want to say another breach of Taoism is the cure for it.[29]

A "breach of Taoism" is a rip in context. If the practice of change in family therapy is somehow destructive of the premises of relationship, so too can be attempts to change this practice of change:

> If you are carrying serious epistemological errors, you will find that they do not work any more. At this point you discover to your horror that it is exceedingly difficult to get rid of the error, that it's sticky. It is as if you had touched honey. As with honey, the falsification gets around; and each thing you try to wipe it off on gets sticky, and your hands still remain sticky.[30]

Having now been sounded, the questions about family therapy will be left to echo through the ensuing pages; however, they will not organize the form or content of what is to follow. Were they to be responded to directly, the premises contextualizing their articulation could not help but be embraced. The alternative is to inspire the imagination of a different class of question.

Taoist and Zen philosophers (as well as comedians, those labeled schizophrenic, and some therapists) are renowned for their deft ability to avoid being pinned down by the contextualizing nature of questions. Through metaphor, stories, absurdity, challenges, humor, and digression, they may offer an answer or pose another question, may indirectly comment on the category of question asked, and/or find ways to pose and answer questions of their own choosing. The Zen stories which follow are illuminating in this regard.

> One day a young novice said to Patriarch Hogen, "My name is Echo, and I would like to ask Your Reverence what is meant by the name Buddha?" Hogen merely said, "Oh so you are Echo are you?"

> A monk once asked Shozan, "Is there any phrase that is neither right nor wrong?" Shozan answered, "A piece of white cloud does not show any ugliness."

> Zuigan called out to himself every day, "Master." Then he answered himself, "Yes sir." And after that he added, "Become sober." Again he answered, "Yes sir." And after that he continued, "Do not be deceived by others." "Yes sir; yes sir," he answered.

> Nobushige, a soldier, came to Hakuin, a famous Zen Master, and asked, "Is there really a paradise and a hell?" "Who are you?" inquired Hakuin. "I am a samurai," Nobushige replied. "You, a samurai!" exclaimed Hakuin. "What kind of a lord would have you as his guard? You look like a beggar!" No-

bushige became so enraged that he began to draw his sword. Hakuin continued, "So you have a sword. It is probably too dull to even cut off my head." Nobushige brandished his weapon. Hakuin remarked, "Here, open the gates of hell." At these words the perceptive samurai sheathed his sword and bowed. "Here, open the gates of paradise," said Hakuin.[31]

There are many correspondences between Taoist and Zen (or, in Chinese, Ch'an) Buddhist thought. A number of writers attribute this to a historical confluence of the two traditions;[32] however, this presumption is open to question. Although reference will be made to some Zen writings in subsequent chapters, most of the focus will be on the Taoist works *Tao Te Ching, Chuang Tzu,* and *I Ching.*

The use of Chinese documents introduces the problem of translation. Never transparent, translation is at its best a transformation, a prism, defracting the original language and ideas in some kind of consistent way—and this, only if the text is interpreted within whatever is known of the cultural and historical context of its inception and with something of the original's linguistic integrity. It is beyond the scope of this work to provide a tour of the thought and language of ancient China; however, essential background will be provided when it contributes to a more thorough understanding of the ideas presented. A brief overview of the texts to be used may prove helpful.

It was the scholars of the Han dynasty (206 B.C.E.–220 C.E.) who first coined the term *Taoism* to encompass the philosophical doctrines of the *Tao Te Ching* and *Chuang Tzu.*[33] The authorship of the *Tao Te Ching* 道 德 經 ("book" 經 "of Tao" 道 "and te" 德) is traditionally attributed to Lao Tzu, said to have been an older contemporary of Confucius, living in the sixth century B.C.E. More recent scholarship suggests that the text should be considered an anthology dating to some time between the fifth and third centuries B.C.E. The *Chuang Tzu* 莊 子 bears the name of its reputed author, Chuang Tzu, who probably lived in the fourth or third century B.C.E. His personal name is thought to have been Chou, but little else is known about him, including the part he played in writing "his" book—it too may be an anthology of sorts; at least some of the text was likely written after his death.

The *I Ching* 易 經 ("book" 經 "of change" 易) is most certainly an assortment of layered texts, with the various parts compiled over the course of a millennium or more. The earliest strata are generally thought to date to remote antiquity, with later sections added at the beginning of the Chou dynasty (circa 1100 B.C.E.) and Confucian appendices written perhaps as late as the beginning of the Han dynasty (circa 200 B.C.E.).[34] It could be argued that this book should not be considered a Taoist text per se; nevertheless, it shares much of the orientation of Taoism and may indeed have been the wellspring for it.

Quotations from Lao Tzu's *Tao Te Ching* 道 德 經 ("book"經 "of Tao" 道 "and te"德) will be mostly drawn from John Wu's rendition; however, I will use other sources and adapt certain phrases in ways which, in my view, better accord with the laconic style of the original Chinese. If the changes become more than just minor tinkering, I will explain my rationale in an endnote. The passages from the *Chuang Tzu* will come from Burton Watson's version, and those from *I Ching* will be from Titus Yü's and my translation.[35]

The etymologies of Chinese characters can often be traced back to pictograms, but there can be significantly different interpretations of what the pictures originally represented. Unless otherwise indicated, my explanations of the meanings and roots of Chinese characters will draw on the scholarship of my teacher Titus Yü, who, in our work together, based his analyses on many etymological dictionaries, most notably

Shuo Wen. Of course, I take responsibility for extrapolations and any omissions or errors.

Three of the characters in the titles of these Taoist texts give a hint of the richness of image found in the original language. The word *Tao* 道, found in the title and throughout the *Tao Te Ching*, depicts a foot 之, which denotes movement, or, more specifically, "going and pausing,"[36] and a head 首, which symbolizes a person. Wieger says that the word as a whole means "to go ahead,"[37] while Watts, exercising a little more panache, suggests that it can be thought of as "intelligent rhythm."[38] *Tao* is usually left untranslated, though it is sometimes referred to as "Way."

The script for the second word of the title, *Te* 德, portrays one acting 彳 with a clear view 直 of one's heart 心. Often rendered as "power" or "virtue," we translated this term in the *I Ching* as "heart-directed actions."

The word *I* 易 in *I Ching* is a picture of the head 日 and body 勿 of a chameleon 蜴. As a living organism it symbolizes change in a number of ways. It is able to change its color in relation to its surroundings; its body temperature changes in response to the ambient temperature; and, perhaps most importantly, its life cycle, from birth to death, is marked by continual change: it grows, sheds skin, breathes, and so on.

This book derives an approach to therapy by subsuming therapeutic issues within more general questions about the relational nature of knowing and not-knowing, acting and not-acting. It combs and interweaves ideas from Bateson, Varela, Berry, and others, with concepts drawn from Taoism, and uses the resulting braided notions to articulate what could be called a relational or systemic orientation to therapeutic practice.

According to Bateson, "the basic of rule of systems theory is that, if you want to understand some phenomenon or appearance, you must consider that phenomenon within the context of all *completed* circuits which are relevant to it."³⁹ A systemic approach to therapy can thus be described in terms of its sensitivity to layered networks of premises and patterns of circular interaction, within and between ideas and people. Some of the various modalities of family therapy could be considered "systemic" within the terms of this definition, particularly those that have explicitly drawn from one or more of the same sources used in this book. The relational orientation notated here, however, makes no attempt to situate itself either within or apart from these other traditions. No apology is offered for either correspondences to, or divergences from, accepted practices of established schools.

The story below is offered as a prelude to what follows. Once told, it, like the questions about family therapy, will be left to echo.

Surly and withdrawn, Alex refused to go to school virtually every day and, if pushed on the issue, would pitch a fit. If his mother did finally manage to get him out the door, his morning would go tolerably well. The grade-six teacher found Alex cooperative and bright, and noted that he got along with his classmates; but it was already late October and he had still made no friends. Alex always came home at noon to eat lunch with his mother, Karen. After the meal, with more school looming before him, he would often throw another tantrum. It was usually effective; he missed a lot of afternoon classes. In the evening, when faced with homework, he would hyperventilate and cry so much that at times his uncle would have to come over to calm him down. The night before Karen called to make an appointment for therapy, Alex told her he no longer wanted to live.

The theme of suicide was familiar to the family. Nine months earlier, with her business bankrupt and marriage of fifteen years crumbling, Karen had taken an overdose of sleeping pills. Her husband, Tim, found her in time to save her life, but it was too late to save the relationship. During her stay in the hospital, she decided she would leave the kids with their father and move in with a friend. But when she was discharged five days later, she came home to find Tim living in their house with another woman. Her outrage galvanized her will and she changed her plans. Taking possession of the two children, she banished her husband from their lives, moved upstate, and secured a new job.

In moving to a new city, Karen hoped to distance herself from the memories and to make a fresh start. But there were problems. The work she found turned sour and she quit. Although she was able to collect unemployment insurance, she felt isolated and depleted. And now, with Alex's tantrums over school and talk of suicide, it wasn't even possible to look for a job, never mind take one. How could she ensure that nothing would happen if she wasn't there to supervise? With Alex becoming harder and harder to handle, Karen began calling Tim, asking for his help in controlling their son. Father, talking to Alex over the phone, could get him to do things—such as go to school—which mother, in person, could not.

As mother and son battled ever more desperately, mother and daughter bonded ever more tightly. Feeling isolated from her adult friends, Karen looked to her eight-year-old daughter, Sandra, for support and companionship. The girl was a model of good manners, and she was doing fine, save for at bedtime. Afraid to sleep alone, Sandra had spent virtually every night since her parents' separation in her mother's bed.

Clearly though, the problem was Alex. If he would obey his mother, go to school, and stop being so depressed and angry, she would be able to find work and get back on her feet. As it was, she felt trapped, sure that the boy would sabo-tage any move on her part to search for a job. Karen, at her wits' end, wanted help for her son so that he would go to school without a major battle, would make friends, and would start feeling better about himself.

The children's father had told them about their mother's suicide attempt when she was still in the hospital, and al-though Karen had since discussed it openly and offered reas-surances, both children continued to worry about her health, her state of mind, and the potential of her trying again. Alex had been told by friends of the family that he was now the "man" of the house, and he should look out for his mom. Karen dismissed this as inappropriate, insisting that as he was only eleven, he shouldn't be burdened with adult responsibili-ties. Nevertheless, Alex would lecture her about smoking and complain that he didn't have more say in how their home was run. Despite her problems with him, Karen viewed her son as a sensitive, creative child who was wise beyond his years.

Sensitive and wise. Sensitive, in fact, to his mother's lone-liness and feelings of failure, and wise enough to be concerned. Too young to be the responsible "man" his mother told him he didn't have to be, he had found a creative way of looking out for her. In refusing to go to school, in coming home every lunch hour, and in not making friends, he had discovered a way to be with her as much as possible.

In fact, together the children managed to be guardians almost around the clock. Alex took the day shift, while San-dra took care of the night, keeping her mother company through sleepless hours. It was likely that Alex wouldn't make any friends until he was sure that his mother could manage without him. Once he knew, really knew, that she was okay, he would find himself wanting to play with other kids at noon and after school. But right now he believed that his mother needed him at home to help her through this difficult period. Similarly, Sandra would no doubt continue being better behaved than most girls her age, and she would find herself wanting to sleep in her mom's bed for as long as she thought Karen needed her to do this.

One day in November Karen received a call from the government, informing her that they had made an error in allowing her unemployment insurance claim. There was no suggestion of impropriety, but since she had technically not been eligible to receive benefits, she would have to pay back everything she had been given over the last several months. Devastated and lost, she once again considered suicide as a way out.

Four hours later a friend happened to phone her and offer her a job. A month earlier she had turned down a similar opportunity, but this time she took it and started working the next day.

Two weeks later Alex was going to school without a fuss, and he had made some friends. He had started whistling around the house, and he was laughing for the first time in months. Sandra's behavior, on the other hand, had become somewhat annoying. She was complaining about Alex's whistling and had started picking on him.

Over the next months, Karen stopped turning to the children's father for help in resolving disputes. She successfully settled Sandra in her own bed, continued to enjoy and thrive in her job, and began a relationship with a new man. Alex continued to whistle.

There is the matter of the four hours—the time between the first and second phone call, the time when Karen had again thought seriously of suicide. She had phoned her brother and cried and talked to him for quite awhile. And, oh yes, Alex had happened to be home from school that day.

Chapter 2 begins with the beginning of knowing—the drawing of a distinction. The complementarity *connection/ separation* is introduced as a way of characterizing the dual function of all boundaries and to help usher in a means of defining the recursiveness of whole-part relations. The juxtaposition of ideas from Bateson and Taoism creates a context in which important double-questions can be asked regarding the fractionation of knowing and the ethics of acting in a participatory universe. The chapter concludes with a discussion of the notion of completion.

Chapter 3 is concerned with the lineality of focus and ignorant divisiveness of conscious knowing. Unmediated consciousness accomplishes much by taking purposeful shortcuts; however, it can easily become a victim of its own success. Two problems closely associated with quick-fix intentionality—the vicious circles of addiction and the paradox of forgetting—are given close attention.

Chapter 4 considers the profession of therapy as a symptom of a societal addiction. As *specialists* of wholeness, therapists are unavoidably defective healers; however, as it is pointed out, this defect can in fact be utilized as a resource in the organization of the therapeutic process. Excerpts from a clinical case serve to highlight some of the recurring themes of the book, and chapter 4 is brought to a close with a return to an issue first raised in the present chapter.

2 | COMPLETION/
(CONNECTION/
separation)

From the first not a thing is.

—Hui-neng

Assertion always implies a denial of something else.

—Charles Sanders Peirce

A universe comes into being when a space is severed or taken apart. By tracing the way we represent such a severance, we can begin to reconstruct, with an accuracy and coverage that appear almost uncanny, the basic forms underlying linguistic, mathematical, physical, and biological science, and can begin to see how the familiar laws of our own experience follow inexorably from the original act of severance.

—G. Spencer-Brown

From the first, not a thing is—but then—from the first not, a thing is. The first *not* makes a severance and a universe comes into being. The introduction of a negation—a *not*—is an act of creation which brings a thing into *existence* (from the Latin *ex-*, "out," and *sistere*, "to stand": "to stand out") and makes the thinking of it possible. But while such created presence is occasioned by absence (by the *not*), the complement of this is also true. If assertion necessarily implies a denial of something else, then it too severs: thus absence is also occasioned by presence. Not only "from the first not, a thing is," but also "from the first thing, a not is." Each side of a distinction—for example, assertion/denial, presence/absence, thing/no-thing—creates, and is created by, the other. Each side exists by virtue of the difference that separates it from, and connects it to, its complement. It is the relationship between the two sides that is primary: "The relationship comes first," says Gregory Bateson, "it *precedes*." [1] In the beginning there is the drawing of a distinction, and the knowing of all things (and no-things) is relationally derivative of that simple and primary act.

Francisco Varela considers the making of distinctions to be "one of the most fundamental of all human activities." [2] Bateson, ever fascinated by the ecological life of mind and the mind-full life of ecologies, views distinctions—or, as he would more commonly say, differences—as essential for any characterization of the living world. Inspired by Jung's separation of *creatura* (the living) and *pleroma* (the nonliving), Bateson distinguishes between "the physical world of pleroma, where forces and impacts provide sufficient basis of explanation, and the *creatura*, where nothing can be understood until *differences* and *distinctions* are invoked." [3] Creatura is "the world seen as mind, wherever such a view is appropriate," [4] and differences are fundamental to its organization. Always in mind there is the distinction, the cut that severs and joins presence and absence.

However, this mind of the living world—that is, the informational processes of perception, communication, learning, evolution, and so on—is a function not only of differences, but also of differences between differences, and differences between these differences between differences: "Every effective difference denotes a demarcation, a line of classification, and all classification is hierarchic. In other words, differences are themselves to be differentiated and classified."[5]

The title of this chapter—"COMPLETION/(CONNEC-TION/separation)"—notates the manner in which difference differentiates levels of classification; its layered form, described below, will be used as a matrix for exploring how Taoist and systemic thinkers characterize the whole/part relations composing the patterned world of mind. The discussion begins with "separation," moves to the relationship between "separation" and "CONNECTION" and the structure of whole/part complementaries (where the rationale for the use of capitalization and different type sizes will be explained), and concludes with "COMPLETION":

COMPLETION / (CONNECTION/separation)

separation

I knew that I was a substance whose whole essence or nature is only to think, and which, in order to be, has need of no locus and does not depend on any material thing, in such a way that this self or ego, that is to say, the soul by which I am what I am, is entirely distinct from the body.

—*René Descartes*

It is the attempt to *separate* intellect from emotion that is monstrous, and I suggest it is equally monstrous—and dangerous—to attempt to separate the external mind from the internal. Or to separate mind from body.

—*Gregory Bateson*

When a judgment cannot be framed in terms of good and evil, it is stated in terms of normal and abnormal. And when it is necessary to justify this last distinction, it is done in terms of what is good or bad for the individual. These are expressions that signal the fundamental duality of Western consciousness.

—*Michel Foucault*

As long as there is a dualistic way of looking at things there is no emancipation.

—*Hui-neng*

A distinction marks a boundary which, in Varela's words, "splits the world into two parts, 'that' and 'this,' or 'environment' and 'system,' or 'us' and 'them,' etc."[6] We in the West are steeped in religious, philosophical, scientific, economic, and political traditions whose manifest doctrines and underlying premises embrace an epistemology of separation—from the transcendence of the Judaeo-Christian God, to Plato's absolute division of the intellect and the senses, to the Cartesian cleavage of mind and body and the Newtonian positivist ideal of objectivity, to the exploitation of the environment and the symmetrical posturing of nuclear powers. Many of us also adhere to a mode of chunklike thinking which is best termed *analytic* (from the Greek *ana-*, "throughout," and *lyein*, "to loosen")—confronted with complexity, we break things down into simpler, more manageable constituent parts. Morris Berman characterizes this disjunctive way of knowing as indicative of "nonparticipating consciousness," where

the knower, or subject "in here," sees himself as radically disparate from the objects he confronts, which he sees as being "out there." In this view, the phenomena of the world remain the same whether or not we are present to observe them, and knowledge is acquired by recognizing a distance between ourselves and nature.[7]

Evidence of this prevailing epistemology can be seen not only *within* traditions and disciplines, but also in the dichotomous separations *between* them. Abraham Maslow describes how both orthodox science and orthodox religion

> have been institutionalized and frozen into a mutually excluding dichotomy. This separation into Aristotelian *a* and *not-a* has been almost perfect, as if a line had been drawn between them in the same way that Spain and Portugal once divided the new world between themselves by drawing a geographical line. Every question, every answer, every method, every jurisdiction, every task has been assigned to either one or the other, with practically no overlaps."[8]

Separation is also inherent in language. To name is to particularize, to define a boundary which distinguishes *this* from *that* which it is not. To name, according to Floyd Merrell,

> is to sort, divide, *differentiate*, order; it is to validate the *differentiating* boundary in which a space is constructed. "Knowledge" derives from the activity of naming and from the possession of names. A boundary cannot be marked off without creating a *difference*, and knowledge is not acquired without marking off boundaries.[9]

The discrete divisions within language—between subject and object, or between static noun and active verb—can seduce us into believing that such separations are not simply the stuff of description, but in fact inhere in the nature of the world. As Benjamin Lee Whorf warns, "we all, unknowingly, project the linguistic relationships of a particular language upon the universe, and *see* them there."[10] Bateson cautions us to beware the human tendency to think and talk as if the world were made up of separable parts:

> All peoples of the world, I believe, certainly all existing peoples, have something like language and, so far as I can understand

the talk of linguists, it seems that all languages depend upon a particulate representation of the universe. All languages have something like nouns and verbs, isolating objects, entities, events, and abstractions. In whatever way you phrase it, "difference" will always propose delimitations and boundaries. If our means of *describing* the world arises out of notions of difference . . . then our picture of the universe will necessarily be particulate.[11]

A particulate understanding, an epistemology of dichotomous separation, derives from a fundamental misunderstanding of the nature of distinctions, and a number of thinkers consider it a serious problem.[12] Maslow, for example, notes how the cloistered insularity of orthodox science and religion has meant that "they are both pathologized, split into sickness, ripped apart into a crippled half-science and crippled half-religion. This either-or split forces a kind of either-or choice between them."[13] The ultimate irony is that a half-science directed toward dominating the environment will betray an assumption identical to that of a transcendent half-religion: that absolute separation is possible. Bateson paints it this way:

> If you put God outside and set him vis-à-vis his creation and if you have the idea that you are created in his image, you will logically and naturally see yourself as outside and against the things around you. And as you arrogate all mind to yourself, you will see the world around you as mindless and therefore not entitled to moral or ethical consideration. The environment will seem yours to exploit.[14]

Wendell Berry similarly argues that our attempted domination and resulting exploitation of nature is grounded in the belief that we are separate from nature and thus in opposition to it.

We are up against an American convention of simple opposition to nature that is deeply established both in our minds and in our ways. We have opposed the primeval forests of the East and the primeval prairies and deserts of the West, we have opposed man-eating beasts and crop-eating insects, sheep-eating coyotes and chicken-eating hawks. In our lawns and gardens and fields, we oppose what we call weeds. And yet more and more of us are beginning to see that this opposition is ultimately destructive even of ourselves, that it does not explain many things that need explaining—in short that it is untrue.[15]

Untrue to nature and untrue to us as humans. As Watts remarks: "Our mistake has been to suppose that the individual is honored and his uniqueness enhanced by emphasizing his separation from the surrounding world, or his eternal difference in essence from his Creator. As well honor the hand by lopping it off!"[16]

Berman observes that "modern scientific thinking, if not the character of contemporary rational-empirical thought in general, remains, in essence, profoundly Newtonian,"[17] and he considers this a threat to our humanity and to our world:

Modern science and technology are based not only on a hostile attitude toward the environment, but on the repression of the body and the unconscious; and unless these can be recovered . . . then what it means to be a human being will forever be lost.[18]

If attempts to solve the problems generated by the dichotomous logic of insular separation do not challenge the rules of that logic, then attempts at adaptation cannot go beyond addiction. According to Bateson, "the 'sobriety' of the alcoholic is characterized by an unusually disastrous variant of the Cartesian dualism, the division between Mind and Matter, or, in this case, between conscious will, or 'self,' and the remainder of the personality."[19] Intoxication is thus a kind of subjective "correction of this error,"[20] but as it fades into hangover, the split is only reconfirmed. It should thus be patently evident that it is also mistaken to suppose that technologically inspired crises of the environment are simply in need of technological solutions. Anthony Wilden is very clear: "The conviction that technology will always find an answer is a capital example of the ideological *hubris* which got us into this mess in the first place."[21] Such hubris is an expression of our either/or orientation to the world, a reflection of the assumption that we can *control* nature. Wendell Berry examines the etymology of the word *control*, finding it

> more than ordinarily revealing, . . . for its root meaning is to roll against, in the sense of a little wheel turning in opposition. The principle of control, then, involves necessarily the principle of division: One thing may turn against another thing only by being divided from it. . . .
>
> As we now know, what we turn against must turn against us.[22]

Indeed, echoes Bateson, "*the creature that wins against its environment destroys itself.*"[23]

Such destruction ramifies from the misconstruing and mishandling of distinctions—between subject and object, self and other, humans and environment, mind and body, good and evil, health and sickness, conscious and unconscious, and so on—as pure separations. A chilling example of this can be found in the late Ayatollah Ruhollah Khomeini's pronouncement of the death sentence on author Salman Rushdie and the publishers of *The Satanic Verses*. The killing of the man and the burning of his books will never produce the removal desired by Khomeini, but must virtually guarantee Rushdie's continued presence in Muslim thought and politics.

A distinction *does* create a boundary which divides, but

that self-same boundary simultaneously and irrevocably *connects* that which it separates. Blindness to this simple realization characterizes not only our tragic relationships to each other and our world, but also our relationships to ourselves. Symptoms are haunting reminders that attempts to eradicate pieces of our lived experience, to banish parts of our minds, can unwittingly create and entrench the very problems we most dread. The parted mind does not, indeed cannot, depart.

A man by the name of Martin consulted me for the purpose of getting a retrospective "proper diagnosis." Two years earlier he had gone to see a psychiatrist for what he was afraid might be a "thought disorder." The doctor had seen him for a number of appointments, had listened to his concerns, and had assured him that he wasn't suffering from such an ailment. Martin remained unconvinced: "I know what I feel, what I had. A lot of people will say, my psychiatrist would say, 'You don't have a thought disorder.' But I know what I feel; nobody else does."

This was a difficult stance for the man to take, given his great trust in the expertise of professionals: "To me a psychiatrist knew how a person is supposed to think and knew what a person is supposed to think. . . . A heart doctor knows exactly how the heart works, a psychiatrist knows exactly how the mind works." He would tell his doctor the sorts of thoughts he had, thoughts that, at least for him, were proof that he was somehow "crazy." The mind expert's attempts to reassure him that such thoughts were normal had only served to confirm for Martin that he must then be crazy after all, for it meant that he himself was obviously unable to clearly distinguish what was crazy from what was not:

MARTIN   When I would go for sessions, as I would talk to him, I would walk away thinking, um, like he'd say, "Martin, that's not crazy," and I would walk away

thinking—he's in my head now—I would walk
away with him thinking in my head [i.e., as if I were
the psychiatrist thinking about me]: "If he [Martin]
thinks that's crazy, then he's not going to know if
jumping off a bridge is crazy, if stabbing somebody's
crazy. He won't know what's crazy." And then I became confused and I didn't know, because I was
thinking that he was thinking that "he won't know
what's crazy anymore." . . . Every time I would go
see him I would get worse.

If Martin fashioned the paradoxical knot that bound
him in this way, it was his psychiatrist who inadvertently
cinched it tight. The Möbius logic that tangled them together
went something like this:

THERAPIST   He [the psychiatrist] thought that you weren't
crazy, but if you thought you were crazy and you
weren't, that would mean you wouldn't know the
difference between what would be crazy and
what wouldn't be crazy, which would mean that
you would be crazy.

MARTIN   Right, exactly.

And again:

THERAPIST   If you said, "Look doctor, I think I have a thought
disorder," and he says, "No, you don't have a
thought disorder," but if you *think* you have a
thought disorder and you don't have a thought
disorder, maybe thinking you do have a thought
disorder is the thought disorder.

MARTIN   Exactly.

Martin's fear of being crazy had not only not been allevi-
ated by the psychiatrist's reassurances, but had been exacer-
bated. As shall be discussed in detail in chapter 3, a distinc-

tion which makes a difference, which matters, cannot simply be dissolved; one side cannot be severed from the other. This man had committed himself to finding out whether or not he had a thought disorder, and his search, organized by the distinction crazy/not crazy, could not be resolved by the psychiatrist voicing the opinion that one side of the distinction did not exist; how appropriate, then, that it was the disembodied voice of the doctor which asserted that it did. The real psychiatrist's voice said the craziness was imagined, and the imagined psychiatrist's voice worried that the craziness was real.

CONNECTION/separation

The boundary of the organism is *also* the boundary of its environment, and thus its movements can be ascribed to the environment as well. . . . We gain better understanding by describing this boundary and its movements as belonging to both the organism and its environment.

—*Alan Watts*

Are there any total divisions between things? Is there a place or time where one thing begins and another ends? If so then clearly there could be no causal or logical interaction between them.

—*Gregory Bateson*

If we represent knowledge as a tree, we know that things that are divided are yet connected. We know that to observe the divisions and ignore the connections is to destroy the tree.

—*Wendell Berry*

The moment it is acknowledged that distinctions join what they divide, it becomes impossible to speak of anything in isolation. The implications of this are far-reaching and will continue to cascade throughout this book. For one thing it means that this section cannot be labeled "Connection" and discussed as an independent topic, as it constitutes only one-half of the pair connection/separation. Connection and separation cannot be considered *apart* from each other, but must be considered *a part*[24] of the distinction which, in separating them, connects them.

Varela points out that the classic—what he calls *hegelian*—way of understanding distinctions rests on an assumption of symmetrical opposition and a logic of negation.[25] Taking the form A/not-A, the two sides of a hegelian pair oppose each other at the same logical level: Good is viewed as the opposite of evil, health as the absence of illness, love as the antithesis of hate. Such distinctions are a clear expression of the Western epistemology of separation described earlier: Each side takes on the appearance of atomistic independence, as if it could exist on its own, and does battle with the other.

Varela offers an alternative framework for understanding distinctions that does not negate a hegelian approach (for to do so would simply invoke a hegelian logic of separation at a meta-level: i.e., hegelian/not-hegelian), but rather enfolds it within the layered relationship between wholes and parts.[26] Taking the form

whole / parts constituting the whole

the two sides of this second type of distinction are asymmetrical across hierarchical levels of organization: "Take any situation (domain, process, entity, notion) which is holistic (total, closed, complete, full, stable, self-contained). Put it on the left side of the /. Put on the right side of it the corresponding processes [parts] (constituents, generators, dynamics)."[27] A whole contextualizes the parts it encompasses and is thus of a higher logical type.[28] Or as Bateson would say: "The contrast between part and whole, whenever this contrast appears in the realm of communication, is simply a contrast in logical typing. The whole is always in a metarelationship with its parts."[29] For example, the relational pattern (whole) of a melodic line contextualizes the individual notes that combine to give it form. Varela explains how these levels of whole and part are coemergent:

> Most discussions place holism/reductionism in polar opposition. . . . This seems to stem from the historical split between empirical sciences, viewed as mainly reductionist or analytic, and the (European) schools of philosophy and social science that grope toward a dynamics of totalities. . . . Both attitudes are possible for a given descriptive level, and in fact they are complementary. On the one hand, one can move down a level and study the properties of the components, disregarding their mutual interconnection as a system. On the other hand, one can disregard the detailed structure of the components, treating their behavior only as contributing to that of a larger unit. . . . We cannot conceive of components if there is no system from which they are abstracted; and there cannot be a whole unless there are constitutive elements.[30]

The shape of this whole/part relationship is described by Varela as *imbricated* (overlapping): "A whole decomposes in parts which generate processes integrating the whole."[31] Such mutual creation, "where one term of the pair *emerges* from the other,"[32] can be described as *recursive,* a circular, self-referential process that Heinz von Foerster defines as "turning upon oneself: . . . run[ning] through one's own path again."[33] Bateson, in fact, uses the idea of recursion to distinguish the generation of, and relationship between, levels of informational organization (e.g., of and between wholes and parts) in the domain of creatura:

> It appears that the idea of "logical typing," when transplanted from the abstract realms inhabited by mathematicological phi-

losophers to the hurly-burly of organisms, takes on a very different appearance. Instead of a hierarchy of classes, we face a hierarchy of *orders of recursiveness.*[34]

The self-referential nature of the connection/separation complementarity provides a way of approaching an understanding of such whole/part recursiveness. The reflexivity pivots on the identity between the terms used to describe the function of the slash (/) and those that comprise the distinction itself: that is, the slash *connects and separates connection and separation*—it does what it describes itself doing.[35] This recursive spinning depicts how the difference in levels between wholes and parts is generated: *The connection of* CONNECTION/separation *evolves in the direction of wholeness, while the separation of* CONNECTION/separation *devolves toward a level of particularity.* The capitalization of the left side of the distinction is intended as an analogic reminder that relationships (connections between) contextualize relata (the results of separation), that wholes encompass parts.

The distinction that separates CONNECTION and separation (thereby constituting them as distinct from one another) also connects them (establishes that they are relationally defined). Thus, the distinction (slash) between CONNECTION and separation

CONNECTION/separation

can itself be distinguished in terms of the two functions it performs; it connects connection and separation—

CONNECTION OF
    CONNECTION/separation

—and it separates connection and separation:

separation of
    CONNECTION/separation

These two phrases are each sides of a more encompassing distinction, one that is a higher order of recursion from the first. The change in level is graphically represented by an enlargement in the type size:

(CONNECTION OF
    CONNECTION/separation) /
      (separation of
        CONNECTION/separation)

The divergence between whole and part becomes more and more pronounced as this self-reference is allowed to blossom. The slash between these two parenthetically enclosed terms creates yet another level of contextual complexity, for the processes on either side of *it* can also be connected and separated. Another order of recursion is thus formed:

(CONNECTION OF
    (CONNECTION OF
      CONNECTION/separation) /
        (separation of
          CONNECTION/separation)) /

    (separation of
      (CONNECTION OF
        CONNECTION/separation) /
        (separation of
          CONNECTION/separation))

And so on.

The reflexive logic of this spiraling of connection/separation can be traced via an analogous distinction—pattern/scatter—within the domain of music. Just as connection/separation folds back, connecting and separating itself, so too the distinction pattern/scatter can be patterned and scattered.

The patterning of PATTERN/scatter—

PATTERNING OF
    PATTERN/scatter

—is heard most often in jazz improvisation, where the structure of a familiar tune can serve as the foundational pattern for melodic, harmonic, and rhythmic variations (scatter). Pattern and scatter are continually brought together and interwoven (patterned) in the composition and performance of each piece.

The scattering of PATTERN/scatter—

scattering of
    PATTERN/scatter

—differentiates (scatters) two distinct musical forms: (1) the regimented precision (pattern) of, say, marching-band music, where all details of composition and performance are accounted for and strictly defined, and (2) the indeterminate nature (scatter) of aleatory music, where various compositional and/or performance decisions (such as pitch, duration, volume, instrumentation) are made through procedures of random selection (throwing dice, flipping coins, consulting random-number charts, etc.).

The distinction between the patterning and scattering of PATTERN/scatter—

(PATTERNING OF
    PATTERN/scatter) /

    (scattering of
        PATTERN/scatter)

—can thus be understood, in musical terms, as:

(JAZZ IMPROVISATION) /
    (marching-band music/aleatory music)

Considered at the next level of recursion, the patterning of the previous distinctions—

(PATTERNING OF
    (PATTERNING OF
        PATTERN/scatter) /
        (scattering of
            PATTERN/scatter))

or

(PATTERNING OF
    (JAZZ IMPROVISATION) /
        (marching-band music/aleatory music))

—would combine, in one compositional form, distinct elements of improvisation, determined structure, and randomness. An illustrative, if somewhat eccentric, example of such a combination comes to mind. Imagine a series of marching tunes played and recorded in an exacting manner. A composer might take the audiotape of such a recording, cut it into hundreds of pieces of varying length, and then resplice the sections in random order. This newly, and strangely, edited tape could then be played in a public performance, with a jazz pianist improvising on its indeterminate syncopations.

On the other hand, the scattering of the lower-level distinctions—

(scattering of
    (PATTERNING OF
        PATTERN/scatter) /
        (scattering of
            PATTERN/scatter))

or

(scattering of
    (JAZZ IMPROVISATION) /
        (marching-band music/aleatory music))

—is descriptive of the separate contexts where these musical forms are most often enjoyed. Jazz tends to be found in clubs, marching-band music on football fields and in parades, and aleatory music on college campuses and in concert halls.

Another way of capturing the imbrication of the CONNECTION/separation relationship is to express it in the form of an injunction:

> (CONNECT SEPARATIONS TO FORM WHOLES) /
> (separate connections to distinguish parts)

The left and right sides of this distinction describe holistic and reductionistic approaches to understanding, respectively. As Varela pointed out above, these two modes of inquiry have been traditionally regarded as dichotomous opposites—an approach to understanding approaches to understanding which is, by virtue of attending only to the separation between the two sides, reductionistic. Varela's alternative—that is, treating holism and reductionism as necessary complements that each have an appropriate and necessary place in the business of knowing[36]—applies the relational principles *within* both traditions to the relationship *between* them. Both are kept separate as unique modalities (a quality derived from reductionism) *and* connected as whole is to part (a derivation of holism):

> (HOLISTICALLY CONNECT
>   HOLISM/reductionism) /
>   (reductionistically separate
>   HOLISM/reductionism)

This is the equivalent of turning the injunction

> (CONNECT SEPARATIONS TO FORM WHOLES) /
> (separate connections to distinguish parts)

back on itself:

> (CONNECT
>> (CONNECT SEPARATIONS TO FORM WHOLES) /
>>> (separate connections to distinguish parts)) /
>
> (separate
>> (CONNECT SEPARATIONS TO FORM WHOLES) /
>>> (separate connections to distinguish parts))

The result is the emergence of a kind of *self-referential completion.*

Not all distinctions lend themselves to such reflexive turning, but because in every case the slash necessarily connects and separates the terms on either side of it, *any distinction can be completed by recursively connecting and separating its two terms.* Connecting the separation between A and not-A enables one to move in the direction of wholeness, to a contextual pattern or premise that reflects the nature of the *relationship between* the parts it encompasses, while separating the connection between A and not-A underscores the uniqueness of the *relata* themselves: A is not not-A; not-A is not A.

This process of completion, of embedding the separations of hegelian dualities within the context of the relationship that connects them, can serve as a model for responding to, and participating in the making of, any and all distinctions in the world of communication. With this in mind, the imbricated complementarity

> COMPLETION / (CONNECTION/separation)

can now be introduced as a compact rendition of the self-referential spiral generated by the whole/part injunction:

> (CONNECT SEPARATIONS TO FORM WHOLES) /
>> (separate connections to distinguish parts)

Its tiered form, once explained, will become the principle organizing pattern for the development of ideas in this and subsequent chapters.

The imbrication of

COMPLETION / (CONNECTION/separation)

can be clearly seen when it is recognized that the first-level distinction within the parentheses is repeated at the second level of recursion. Thus,

(CONNECTION/separation)

spirals to become:

COMPLETION / (CONNECTION/separation)

COMPLETION connects CONNECTION/separation, and CONNECTION/separation separates COMPLETION. The capitalization of COMPLETION distinguishes it as a higher-order connection, the context of connection and separation. It is not a connection that precludes separation, not a holism that opposes reductionism, but a cycling that incorporates both—a unity of "not one, not two,"[37] an expression of the Mahayana Buddhist phrase "Difference is identity; identity is difference."[38]

Thus,

COMPLETION / (CONNECTION/separation)

encapsulates both the first-order distinction,

(CONNECTION/separation)

and its second-order recursion:

(CONNECTION OF CONNECTION/separation) /
      (separation of CONNECTION/separation)

The layered form of COMPLETION / (CONNECTION/ separation) is intended as a matrix for orienting to distinctions, for contextualizing them in terms of the connections of their separations and the separations of their connections. Consider, for instance, the crazy/not crazy difference that organized the relationship between Martin and his psychiatrist. The connection between the two sides of the distinction (metaphorically embodied in the relationship between patient and doctor) was reinforced every time an attempt was made to separate them, to define one as the negation of, or in opposition to, the other. The "thought disorder" thus proved most intractable. Recognizing that the relationship between A and not-A can never be simply an entrenched division, that the separation between them *is* a connection, is the first step toward relating such dichotomies as parts of a context which encompasses them both.

Sanity cannot be achieved by casting out disordered thoughts: As Carl Whitaker likes to remind us, "We are all schizophrenics . . . in the middle of the night when we're sound asleep."[39] The question is not how to successfully sever order and disorder, but how to complete them in such a way that their separation is contextualized by their connection. As any creative artist or scientist could have told the dichotomously distinguished men (patient/psychiatrist) struggling with their dichotomous distinction (crazy/not crazy), the successful *combination* of order and disorder is the essence of creative process. Bateson differentiates "rigor and imagination, the two great contraries of mental process, either of which by itself is lethal. Rigor alone is paralytic death, but imagination alone is insanity."[40]

Mapped onto the model

COMPLETION / (CONNECTION/separation)

this idea can be expressed as

RIGOROUS IMAGINATION /
    (ORDERED THOUGHTS / disordered thoughts)

with the lower-case "disordered thoughts" indicative of separation, the small capitals of "ORDERED THOUGHTS" designat-
ing a process of connection, and the upper-case "RIGOROUS
IMAGINATION" referring to the generative connection of
the separation between order and disorder.

The wholeness generated by recursive completions is
never conclusive, never a closure, precisely because it is not
exclusive of its own decomposition: Completion is a connection that embraces the partitioning of itself. Separation only
becomes problematic when it is established as the *context* of
relationship, rather than as a subsumed aspect of it—as when,
for example, the environment is thought of and treated as
other. The result of such *alienation* (from the Latin *alis-us*,
"other") is expressed in the West as symmetrical confrontation—"the mountain must be conquered"—or as exploitation: "This mountain can be leveled for its timber and its
limestone, and the resulting pit will serve as a sterling garbage
dump." But the marking of a boundary between self and environment needn't create an epistemological chasm; the distinctiveness of each can be honored when their connection as
interactive components in an inclusive ecosystem is underscored. Thus,

COMPLETION / (CONNECTION/separation)

becomes:

ECOSYSTEMIC RELATIONS / (ENVIRONMENT/humans)

Such a pattern illustrates Wendell Berry's contention that "by
diminishing nature we diminish ourselves, and vice versa,"[41]
and that

nature and human culture, wildness and domesticity, are not opposed but are interdependent. Authentic experience of either will reveal the need of one for the other. In fact, examples . . . prove that a human economy and wildness can exist not only in compatibility but to their mutual benefit.[42]

Not all distinctions can be so directly configured, however. The terms *order* and *disorder* respectively describe processes of connection and separation and thus lend themselves naturally to such whole/part stacking; but, if a difference defines a relationship between two *parts,* then the process of transforming them onto the matrix of COMPLETION / (CONNECTION/separation) must include one additional step. Anticipating a discussion later in the chapter, ponder, for illustration, the distinction knower/known.

Both knower and known are "things," abstracted from the relationship of knowing. There is nothing inherent in their relationship that suggests one be thought of as contextually more encompassing than the other, and neither term is necessarily descriptive of a process of either joining (connection) or dividing (separation). In situations such as this— that is, where a distinction marks a relationship between two *parts—both* terms are placed on *both* sides of the parenthetically enclosed side of the COMPLETION / (CONNECTION/separation) distinction. That is, knower/known is arrayed on COMPLETION/(CONNECTION/separation) as:

COMPLETION / ((KNOWER/KNOWN) / (knower/known))

These two parenthetical terms can now be treated as distinct descriptions of the relationship between knower and known. The process of knowing is represented as either a connection of knower and known—(KNOWER/KNOWN)—or as a separation between them: (knower/known). The separation of knower and known is characteristic of the Cartesian belief that knowledge is obtained by objectively distancing the observer from the observed; the connection of knower and known, on the other hand, is descriptive of the constructivist belief (to be discussed later) that the knower is implicated in the known, that there is no separation between them:

COMPLETION /
    ((CONNECTED, CONSTRUCTIVIST KNOWING) /
      (disjunctive, cartesian knowing))

Completing the distinction between these two orientations ensures that they not be dichotomized, but rather contextually enfolded within an approach to knowing that is inclusive of them both:

CONTEXTUAL KNOWING /
    (CONNECTED KNOWING / separated knowing)

The separation of knower and known needn't remain separate from the connection of knower and known, as Wendell Berry's poem "The Cold" relates:

How exactly good it is
to know myself
in the solitude of winter,

my body containing its own
warmth, divided from all
by the cold; and to go

separate and sure
among the trees cleanly
divided, thinking of you

perfect too in your solitude,
your life withdrawn into
your own keeping

—to be clear, poised
in perfect self-suspension
toward you, as though frozen.

And having known fully the
goodness of that, it will be
good also to melt.[43]

To reiterate: The spirial matrix COMPLETION / (CONNEC-
TION/separation) can be used to take the two sides of any given
distinction—whether whole/part or part/part—and to consider ways in which they mutually define, propose, create, and/
or maintain one another in an encompassing pattern of interaction. Whole/part distinctions—such as context/text, envi-
ronment/species, melody/note—or those that are descriptive
of processes of connection/separation—such as integrate/dis-
integrate, information/noise, gather/scatter—can be mapped
directly onto the right side of the pattern:

COMPLETION / (CONTEXT/text)
COMPLETION / (ENVIRONMENT/species)
COMPLETION / (MELODY/note)
COMPLETION / (INTEGRATE/dis-integrate)
COMPLETION / (INFORMATION/noise)
COMPLETION / (GATHER/scatter)

Part/part distinctions—such as front/back, presence/absence,
sound/silence, warp/woof—are doubly placed on the right
side of the larger distinction, in order that a CONNECTION/sep-
aration relationship can be created:

COMPLETION / ((FRONT/BACK) / (front/back))
COMPLETION / ((PRESENCE/ABSENCE) / (presence/absence))
COMPLETION / ((SOUND/SILENCE) / (sound/silence))
COMPLETION / ((WARP/WOOF) / (warp/woof))

In all cases, the far left side of each tiered relation can be considered a context or completion: a connection of connection and separation.

COMPLETION /
(CONNECTION/separation)

A Mind Poet
Stays in the house.
The house is empty
And it has no walls.
The poem
Is seen from all sides,
Everywhere,
At once.

—Gary Snyder

The matrix COMPLETION / (CONNECTION/separation) will now be used as a pattern with which to encounter the textured grain of Taoism, systemic thought, and the practice of therapy. In this process it will produce moiré phenomena— forms created by the rhythmic interface of patterns[44]—which will be both related and distinct from their sources. As these interactive patterns are then brought to bear upon one another, multilevel moirés can be expected to develop, providing the sorts of double or multiple descriptions which Bateson considers necessary for an in-depth view and understanding.[45] Such contrapuntal weaving can be understood as an exercise in what Bateson terms *abduction*, that is, "the lateral extension of abstract components of description." Abduction is a necessary attribute of all mind-full activities: "Metaphor, dream, parable, allegory, the whole of art, the whole of science, the whole of religion . . . are instances or aggregates of instances of abduction." [46]

The first moiré to emerge derives from an initial exploration of Taoism; however, the shape of this pattern will very soon thereafter be used to broach Bateson's notions of Mind. A circling between these two domains of thought will then ensue, giving rise to issues regarding the relationship between the nature of mind and the Mind of Nature.

TAO / ((YIN/YANG) / (yin/yang))

STUDENT Where is Tao?
TEACHER Right before us.
STUDENT Why don't I see it?
TEACHER Because of your egoism you cannot see it.
STUDENT If I cannot see it because of my egoism, does your Reverence see it?
TEACHER As long as there is "I and thou," this complicates the situation and there is no seeing Tao.
STUDENT When there is neither "I" nor "thou" is it seen?
TEACHER When there is neither "I" nor "thou," who is here to see it?

—Yen-kuan Ch'i-an

The Taoists never dichotomized their contraries (i.e., they conceived of them as YIN/YANG rather than yin/yang). As the *T'ai Chi* ("grand" 太 "polarity" 極) symbol elegantly portrays, the shaded side (yin 陰) of the circle is dark only to the extent that the light side (yang 陽) is bright; the boundary they share exists by virtue of their relationship, and each "side" contains within it the seed of the other (see figure 1). This creates a continually moving, circling balance wherein one side of the distinction is always proposing the existence of the other.

Figure 1. The T'ai Chi Symbol

The archaic form of the Chinese character *yin* 𝘫 is a picture of clouds, while the ancient form of *yang* 㼒 depicts the sun ○ shining ⋒ from above the horizon —. Each has qualities or attributes associated with it, but only in relation to its complement. Thus, for example, yin withdraws inward and down as yang moves outward and up; yin is empty in relation to yang's fullness, yin is soft to the extent that yang is hard, and so on. The emphasis is always on the recursive balance created by their mutual definition, as can be seen in the following passage from chapter 2 of Lao Tzu's *Tao Te Ching:*

> Presence and absence reciprocally grow
> Difficult and easy reciprocally complete
> Long and short reciprocally shape
> High and low reciprocally contrast
> Sound and notes reciprocally harmonize
> Back and front reciprocally follow.[47]

Where is the Tao in all of this? Abductively extrapolating from the pattern

TAO / ((YIN/YANG) / (yin/yang))

we will be poised to look for it in the *reciprocal relationship between* the connection and separation of yin and yang, in the circuitous way their twoness is one and their oneness is two. Front can follow back only if they are cyclically connected, and indeed Lao Tzu does make reference to the Tao in terms of circular motion:

反 者 道 之 動

"Returning: Tao's moving[48]

Tao is not a thing, or a conglomerate of parts, but a process of recursive relationship, emergent from the connected separation of yin and yang. The imbricated complementarity of Taoism—TAO / ((YIN/YANG) / (yin/yang))—is not so much a body of ideas to be learned as an orientation to knowing and not knowing, a continual reminder to connect one's separations and separate one's connections in recursive ways. The Tao is inclusive of, and dependent on, the distinction yin/yang as a necessary part of its wholeness.

The poet Lionel Kearns manages to convey something of this self-referentiality in his visual poem "The Birth of God" (see figure 2).[49] The gestalt of the whole is different from, yet derivative of, the layered crossover of the parts. It all happens in the relations between.

Layered complementarities provide an avenue for approaching what Bateson refers to as *Mind*. He considers "mental function" to be immanent in the interaction of differentiated parts,[50] that is, "in the ensemble as a *whole*."[51] Wholes are constituted by the combined interaction of the parts,[52] and this interaction is circular: the simplest unit of mind is "the elementary cybernetic system with its messages in circuit."[53] Expressed in spiral form, Mind thus becomes:

MIND /

    (CIRCUITOUS INTERACTION BETWEEN PARTS /

      differentiation of parts)

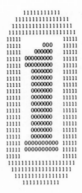

Figure 2. The Birth of God

As we shall see, there is a resonance between Tao and Mind, an abductive relationship that recalls Watts's analysis of the etymology of Tao as "intelligent rhythm."[54] The Tao's rhythmic (patterned)—and immanent (relational)—nature is suggested in chapter 5 of the *Tao Te Ching*, where Lao Tzu likens it, by implication, to the action of a bellows:

> Between Heaven and Earth,
> There seems to be a Bellows:
> It is empty, and yet it is inexhaustible;
> The more it works, the more comes out of it.
> No amount of words can fathom it:
> Better look for it within you.[55]

Chang explains that

> the understanding of *Tao* is an inner experience in which distinction between subject and object vanishes. It is an intuitive, immediate awareness rather than a mediated, inferential, or intellectual process. *Tao* does not blossom into vital consciousness until all distinctions between self and nonself have disappeared.[56]

The immanence of Tao makes it possible to look for it within;[57] however, it also demands the converse search—that is, to follow it (as Mind) as it extends outward, beyond the confines of our "skin encapsulated ego"[58] to its encompassment in the ecosystemic relations of which we are a part. In the words of Bateson:

> The individual mind is immanent but not only in the body. It is immanent also in pathways and messages outside the body; and there is a larger Mind of which the individual mind is only a subsystem. This larger Mind is comparable to God and is perhaps what some people mean by "God," but it is still immanent in the total interconnected social system and planetary ecology.[59]

This embedding of mind within Mind—like Chinese box within Chinese box—is also apparent in the work of Varela, who uses the metaphor of "conversation" to talk about the recursive layering of parts and whole:

> There is a sense in which we must consider individual organisms and their (internal) cognitive processes. However, it is equally true . . . to realize that cognitive processes can also be seen as operating at the *next higher level*, that is, the cognitive processes of the autonomous unit of which *we* are participants and components. . . . To this next higher level belong the characteristics of mind we attribute to ourselves individually; in fact, what we experience as our mind cannot truly be separated from this network to which we connect and through which we interdepend. . . .
>
> From this point of view, then, mind is an immanent quality, of a class of organizations including individual living systems, but also ecological aggregates, social units of various sorts, brains, conversations, and many others, however spatially distributed or short-lived. There is mind in every unity engaged in conversationlike interactions.[60]

Given such a conception of Mind, what then is *knowing*? In order to find an appropriately relational answer, it will help to orient our inquiry in relational terms. A template can be found in Warren McCulloch's famous double question: "What is a number, that a man may know it, and a man, that he may know a number?"[61] Asked of the relationship between knower and known, the query becomes: What is the known that a knower may know it, and what is a knower that it may know a known?

KNOWING /
((KNOWER/KNOWN) / (knower/known))

We subtract or repress our awareness that perception is active and repress our awareness that action is passive.
—*Gregory Bateson*

Mind is immanent in "the pattern which connects all the living creatures";[62] it is a pattern of patterns "which defines the vast generalization that, indeed, it is patterns which connect."[63] This assertion aptly illustrates the fine line Bateson treads between the concerns of ontology—"problems of how things are, what is a person, and what sort of a world this is"[64]—and issues of epistemology—"how we know anything, or more specifically, how we know what sort of a world it is and what sort of creatures we are that can know something (or perhaps nothing) of this matter."[65]

Alasdair MacIntyre credits Christian Wolff (1679–1754) with canonizing *ontologia* as a philosophical term. Wolff "argued a priori that the world is composed of simple substances, themselves neither perceived nor possessing extension or shape."[66] Thus, ontology has to do with "being," with how things "really" are, independent of an observer. Ontologically speaking, knower and known are distinct entities (i.e., the relationship between them is one of knower/known rather than KNOWER/KNOWN); both maintain an existence and identity before, during, and after taking part in the particular activity of knowing that brings them together. From an epistemological standpoint, the connection between knower and known (i.e., KNOWER/KNOWN) bestows existence upon the known. However, Gregory Bateson and Mary Catherine Bateson argue that "because what *is* is identical for all human purposes with what can be known, there can be no clear line between epistemology and ontology."[67] In other words, because the known world is a world of knowing, ontology is subsumed within epistemology: KNOWING / (EPISTEMOLOGY/ontology). Bateson insists that the definition of a reality is dependent upon an observer doing the defining, imposing a meaning: "Bishop Berkeley was right, at least in asserting that what happens in the forest is *meaningless* if he is not there to be affected by it."[68] Further, he reminds us that "'parts,' 'wholes,' 'trees,' and 'sounds' exist as such only in quotation marks. It is *we* who differentiate 'tree' from 'air' and 'earth,' 'whole' from 'part,' and so on."[69]

In this, Bateson is in accord with the Heisenberg transformations taking place in a variety of disciplines.[70] Alan Watts relates that "from physics to psychology, every department of science is realizing more and more that to observe the world is to participate in it, and that, frustrating as this may first seem to be, it is the most important clue of all to further knowledge."[71] Morris Berman captures it most eloquently: "We are sensuous participants in the very world we seek to describe."[72] In a word, we *construct* reality.

The foundation of such a participatory world is not lost in the ephemeral instability of solipsistic hallucination, nor found in the supposed stability of an ontologically distinct reality. Rather, as Varela indicates, it is grounded in *experience,* in the relationship of knowing:

> It should now be clear that the first cut, the most elementary distinction we can make, may be the intuitively satisfactory cut between oneself *qua* experiencing subject on the one side, and one's experience on the other. But this cut can under no circumstances be a cut between oneself and an independently existing world of objective objects. Our "knowlege," whatever rational meaning we give that term, must begin with experience, and with cuts *within* our experience—such as, for instance, the cut we make between the part of our experience that we come to call "ourself" and all the rest of our experience, which we then call our "world." Hence, this world of ours, no matter how we structure it, no matter how well we manage to keep it stable with permanent objects and recurrent interactions, is by definition a world codependent with our experience, and not the ontological reality of which philosophers and scientists alike have dreamed.[73]

As the left side of the imbricated complementarity

CONSTRUCTED EXPERIENCE /
((KNOWER/KNOWN) / (knower/known))

the notion of CONSTRUCTED EXPERIENCE accounts for the connection between the connection and separation of knower and known. The ontological splitting of knower and known—knower/known—is itself an epistemological act. The separation of knower and known is not, in this sense, objectively real, but rather a necessary and helpful distinction drawn within the context of an epistemological connection (i.e., within the context of KNOWER/KNOWN).

Formalized as a philosophical stance, such a constructivist view focuses concern on the implications and ethics of connected knowing, thus bridging the schism separating the equally dichotomous epistemologies of solipsism and naive realism:

KNOWING / ((CONSTRUCTIVISM) / (subjectivism/objectivism))

Ernst von Glasersfeld, a leading proponent of constructivist thinking, explains that

> radical constructivism . . . is radical because it breaks with convention and develops a theory of knowledge in which knowledge does not reflect an "objective" ontological reality, but exclusively an ordering and organization of a world constituted by our experience. The radical constructivist has relinquished "metaphysical realism" once and for all and finds himself in full agreement with Piaget, who says, "Intelligence organizes the world by organizing itself." [74]

Bateson does not limit such intelligence (mind) to the strictly human, and thus he makes what sound to be ontological statements about the knowing of other members of Creatura. He will assert that a tree exists only in quotation marks, but will then also maintain that this quotationed biological form is involved in its *own* knowing, its own constructions: "Do not forget that the 'tree' is alive and therefore itself capable of receiving certain sorts of information. It too may discriminate 'wet' from 'dry.'" [75] And when the tree dies and falls, it becomes part of the knowing of the forest: "Bishop Berkeley always forgot the grass and the squirrels in the woods, for whom the falling tree made a *meaningful* sound" [76]—or, if not a sound, at least a meaningful difference.

If Bateson is right, the tree will not know how to recognize "moisture" per se, but rather the *difference between* moisture and the lack thereof: "All receipt of information is necessarily the receipt of news of *difference,* and all perception of difference is limited by threshold. Differences that are too slight or too slowly presented are not perceivable."[77] Bateson's *difference,* like Spencer-Brown's *distinction,*[78] proposes *relationship* as the fundamental building block of Mind. However, a "building block" metaphor is inappropriate, for it implies the foundation is solid. Such permanence is not possible, given that a difference is not a concrete thing with dimensions in space and time—it is a relationship in mind, and mind, says Bateson, "is empty; it is no-thing. It exists only in its ideas, and these again are no-things."[79]

Ideas (and here we return to the notion of circular process) are, according to Bateson, the transforms of difference traveling in a circuit;[80] the whole of Mind, then, from difference on up, is change upon change upon recursive change:

> Our sensory system—and surely the sensory systems of all other creatures (even plants?) and the mental systems behind the senses (i.e., those parts of the mental systems inside the creatures)—can only operate with *events* which we can call *changes.*[81]

Varela concludes:

> All of this boils down, actually, to a realization that although the world *does* look solid and regular, when we come to examine it there is no fixed point of reference to which it can be pinned down; it is nowhere substantial or solid. The whole of experience reveals the co-dependent and relative quality of all knowledge.[82]

And yet, are these statements about the impossibility of ontology not ontological in form? Is the assertion about there being no fixed point of reference not itself such a point? If it is, then it self-referentially proves itself wrong; and if it isn't, then clearly fixed points of reference *are* possible and again it is wrong. Such paradoxes are comfortably familiar to Taoists, who welcome them into the fabric of their thought, and we shall be examining some of these shortly. Suffice it to say at this point that such oscillations need never, and can never, be contained. As soon as the knower is figured into his or her knowing, there will be self-reference; in fact, there would be no "self," no conscious mind without it. Consciousness is defined by Bateson and Bateson as "a reflexive aspect of mental process that occurs in some but not all minds, in which the knower is aware of some fraction of his knowledge or the thinker of some fraction of his thought."[83]

The paradox of ontologically denying ontology can be mapped as part of

EXPERIENCE /
((EPISTEMOLOGY/ONTOLOGY)/(epistemology/ontology))

where any definitive statement about the epistemological nature of knowing necessarily becomes an ontological assertion of "the way things really are." A denial of ontology is an assertion of the dichotomous split—(epistemology/ontology)—between the two. But as has been said many times, the act of separating is itself a connection; in making the assertion of the denial, the denied is asserted, and the connection between the two—(EPISTEMOLOGY/ONTOLOGY)—is forged.

This need not be marked as a problem to be eschewed, but can be welcomed as a *koan* to be chewed.[84] If knowing begins in relationship, then ontological statements are always properly contextualized as a part of experience, not apart from it as an ontology, left to its own devices, would insist. Conversely, epistemological statements can never be taken as assertions about some kind of internalized knowing. Experience is relational and knowing is circular—there is no settled place from which to start or for which to head. Varela constructs an orientation we might term "not inside, not outside":[85]

> EXPERIENCE /
>> ((INSIDE/OUTSIDE) / (inside/outside))

Reality is not just constructed at our whim, for that would be to assume that there is a starting point we can choose from: inside first. It also shows that reality cannot be understood as given and that we are to perceive it and pick it up, as a recipient, for that would also be to assume a starting point: outside first. . . .

[This] reveals to us a world where "no-ground," "no-foundation" can become the basis of understanding.[86]

The pattern EXPERIENCE / (EPISTEMOLOGY/ontology) also surfaces in Bateson's work in a slightly altered form—EPISTEMOLOGY / (EPISTEMOLOGY/ontology)—as an attempt to describe relationally, at many different levels, the knowing, the epistemology, of Creatura. That is, he begins with an ontological assertion that all minds have their own local epistemologies, their own ways of participating in the patterning of differences (as in the knowing of trees and grass). But he then goes on to assume that these patterns are subsumed in a pattern which connects them in an inclusive epistemology of Mind.[87] This whole/part stacking of knowing gives form to a layered version of the McCulloch question: What is Mind that a mind may know it, and a mind that it may know Mind?

Or can Mind be known? Can the part know the whole? Spencer-Brown characterizes the situation this way:

> We cannot escape the fact that the world we know is constructed in order (and thus in such a way as to be able) to see itself. . . .

This indeed is amazing. . . .

But *in order* to do so, evidently it must first cut itself up into at least one state which sees, and at least one other state which is seen. In this severed and mutilated condition, whatever it sees is *only partially* itself. We may take it that the world undoubtedly is itself (i.e., is indistinct from itself), but, in any attempt to see itself as an object, it must, equally undoubtedly, act so as to make itself distinct from, and therefore false to, itself. In this condition it will always partially elude itself.[88]

Our double question must thus become: What is the knowing of mind that it cannot know the knowing of Mind, and the knowing of Mind that it cannot be known by the knowing of mind? Bateson sheds further light:

If, as we must believe, the total mind is an integrated network (of propositions, images, processes, neural pathology, or what have you—according to what scientific language you prefer to use), and if the content of consciousness is only a sampling of different parts and localities in this network; then, inevitably, the conscious view of the network as a whole is a monstrous denial of the *integration* of that whole. From the cutting of consciousness, what appears above the surface is *arcs* of circuits instead of either the complete circuits or the larger complete circuits of circuits.[89]

We are, in part, constrained by language with its cursed pleromatic touch. How can one characterize the relational Mind of Creatura when everything language touches is turned into a "thing"? Bateson and Bateson lament:

If it is true that there are *things* in Pleroma, then nouns (which are not things) are a useful invention for thinking about things —but with nouns we have invented the capacity for false reification. There are no things in Creatura—only ideas, images, clusters of abstract relations—but the vast convenience of talking about things leads us to treat any available idea—truth, God, charisma—as if it were thing-like.[90]

This peculiarity of language is not newly recognized; 2,500 years ago Lao Tzu introduced the *Tao Te Ching* with this *caveat orator* (let the speaker beware!):

道 可 道 非 常 道

The Tao that can be told of is not the eternal Tao.[91]

It seems there are places where language, perception, and knowing cannot, and perhaps should not, reach if wholeness is to be protected. Bateson clarifies the constraints: "There is always, of course, violence to the whole system if you think about the parts separately; but we're going to do that if we want to think at all, because it's too difficult to think about everything at once."[92] Confronted with such impossibility, the challenge is to construct an imaginative and playful response. Lao Tzu is a wonderful exemplar in this regard.

TAO / (KNOWING/not-knowing)

Emptiness constantly falls within our reach; it is always with us and in us, and conditions all our knowledge, all our deeds, and is our life itself. It is only when we attempt to pick it up and hold it forth as something before our eyes that it eludes us, frustrates all our efforts, and vanishes like vapour.

—D. T. Suzuki

After telling us that "the Tao that can be told of is not the eternal Tao," Lao Tzu continues with a parallel phrase, again comprised of six characters. Wing-Tsit Chan's translation reads:

名 可 名 非 常 名

The name that can be named is not the eternal name.[93]

Once caught in language Tao is bound, and its identity is predicated on its being distinct from that which it is not—against which it can stand in relief. However, there is nothing that is not Tao; because it is already complete, there is no necessity for an other-than-Tao to complement it. Tao is not an "it," but an inclusive unity, a process that encompasses its own absence. Thus, for Tao to remain integral, to not be cleft by the distinctions and differences of thought and perception, it must remain unnamed 無 名,[94] as well as unseen 不 見, unheard 不 聞, and ungrasped 不 得.[95]

Uncaptured in language, Tao remains unknown: As was explained earlier, this is not a separation of transcendence, but of necessity. As Bateson recognizes, "Those distinctions that remain undrawn are *not*."[96] By not being distinguished, by remaining *not,* the Tao stays whole. Rather than being split in two—a Tao and an other-than-Tao—it embraces its otherness by not being differentiated from it in the first place.

Or is that true? Can Tao *not* not be whole? Deny it or not, Tao *is* named—it is Tao. Can it then not fail to not be whole? Is it possible to snatch the name away after the fact—that is, can a distinction, once drawn, be undrawn?[97] But without naming it in the first place there could be no Tao to not name. At issue are the threats to the holiness and health of wholeness[98] when confronted in language by a knowing that is partial and partialing. Like plucking a budding flower to understand the beauty of its developing form and contextual fit, subjecting the Tao to scrutiny can isolate and kill it. "It is very difficult," Bateson remarks,

> to talk about those living systems that are healthy and doing well; it's much easier to talk about living matters when they are sick, when they're disturbed, when things are going wrong. Pathology is a relatively easy thing to discuss, health is very difficult. This, of course, is one of the reasons why there is such a thing as the sacred, and why the sacred is difficult to talk about, because the sacred is peculiarly related to the healthy. One does not like to disturb the sacred, for in general, to talk about something changes it, and perhaps will turn it into a pathology.[99]

If language falters when approaching the sacred ground of wholeness, how can the *Tao Te Ching* fail to fail at speaking the unspeakable, fail to pathologize the Tao? How do we reconcile Lao Tzu's five-thousand-word exposition on something that should not—indeed cannot—be exposed? The ninth-century Tang poet P'o Chü-i clearly had this in mind when he teased:

> Those who speak do not know
> Those who know do not speak—
> So says Lao Tzu
> If Lao Tzu is a knower
> Why did he write 5000 words?[100]

Why indeed. Would it not have been more Taoist to not have written a word? After all:

> Good walking leaves no track behind it;
> Good speech leaves no mark to be picked at.[101]

But Lao Tzu is advocating something different here than not walking or not speaking in the first place. Rather, he suggests the possibility of not getting imprisoned in the distinctions we must inevitably draw. Bateson reminds us that "of necessity we shall split our descriptions when we talk about the universe. But there may be better and worse ways of doing this splitting of the universe into nameable parts."[102] And there may be better and worse ways of gathering the parts into forms of expression; perhaps there are ways of adapting the limitations of language as resources for saying what can't be said.

Despite inevitable whole/part separations, Bateson does locate opportunities for resonance between the Mind of Creatura and the expression of mind in language, and this opens the possibility for shaping our descriptions to accord with the patterned ways in which Creatura describes itself to itself. The bridge lies in those aspects of language and thought that themselves are fundamentally relational—metaphor and story. Metaphor is not simply a literary form; it "runs right through Creatura"[103] and is thus "right at the bottom of being alive."[104]

The biological world, organized relationally, is metaphorically composed: the petals and sepals of a flower are metaphors of leaves; the elephant's trunk is a metaphor of the human nose; the wombat, a marsupial, is a metaphor of the mammalian woodchuck; and so on. The metaphor of metaphor is a way of addressing the connected separation of biological forms, the pattern of their corresponding distinctiveness. Octavio Paz explains how metaphor maintains the integrity of "not one, not two":

> Analogy is the science of correspondences. It is, however, a science which exists only by virtue of differences. Precisely because this is not that, it is possible to extend a bridge between this and that. The bridge is the word like, or the word is: this is like that, this is that. The bridge does not do away with distance: it is an intermediary; neither does it eliminate differences: it establishes a relation between different terms. . . . Analogy says that everything is the metaphor of something else.[105]

Bateson defines *story* as "an aggregate of formal relations scattered in time to make a sequence having a certain
sort of minuet formal dance to it."[106] In the connections between characters, in the development of plot and the time of
its telling, it weaves a pattern. Story and thought are one and
the same.

> [This] is in fact how people think, and it is . . . the only way in
> which they could think. There are no other ways of dealing
> with this problem of relations in a succinct form in which all
> the relations you want to think about sort of simultaneously
> can get into the picture together or get into the picture piled on
> top of each other so they pull on each other the right way. This
> is the function of stories. . . . What is true is the relations
> within the story.[107]

William Carlos Williams adds a layer of self-referential grace
to the expression of this relational view by gathering mind
and poem together in a poem mindful of itself.[108]

> Be patient that I address you in a poem,
>   there is no other
>   fit medium.
> The mind
>   lives there. It is uncertain,
>   can trick us and leave us
> agonized. But for resources
>   what can equal it?
>   There is nothing. We
> should be lost
>   without its wings to
>   fly off upon.
> . . . .
>   A new world
>   is only a new mind.
>   And the mind and the poem
> are all apiece.[109]

The story, as Bateson tells it, is not unique to human thought, but rather joins our mind with the Mind of Creatura:

> The fact of thinking in terms of stories does not isolate human beings as something separate from the starfish and the sea anemones, the coconut palms and the primroses. Rather, if the world be connected, if I am at all fundamentally right in what I am saying, then *thinking in terms of stories* must be shared by all mind or minds, whether ours or those of redwood forests and sea anemones.[110]

This opens the possibility of modeling our storied descriptions on the organization of the living stories described: "A scientist describing an earthworm might start at the head end and work down its length—thus producing a description iconic in its sequence and elongation."[111] In the same spirit, Bateson praises the poet (and botanist) Goethe[112] for straightening out

> the gross comparative anatomy of flowering plants. He discovered that a "leaf" is not satisfactorily defined as "a flat green thing" or a "stem" as "a cylindrical thing." The way to go about the definition—and undoubtedly somewhere deep in the growth processes of the plant, this is how the matter is handled—is to note that buds (i.e., baby stems) form in the angles of leaves. From that, the botanist constructs the definitions on the basis of the relations between stem, leaf, bud, angle, and so on.
> "*A stem is that which bears leaves.*"
> "*A leaf is that which has a bud in its angle.*"
> "*A stem is what was once a bud in that position.*"[113]

Thus, the biologist's descriptions have the potential for some sort of valid "fit," in that they

> may follow the classification of parts and relations which the DNA and/or other biological systems of control themselves

use. . . . In any case, [the biologist] has the possibility of being right in a sense the physicist can never achieve.[114]

We see here the ontological edge of Bateson's epistemological knife, and why he would consider himself "almost a positivist."[115] If this be positivism, it is at least of a biological variety, and, informed by the metaphorical notion that mind is synecdochical of Mind, it pays heed to the gaps. Knowing subjected to knowing will never be represented and never be whole; the most that can be achieved is a moiré pattern reflective of the encounter and an appreciation for what must be left unspoken. William Carlos Williams:

How shall we get said what must be said?

Only the poem.
. . . .
                    Only the poem
only the made poem, to get said what must
be said, not to copy nature, sticks
in our throats .[116]

Were Bateson working purely within a positivist tradition, he would view such gaps in knowledge and description—what sticks in the throat—as temporary potholes to be filled in and paved over as soon as possible. This is clearly not the case. He, like the Taoists, recognizes that one who approaches Mind or Tao in this way—rushing after it, striving diligently forward and attempting to learn more and more—will inevitably come up empty-handed. An empty hand is, however, a fine place to start. Lao Tzu advises:

fussing spoils
grasping loses
The Sage doesn't fuss—thus doesn't spoil
            doesn't grasp—thus doesn't lose[117]

Since Tao is empty 虛,[118] there is nothing to grasp; and like an empty bowl 用, it can never 不 be brimmed 盈:[119]

> Practicing learning: daily accumulating
> Practicing Tao: daily diminishing[120]

Poets and Taoists alike honor what sticks in the throat, what can't be said: "There are many matters and many circumstances in which *consciousness* is undesirable and silence is golden," Bateson and Bateson advise, "so that secrecy can be used as a *marker* to tell us that we are approaching holy ground."[121] Words fill; in silence the emptiness of Tao remains pristine. The Zen poet Ryota whispers:

> They spoke no word.
> The visitor, the host
> And the white chrysanthemum.[122]

But for silence to be silence, sound must be in the air. Each is a request for the other, as John Cage so eloquently says (and, in the gaps, doesn't-say) in his "Lecture on Nothing":[123]

I am here   ,   and there is nothing to say   .

                                                                If among you are
those who wish to get somewhere   ,   let them leave at
any moment   .   What we re-quire   is
silence   ;   but what silence requires
            is   that I go on talking .
[. . . . .]

                                                                            But
now   there are silences   and the
words   make   help make   the
silences   .

                                                I have nothing to say
            and I am saying it   and that is
poetry   as I need it   .

There is no getting away from the schisms of language, perception, and knowing. And, in fact, no need to. The point is to not get caught inside the distinctions we create, and that won't happen as long as our separations are connected and our connections can be separated: There is always a way out. Of course the way *out* will always simultaneously be a way *inside* another boundary. Freedom from limitation is not an escape from distinctions—that would only be death—but a playful movement between, a continual oscillation between, connection and separation. If Taoism were only connection it would not exist; as Varela attests, there must be whole *and* parts:

> There is a strong current in contemporary culture advocating autonomy, information (symbolic descriptions), and holism as some sort of cure-all and as a radically "new" dimension. This is often seen in discussions about environmental phenomena, human health, and management. . . . We take a rather different view. We simply see autonomy and control, causal and symbolic explanations, reductionism and holism as complementary or "cognitively adjoint" for the understanding of those systems in which we are interested. They are intertwined in any satisfactory description; each entails some loss relative to our cognitive preferences, as well as some gain.[124]

Cage's talking about nothing is a way of not-talking about the something of emptiness; much gets said in the spaces between. Let us take another look at the first line of the *Tao Te Ching*, at how Lao Tzu uses a poetic sensibility to not-say what needs saying; he employs what we might call a strategy of con-volution. Chan's rendition of the line—"The Tao that can be told of is not the eternal Tao"[125]—does not make clear the threefold repetition of the word *Tao* in the original Chinese. Word for word it reads:

Tao   able to Tao   not   forever[126] Tao

The second *Tao* can be partially retained in translation by embedding it within a pun: "Tao endowed is not forever Tao."[127] The Tao that is able to be endowed with attributes is not the Tao of pure ongoing process. And yet the word *forever,* used to describe the nature of the "real" Tao, functions in the sentence as an adjective—it is an attribute. Thus the sentence affirms and denies itself in continual oscillation. The Möbius pattern can be depicted as:

TAO /

    ((FOREVER TAO / ENDOWED TAO) /

      (endowed Tao / forever Tao))

The denial of the connection (i.e., the separation) between the endowed Tao and the forever Tao—"Endowed Tao not forever Tao"—is depicted by the enclosed distinction on the far right—(endowed Tao / forever Tao). The denial of the denial (i.e., the connection)—that the forever Tao is *not* not endowed—is shown by the distinction (FOREVER TAO / ENDOWED TAO). The Tao reflexively completes these two terms.

It is this, the oscillation, that speaks to both the presence and absence of the Tao in a way in which the words written as technical prose—that is, where all attention is directed toward describing the presence of what is, without the necessary self-consciousness to not-say what is not—could not. The endless turning generated by the internal paradox of the sentence is analogous to the recursive, empty process of the Tao.

The separations between the thought and the unthinkable reflect the necessary disjunction between whole and part, and a respect for not-knowing is a respect for the integrity of what Wendell Berry calls *mystery:*

> To call the unknown by its right name, "mystery," is to suggest that we had better respect the possibility of a larger, unseen pattern that can be damaged or destroyed and, with it, the smaller patterns. . . .
>
> If we are up against mystery, then we dare act only on the most modest assumptions. The modern scientific program has held that we must act on the basis of knowledge, which, because its effects are so manifestly large, we have assumed to be ample. But if we are up against mystery, then knowledge is relatively small, and the ancient program is the right one: Act on the basis of ignorance. Acting on the basis of ignorance, paradoxically, requires one to know things, remember things—for instance, that failure is possible, that error is possible, that second chances are desirable.[128]

As a variation of the imbricated complementarity COMPLETION / (CONNECTION/separation), Berry's position can be presented as MYSTERY / (RESPECT/ignorance), where the connection between respect (a sign of connection to the whole) and ignorance (a recognition of necessary separation from the whole) becomes a guide for action.

The informative loop between the limits of knowing and the ethics of acting is also found in constructivist circles, where Heinz von Foerster's "aesthetical imperative" rings forth: "If you desire to see, learn how to act."[129] Taoists would not disagree, but would complete the idea by proposing the inverse and reverse. While Berry would have us found our action in not-knowing, Lao Tzu would have us find our knowing in not-acting. Such is the notion of *wu wei,* to which we now turn.

WEI WU WEI / (KNOWING/not-acting)

The term *wu wei* 無 爲, one of the most pivotal in Taoist thought, has commonly been translated in English as "non-action." This is unfortunate, for it can be misinterpreted to mean "not doing anything at all." Richard Wilhelm explains that *wu wei* "is not quietism in our sense, but is the readiness to act the part in the phenomenal world assigned to man by time and his surroundings."[130] In other words, *wu wei* has to do with acting in accord with context.

Wu 無 means "no," a negation which originally meant "to vanish."[131] It conveys the sense of emptiness, immanence, and boundlessness, and is thus closely associated with the Tao. Ezra Pound, a poet known more, perhaps, for his uncanny intuitive grasp of Chinese pictograms than for his exhaustive scholarship, and more for luminescent than definitive renderings of Chinese poetry, made the following speculations about the character *wu* 無: "*Not Possessing.* Morrison [editor of a seven-volume Chinese-English dictionary] says: 'Etymology not clear.' It is certainly fire [⺀⺀⺀] under what looks like a fence [無], but primitive sign does not look like fire but like *bird*. At a wild guess I should say primitive sign looks like 'birdie has flown' (off with the branch). F[enollosa] gives it as 'lost in a forest.'"[132]

Wei 爲 means "activity," but it has a double meaning, captured in part by the word "act." *To act* can simply mean "to do," or it can imply a certain artificiality or forced quality. Combining *wu* and *wei* in the phrase *wu wei*, we have the beginnings of a translation: "not acting." Benjamin Hoff achieves an ingenious rendering of *wu wei* by incorporating the pictoral etymology of *wei* in the following manner:

Practically speaking, [*Wu Wei*] means without meddlesome, combative, or egotistical effort. It seems rather significant that the character *Wei* developed from the symbols for a clawing hand and a monkey, since the term *Wu Wei* means not going against the nature of things; no clever tampering; no Monkeying Around.[133]

Hoff's translation—"no monkeying around"—works well for *wu wei*, but it fails to live up to the demands of *wei wu wei* 為 無 為 (found, for example, at the beginning of chapter 63 of the *Tao Te Ching*), where the first *wei* carries no negative connotations; "monkeying without monkeying around" does not do justice to the original. John Wu comes closer to conveying the doubleness of *wei* by rendering it as both "do" and "ado" as the occasion requires; *wu wei* becomes "no ado," and the phrase *wei wu wei*, meaning "to act without acting" or "to act without straining," then becomes "doing without ado."[134] In English, our spiral moiré thus reads: DO WITHOUT ADO / (KNOWING / no ado).

There is yet another way of getting the gist of it. John Cage's layering of sound and silence in his "Lecture on Nothing" and Lao Tzu's use of paradox in the first line of the *Tao Te Ching* were earlier described as means of not-saying what needed saying. Different from *not saying*, which, like *nonaction*, suggests only the indifferent absence of something, *not-saying* is an *involved or absorbed absence*, a *necessary gap*. It speaks of the connected absence of the Tao and reflects the complementarity of respect and ignorance mentioned earlier by Berry. Likewise, the "no ado" of *wu wei* can be thought of as not-acting, an action responsive to the demands of the context. As *active emptiness*, *wu wei* is relationally fitting; it accords with the encompassing (and empty) pattern of the whole.

Two lines in the thirty-seventh chapter of the *Tao Te*

Ching concern themselves with the connection between Tao and *wu wei*. But in order to tease out an understanding of Tao's *not-acting* we must ease in again to the con-volutions of Lao Tzu's *not-saying*. Wu translates the passage as:

Tao never makes any ado,
And yet it does everything.[135]

Missing from the English version are the two negations in the second sentence: *wu* 無 and *pu* 不. The translator presumably decided that they canceled each other out and chose to render the phrase positively: "And yet it does everything." But saying something with a double negative is much different from just stating it in the affirmative.

Hypnotists have long known that to make sense of a simple negation one has to first represent whatever is negated. Because "negation exists only in language and not in experience,"[136] a person cannot experience the suggestions "don't get too comfortable" or "I wouldn't ask you to relax" without imagining the feelings of comfort and relaxation. The hypnotist makes use of this phenomenon to facilitate trance induction.

If a simple negation sends us to its opposite in order to make sense of it, then a double negation sends us in a circle, to both poles of what is being said and not said. Like the reciprocal definition of yin and yang, a double negation involves an assertion and its counter in a mutual proposing that never resolves to one side of the distinction. Lao Tzu's use of negation, like his use of paradox, is a strategy of con-volution for talking in the gaps, for not-talking about the recursiveness of Tao. Something of the spirit in the Chinese can be retained by modifying Wu's second line in the following way:

> Tao never makes any ado,
> But is never not doing.

However, the original's crisp flow, parallel structure, and not-saying can be more fully appreciated if both lines are re-translated as:

Tao forever not-acts
But never not acts

As was mentioned earlier, the not-acting of *wu wei* is a means of participatory knowing. This stands in stark contrast to the traditional scientific orientation wherein the knower stands apart and researches by means of duress. Morris Berman characterizes this legacy of the Scientific Revolution: "Knowledge of nature comes about under artificial conditions. Vex nature, disturb it, alter it, anything—but do not leave it alone. Then, and only then, will you know it." [137] For a Taoist, knowledge is a question of fit—it comes about not by manipulating nature, but by attuning 正 to it, by adapting 柔 to its course. The famous Taoist philosopher Chuang Tzu (circa 300 B.C.E.) aptly illustrates the point in a fictional story about Confucius and a man who has mastered the art of *wu wei*:

> Confucius was seeing the sights at Lü-liang, where the water falls from a height of thirty fathoms and races and boils along

for forty li, so swift that no fish or other water creature can swim in it. He saw a man dive into the water and, supposing that the man was in some kind of trouble and intended to end his life, he ordered his disciples to line up on the bank and pull the man out. But after the man had gone a couple of hundred paces, he came out of the water and began strolling along the base of the embankment, his hair streaming down, singing a song. Confucius ran after him and said, "At first I thought you were a ghost, but now I see you're a man. May I ask if you have some special way of staying afloat in the water?"

"I have no way. I began with what I was used to, grew up with my nature, and let things come to completion with fate. I go under with the swirls and come out with the eddies, following along the way the water goes and never thinking about myself. That's how I can stay afloat." [138]

Wu wei is knowing via *immersement*. Like the action of an artist who soaks into his or her work, it is undertaken for its own sake, rather than for some removed purpose. Gary Snyder relates the story of one of Basho's disciples,

who took down something Basho once said to a group of students. He said, "To learn about the pine, go to the pine. To learn about the bamboo, go to the bamboo. But this *learn* is not just what you think learn is. You only learn by becoming totally absorbed in that which you wish to learn. There are many people who think that they have learned something and willfully construct a poem which is artifice and does not flow from their delicate entrance into the life of another object." [139]

This full involvement is not, however, an expression of connection alone. In contrast to the "ex-orbitance" of purposeful attainment (which hangs onto only one side of a distinction), the emptiness of *wei wu wei* strikes a fundamental balance between the connection of knowing *and* the separation of not-acting—WEI WU WEI / (IMMERSED KNOWING / not-acting)—as this passage from the *I Ching* conveys:

> "ex-orbitant" speaks of:
> knowing when to step forward but not backward
> accepting life but not death
> knowing when to grasp but not to let go
> only sages know when to step forward and backward
> how to accept life and death
> do not slip from attunement
> only sages [140]

In recursively joining both sides of the connection/separation distinction, both sides of life and death, *wu wei* is not-one-not-two action, a *knowing (no-ing) act of completion* and a *complete act of knowing (no-ing)*.

The *circularity* of completion is of especial importance in Taoist thought and warrants a section devoted to its elucidation. The discussion will begin with an investigation of the root meanings of four Chinese characters that appear at the beginning and throughout the *I Ching*. The final, fourth, word of the series is particularly puzzling—its meaning in this context has stumped commentators of the book for centuries. The interpretation developed here hinges on a piece of abductive reasoning: a critical clue is sought, and found, in the work of Bateson.[141] The resulting understanding provides the necessary groundwork for completing the chapter—with a discussion of the mind of knowing, the Mind of Nature, and the nature of wisdom.

COMPLETION / (LIFE/death)

Within the circles of our lives
we dance the circles of the years,

the circles of the seasons
within the circles of the years,
the cycles of the moon
within the circles of the seasons,
the circles of our reasons
within the cycles of the moon.

—*Wendell Berry*

If our explanations or our understanding of the universe is in some sense to match that universe, or model it, and if the universe is recursive, then our explanations and our logics must also be fundamentally recursive.

—*Gregory Bateson*

There are four words in the *I Ching*—*yüan*, *heng*, *li*, and *chen*—that together compose what Iulian Shchutskii calls a "mantic formulae."[142] They occur frequently in different combinations throughout the book, but first appear at the very beginning, immediately following the title of the first chapter, "*Ch'ien*."

乾　Ch'ien

元　yüan

亨　heng

利　li

貞　chen

Shchutskii believes that these mantic terms belong to the oldest strata of the book, "remnants of a much earlier system of divination,"[143] but that their original meanings have been lost. Because of the ambiguous nature of ancient Chinese, there is no way of determining exactly how the phrase should be punctuated, and thus interpreted. It can be read as a single sentence: *Ch'ien yüan heng li chen.* Or, alternatively, it can be understood as a kind of list—*Ch'ien: yüan, heng, li, chen*—where the latter four words, each relatively independent, explicate the meaning of the first.

Richard Wilhelm, choosing the first alternative, translates the phrase as:

> THE CREATIVE works sublime success,
> Furthering through perseverance.[144]

Shchutskii finds it "difficult to agree with such an interpretation since a construction so highly developed in grammatical relations would hardly be possible in such an archaic text."[145] It also produces a sentence so abstract that it is virtually meaningless. The alternative—treating the terms as different dimensions or aspects of *Ch'ien*—is more in keeping with the paratactic structure of ancient Chinese, and it correctly confers equal importance on all four words.[146] By looking closely at the etymologies of *Ch'ien* and the other four characters, it is possible to recover something of their original meanings and to suggest an interpretation of the phrase as a whole.

Wilhelm's translation of *Ch'ien* 乾 as "The Creative" is accurate, but incomplete. The archaic form of the character 乾 depicts the sun 日 (heat, light, creativity) between the roots 丂 and branches 屮 of a plant (the beginning and end of growth). The symbol on the right 乙 is an abbreviated form of *ch'i* 氣, or "life-breath." The translation "Enflaming[147] Inspiration" suggests the combination of the elemental light of the sun and the breath-like nature of *ch'i* (*inspiration* is from the Latin *in* and *spirare*—"to breathe in"); it speaks of the complete life process, from beginning (roots) to end (branches).

The top stroke — of *yüan* 元 means "one" or "first" and

thus suggests the notion of inception or beginning. The lower portion of the character 兀 probably depicts the foundation from which the "originating" begins. The second word of the four, *heng* 亨, speaks of unobstructed process and development: a smooth flow 了 issues from an opening 口: it "flows freely." *Li* 利 is a picture of the fruit / of mature crops 禾 being harvested with a cutting implement 刂. It thus refers to a ripeness of a situation, a time when one's effort "bears fruit."

Chen 貞, the last of the four mantic terms, is very curious: It literally means to divine ⼘ with a tortoise shell 貝, a practice dating to the Shang dynasty (1766–1122 B.C.E.). Having been asked a question of import, a diviner would heat a tortoise shell over a fire until it cracked and then interpret the resultant random scattering of lines. However, within the context of "Enflaming Inspiration" and the other three characters, it is clear that *chen* is not being used in its literal sense (i.e., as "to divine"):

Enflaming Inspiration
  originates
  flows freely
  bears fruit
  chen

The sequence "originates/ flows freely/ bears fruit" appears to describe the phases of a life process, from the beginning, through development, and on to maturation. What then is the fourth phase of "Enflaming Inspiration," and how does divination fit into this cycle? Looking beyond the perimeters of Taoism, we find an important hint in Bateson:

Ross Ashby long ago pointed out that no system (neither computer nor organism) can produce anything *new* unless the system contains some source of the random. In the computer, this will be a random-number generator which will ensure that the

"seeking," trial-and-error moves of the machine will ultimately cover all the possibilities of the set to be explored.

In other words, all innovative, *creative* systems are . . .
divergent.[148]

The essential element in divination is its *unpredictability*,
its incorporation of the *random* in the formulation of answers. The diviner has no control over the way in which the
tortoise shell will crack. And it is to this notion of *divergence*
that *chen,* in this context, most probably refers. In order for
the creative cycle of Enflaming Inspiration to return to an
original beginning, there must be a period of dis-integration,
a time following maturation where seeds scatter and organic
matter breaks down and returns to the soil. As Bateson puts
it, "The ongoing processes of change *feed on the random.*"[149]
And again:

> For the creation of new order, the workings of the random, the
> plethora of uncommitted alternatives (entropy) is necessary. It
> is out of the random that organisms collect new mutations,
> and it is there that stochastic learning gathers its solutions.
> Evolution leads to climax: ecological saturation of all the pos-
> sibilities of differentiation. Learning leads to the overpacked
> mind. By return to the unlearned and mass-produced egg, the
> ongoing species again and again clears its memory banks to be
> ready for the new.[150]

The sequence is now complete:

元　originates

亨　flows freely

利　bears fruit

貞　diversifies

The scattering denoted by "diversifies" is the unravelling of pattern, the separation of death that brings life to completion and makes it possible for it to begin again. In Chuang Tzu's words:

> Life is the companion of death, death is the beginning of life. Who understands their workings? Man's life is a coming-together of breath. If it comes together, there is life; if it scatters, there is death. And if life and death are companions to each other, then what is there for us to be anxious about? [151]

When the cyclic process of renewal elaborated by the four terms *yüan, heng, li,* and *chen* is laconically expressed as the imbricated moiré COMPLETION / (LIFE/death), a correspondence can be marked between this pattern of living process and the pattern of mind delineated in the complementarity COMPLETION / (CONNECTION/separation). There is resonance between the organization of knowing and the organization of the living—each is metaphoric of the other. Just as the wholeness of knowing is a process of completing the connections and separations of drawn distinctions, so the wholeness of an ecosystem is a process of completing the connections and separations of life and death. The mind of knowing must sever in order to connect; the Mind of Nature must sever in order to live: Nature knows itself (i.e., recursively sets the limits of its organization, defines the thresholds of its structure) by drawing distinctions with the knife of death. [152] And just as the mind of knowing is threatened if unconnected separations hold sway, so too, as Bateson articulates below, the survival of the Mind of Nature rests entirely on its continued success at *encompassing* death.

> Nature avoids (temporarily) what looks like irreversible change by accepting ephemeral change. "The bamboo bends before the wind," in Japanese metaphor; and death itself is avoided

by a quick change from individual subject to class. Nature, to personify the system, allows old man Death (also personified) to have his individual victims while she substitutes that more abstract entity, the class of taxon, to kill which Death must work faster than the reproductive systems of the creatures. Finally, if Death should have his victory over the species, Nature will say, "Just what I needed for my ecosystem." [153]

Left to its own devices, an ecosystem evolves in the direction of complexity, weaving life and death in a regenerative balance known as *climax*. Gary Snyder describes it this way:

This condition, called "climax," is an optimum condition of diversity—optimum stability. When a system reaches climax, it levels out for centuries or millennia. By virtue of its diversity it has the capacity to absorb all sorts of impacts. Insects, fungi, weather conditions come and go; it's the opposite of monoculture. . . . Another aspect of a climax situation is that almost half of the energy that flows in the system does not come from annual growth, it comes from the recycling of dead growth. . . . This is also what is called "maturity." By some oddity in the language it's also what we call a virgin forest, although it's actually very experienced, wise, and mature. [154]

The Mind of Nature is wise and healthy when its cycles are complete, when it enfolds death as a part of the ongoing renewal and complexity of its wholeness. There are no monotone or transitive "values" in biology, says Bateson, nothing of which there can always be more. Death is the calibration that establishes the thresholds and thus regulates the living balance of the whole:

Desired substances, things, patterns, or sequences of experience that are in some sense "good" for the organism—items of diet, conditions of life, temperature, entertainment, sex, and so forth—are never such that more of the something is always better than less of the something. Rather, for all objects and experiences, there is a quantity that has optimum value. Above that quantity, the variable becomes toxic. To fall below that value is to be deprived.[155]

There can even be too much "life." Cancer cells don't know when to die and thus they undermine the balance of the system of which they are a part. In trespassing beyond the thresholds of the organism, they trigger its death.

The mind of knowing, in turn, is wise—that is, in Bateson's terms, it has "a sense or recognition of the fact of circuity"[156]—and healthy (i.e., whole) when dichotomous distinctions are joined and actions are complete:

Half then whole
Bent then straight
Hollow then full
Worn then new
Little then gains
Plenty then perplexed[157]

Commenting on the last two lines of this passage from the *Tao Te Ching*, Wang Pi (226–249 C.E.) highlights the problem of not attending to cyclic balance:

The Tao of *Tzu-jan* [i.e., being true to one's nature] is like a tree. The more it grows (to have plenty), the more distant it is from the roots; the less it grows (to have little), the less distant it is from the roots. If one always increases, then one becomes removed from the true essence.[158]

Wu wei is the not-acting of this circuitous knowing. The wisdom is reflected in knowing *how* to complete and knowing *when* the completion has been reached. Wendell Berry tells the story of a barber he once knew who refused to give a discount to a bald client, explaining that his artistry consisted, not in the cutting off, but in the knowing when to stop. He spoke, I think, as a true artist and a true human. The lack of such knowledge is extremely dangerous in and to an individual. But ignorance of when to stop is a modern epidemic; it is the basis of "industrial progress" and "economic growth."[159]

Despite its cyclic timing—knowing when to stop and when to begin—the complete knowing of *wu wei*, however participatory, is necessarily a not-knowing of completion. This ensures a certain humility and respect in encountering the wholes of which one is a part. Lao Tzu warns:

> The world is a sacred vessel, which must not be tampered
> with or grabbed after.
> To tamper with it is to spoil it, and to grasp it is to lose it.[160]

The ideas set forth in this chapter, unpacked from the spiral complementarity COMPLETION / (CONNECTION/separation), have made many connections and left much not-said. The moirés—and the moirés of moirés—that have emerged will, in the next chapter, be used as guides for contextually patterning the shortcut intentionality of conscious mind and the problems that swirl in its wake.

3 | CONTRACTION
[SEPARATION \
connection]

Take heed of hating me,
Or too much triumph in the victory;
Not that I shall be mine own officer,
And hate with hate again retaliate;
But thou wilt lose the style of conqueror,
If I thy conquest, perish by thy hate.
Then, lest my being nothing lessen thee,
If thou hate me, take heed of hating me.
—John Donne

Unaided consciousness must always tend toward hate; not only because it is good common sense to exterminate the other fellow, but for the more profound reason that, seeing only arcs of circuits, the individual is continually surprised and necessarily angered when his hardheaded policies return to plague the inventor.
—Gregory Bateson

Any organism that destroys what it takes to be its other, not recognizing itself in that other, lays a firm foundation for self-destruction.
—Edward E. Sampson

Desire is the presence of an *absence*.
—Alexandre Kojeve

A person who thinks of a boomerang as just a slab wood will be puzzled when attempts to throw it away continually fail. Similarly, a person who thinks of hate as pure *repulsion* (from the Latin *re-*, "back," and *pellere*, "to drive") will be repeatedly perplexed at how *compelling* (from the Latin *com-*, "together," and *pellere*, "to drive") the object of hate becomes.

The mirror reflection of hate is desire. Whereas the separation of hate effects a connection, the connection of desire is an effect of separation: Once the object of desire is gained the desire of the object is lost.

Common to both hate and desire is the *inversion of wholeness* indicated in the title of this chapter. In contradistinction to the imbricated shape of *health* formalized in the whole/part matrix COMPLETION / (CONNECTION/separation), the model CONTRACTION \ [SEPARATION\connection] defines the inverted, fractionated shape of *defection* (from the Latin *defect-us*, "defect," "want"). The *Oxford English Dictionary* defines *defection* as "the action or fact of . . . falling short."[1] A *defect* has to do with "the fact of being wanting or falling short; lack or absence of something essential to completeness."[2] The pattern of contraction—

CONTRACTION \ [SEPARATION\connection]

—is, in this sense, a *defective* version of

COMPLETION / (CONNECTION/separation)

Contraction falls short of completion. The word *contraction* (from the Latin *con-*, "together" + *trahere*, "to pull, draw") means to draw together, to narrow, limit, or shorten. As when a muscle contracts, such shortening is accompanied by an attendant tightness. Similarly, in the world of grammar, *contraction* refers to a word that has been shortened by the omission of medial letters or sounds. As the contrary of completion, contraction is not simply noncompletion or incompletion; it is used here to connote a tightened, shortened *connection,* a constriction that, in falling short of health, *precludes* completion. As we shall see below, contraction is a short-circuited parody of the long-circuited wholeness of completion.

The order and capitalization of items in COMPLETION / (CONNECTION/separation) denotes the spiral of their whole/part layering. CONNECTION contextualizes separation, and COMPLETION, which connects CONNECTION and separation, contextualizes them both. In the wound-up dichotomy CONTRACTION \ [SEPARATION\connection], *the contextual stacking of connection and separation is inverted,* with the latter now embedding the former. This difference is highlighted by the reversal of the direction of the slashes and the placement of SEPARATION\connection in square brackets.

With completion, connections relax and resolve to dissolution. Separation (the scattering of patterns) follows (and thus precedes) connection in continual recursive process:

元　originates

亨　flows freely

利　bears fruit

貞　diversifies

But contraction is always a "shortcoming," and thus such resolution is never reached—the denial of the *simultaneity* of connection and separation (i.e., treating distinctions only as severance) denies their *succession* and thus precludes their success. This is the pattern of paradox that Bateson terms the *double bind.*[3] The schismatic bond that binds is one that cannot complete—within contraction, separation and connection continually undermine each other: The moment they succeed they fail. *Hate prevents the separation it desires and desire invents the separation it hates.*

Confronted with the short-circuits of symptoms such as hate and desire, family therapists are accustomed to reflecting on their underlying purpose. As interesting as this line of reasoning can be, an even more intriguing proposition emerges if we reverse the logic of the formulation: rather than explore the purpose of symptoms, this chapter considers problems as symptoms of purpose. Intricately lacing the unconnected separations of all contractions is the peculiar ig-norance of conscious knowing.

SHORT-CIRCUIT \
[CONSCIOUS KNOWING \
purpose]

不知 知不 Knowing ignorance: tiptop
知病 知上 Ignorant knowing: defective

—*Lao Tzu*

La peste de l'homme, c'est l'opinion de savoir.
(Mankind's plague is the conceit of knowing.)
—*Michel de Montaigne*

It may well be that consciousness contains systematic distortions of view which, when implemented by modern technology, become destructive of the balances between man, his society, and his ecosystem.
—*Gregory Bateson*

Properly embedded in the total weave of Mind, consciousness functions much as its position in this whole/part pattern of mental process would suggest:

MIND / (UNCONSCIOUS/conscious)

Consciousness, which takes the place of "separation" in the matrix COMPLETION / (CONNECTION/separation), knows by dissecting and analyzing, by *separating*.

Included within and connected to relational knowing (i.e., to "unconscious" or "primary" processes such as dreams, art, and "feelings"),[4] such divisiveness adaptively fits and contributes to the completion of Mind. Indeed, Roy Rappaport believes that purposefulness (which he takes to be a concomitant of consciousness) has undoubtedly contributed substantially to humankind's survival during our three million years' residency on the planet.[5] However, it is perhaps to be expected that conscious knowing—predicated as it is on separation—should tend to self-reflexively split itself off from the balance of Mind, from the body and its social and biological contexts. Bateson discusses how unmediated consciousness necessarily distorts the interactive circularity of mental process. When the sense of participatory knowing is deposed, the non-sense of divisive knowing is imposed.

> If the total mind and the outer world do not, in general, have this lineal structure, then by forcing this structure upon them, we become blind to the cybernetic circularities of the self and the external world. Our conscious sampling of data will not disclose whole circuits but only arcs of circuits, cut off from their matrix by our selective attention.[6]

Unfortunately, any goal-directed (purposeful) action taken within such a context of fissured knowing will necessarily fall short of wisdom. Purpose is rather like a race horse with blinders: chiefly concerned with getting from point A to point B in the most direct way and in the shortest possible time, it suffers the effects of tunnel-vision. Consciousness, says Bateson,

> is organized in terms of purpose. It is a short-cut device to enable you to get quickly at what you want; not to act with maximum wisdom in order to live, but to follow the shortest logical or causal path to get what you next want. . . .
>
> Purposive consciousness pulls out, from the total mind, sequences which do not have the loop structure which is characteristic of the whole systemic structure. If you follow the "common-sense" dictates of consciousness you become, effectively, greedy and unwise.[7]

With single-focused attention riveted on end goals, consciousness grasps for only one side of distinctions, as opposed to clinging to both sides:[8] A desired "good" is isolated and pursued as if it were an independent entity, as if there were no limit to it, no threshold beyond which it stops being good, and no recognition that there is *always* another side to the coin. Such lopsided logic renders consciousness ig-norant of the simple wisdom of Lao Tzu:

物 或 損 之 而 益
或 益 之 而 損

things may gain by losing
　　may lose by gaining[9]

Gary Snyder tells a story of when he was a student of Zen in Japan:

> During the first year or two that I was at Daitoku-ji Sodo . . . I noticed a number of times little improvements that could be made. Ultimately I ventured to suggest to the head monks some labor- and time-saving techniques. They were tolerant of

me for a while. Finally, one day one of them took me aside and said, "We don't want to do things any better or any faster, because that's not the point—the point is that you live the whole life. If we speed up the work in the garden, you'll just have to spend that much more time sitting in the zendo [meditation hall], and your legs will hurt more." It's all one meditation. The importance is in the right balance, and not how to save time in one place or another.[10]

Lao Tzu's recursive logic and the monk's wisdom are echoed in Bateson's descriptions of biological systems as balanced, *multipurposed* circuits.

There is no single variable in the redwood forest of which we can say that the whole system is oriented to maximizing that variable and all other variables are subsidiary to it; and, indeed, the redwood forest works toward optima, not maxima. Its needs are satiable, and too much of anything is toxic.[11]

The poet e. e. cummings weaves it this way:

whatever's merely wilful,
and not miraculous
(be never it so skilful)
must wither fail and cease
—but better than to grow
beauty knows no[12]

The "no" beauty knows is *threshold,* a boundary within a whole, a separation contextualized by the connection of "yes." By saying no to the skillful purpose of the particular, the whole says yes to the miraculous, to the aesthetic balance of the relational pattern which connects:

BEAUTY / (YES/no)

But like Faust, consciousness becomes narcissistically intoxicated by the "beauty" of its own short-term successes.

Losing sight of "no," of what it cannot know, consciousness does not keep its place in Mind in mind. If left uncalibrated, its lineality of focus and action will, in the service of expediency, clear-cut a swath through the delicate complexity of living relationships as it invades and colonizes domains of Mind beyond its ken.

"If a man entertain false opinions regarding his own nature," Bateson cautions, "he will be led thereby to courses of action which will be in some profound sense immoral or ugly." [13] Ugliness knows the "no" of ig-norance and the "yes" of unrestricted growth:

UGLINESS \ [NO\yes]

Such "per-version" of beauty is a short-circuited contraction reflecting the severance (separation) of consciousness from the larger Mind and the attachment (connection) of purpose to singular goals:

SHORT-CIRCUIT \ [CONSCIOUS KNOWING \ purpose]

Bateson provides illustration:

> We will imagine a steady state process going along on the hillside of Ponderosa pines, and the pines are balancing out with the deer and the cactuses and all the rest of the living things there. What are they called? "Sentient beings." Now in come you and I, and of the various variables on that hillside, we decide to maximize one. . . .
>
> Now what happened? What happened was that the human beings identified *a* variable, looked at the immediate predecessors of that variable in the general train, and started with what sophistication they could to maximize these in order to maximize the one they wanted. But they have totally ignored three quarters of the whole circle, you see. . . . [which means they] are going to wreck the balances. [14]

Not knowing its ignorance, consciousness becomes ignorant knowing, and this, as Lao Tzu correctly diagnoses in the quotation at the beginning of this section, is defective.[15] Bateson offers a diagnosis:

> Mere purposive rationality unaided by such phenomena as art, religion, dream, and the like, is necessarily pathogenic and destructive of life; and . . . its virulence springs specifically from the circumstance that life depends upon interlocking *circuits* of contingency, while consciousness can see only such short arcs of such circuits as human purpose may direct.[16]

Even when the discord between Mind and unmediated consciousness is recognized, it is very difficult to do anything that does not simply make matters worse. Solutions that do not escape the dualistic assumptions of conscious knowing will themselves become symptomatic expressions of purpose, hopelessly entangled in the problems they are helplessly trying to eradicate.[17] In fact, it is precisely this attempt to *eradicate problems* that secures the failure of dichotomous solutions and guarantees an exacerbation of the original situation. Solution and problem are mutually defined; it is impossible for one side of a distinction to destroy the other side—*any* oppositional response only highlights the relationship, thus intensifying the problem and reiterating its intractability:

SHORT-CIRCUIT \

[DISJUNCTIVE SOLUTION \ conjunctive problem]

This transform of the analytic matrix CONTRACTION \ [SEPARATION \ connection], where repelling (disjunctive) solutions circle endlessly with compelling (conjunctive) problems, defines a pattern commonly identified as *addiction*.

ADDICTION \

[DISJUNCTIVE SOLUTION \ conjunctive problem]

What then is a shortcut? What is wrong with the proposed shortcuts in evolution and in the resolution of guilt? What is wrong, in principle, with shortcuts?

—*Gregory Bateson*

Mastery as the remedy becomes the poison.

—*Edward Sampson*

Vicious circles are what biology lives on, but you've got to have a world in which that is all the time being held in control.

—*Gregory Bateson*

People who respond to the close presence of bees by flailing their arms and trying to slap them away are not only usually unsuccessful in ridding themselves of the source of their fear, but their actions attract the bees, thus heightening their danger of being stung. All disjunctive solutions—where one tries to quickly destroy or banish or defeat a problem—have something of this flailing-at-bees quality about them, and all conjunctive problems are rather bee-like in character: that is, such problems hover around those who attempt to repel them, and their sting can be painful and dangerous.

The dichotomous definition of a problem as something in need of a quick and complete solution establishes the very context of separation that precludes the possibility of completion. It is in this way that the tight, addictive circles of problem and solution are continually respun:

SHORT-CIRCUIT ADDICTION \
    [DISJUNCTIVE SOLUTION\conjunctive problem]

As will be discussed in the next chapter, completion is only possible within a context of connection, where the relaxed immersement of long-circuit adaptation replaces the frantic drowning of short-circuit addiction:

LONG-CIRCUIT ADAPTATION / (IMMERSEMENT/dispersement)

The short-circuit of addiction is an adaptation of sorts, but one that does not complete. It is, by definition, a vicious circle. In adapting to some item of experience—be it a relationship with a person, object, chemical, behavior, attitude, or belief—addiction provides short-term benefits; but when continued beyond a certain threshold (of time or quantity) it is destructive of more inclusive levels of systemic organization (e.g., physiological, psychological, social, and ecological relationships):

ADDICTION \
    [FISSION OF SYSTEMIC RELATIONSHIPS \
        fusion to particular item of experience]

According to Bateson, adaptation and addiction "are *very* closely related phenomena."[18] For example, drugs such as alcohol, nicotine, cocaine, and tranquilizers can alter the metabolism of a person in a way that is experienced as "pleasurable." If usage continues over time, the metabolism may adapt in such a way that the *absence* of the drug is experienced as "painful." The continuation (or increase) of the drug level has immediate adapative advantages (avoidance of pain, experience of relief or pleasure) but extended addictive drawbacks: In addition to destroying organs in the body system, the addiction can also undermine relationships with family members, co-workers, friends, and so on, who organize their behavior around the person's intake of the drug. In striving to deal effectively (purposefully) with the situation, other people get inducted into the cycle of addiction—they too are caught in the creation and maintenance of the vicious cycle.

It should not be surprising that addiction commonly entails an *escalating* process, given that it is grounded in the transitive values of purpose. Addiction is a solution that is ignorant of thresholds: Like money, more is always thought to be better than less. For instance, the adaptive development of nuclear weaponry that so expediently brought World War II to an end has become a systemic addiction infecting America's economy, military strategy, and foreign policy. Gregory Bateson and Mary Catherine Bateson inscribe the spiral: "The armaments boys are addicted to feeling not just strong but stronger—stronger than yesterday and stronger than the Russians. The arms race both leaves us vulnerable to war and tends to escalate."[19]

If a system positions itself toward maximizing or minimizing one variable in its repertoire, the balance maintained by interactive complexity will be lost. Our consumer economy, what Wendell Berry refers to below as a "little economy," is a case in point. Addicted to increasing "wealth," individuals and businesses adapt in order to grow richer, and in so doing trivialize the natural environment (a more encompassing system than human society) from which the wealth is ultimately drawn.

> An explosive economy . . . is not only an economy that is dependent upon explosions but also one that sets no limits on itself. Any little economy that sees itself as unlimited is obviously self-blinded. It does not see its real relation of dependence and obligation to the Great Economy; in fact, it does not see that there *is* a Great Economy. Instead it calls the Great

Economy "raw material" or "natural resources" or "nature" and proceeds with the business of putting it "under control." [20]

In order to maximize the earnings of our little economy, we minimize controls on the waste we return to the Great Economy, producing such symptoms as acid rain and acid lakes. In applying solutions to these perceived problems, we, like all addicts, fail to question our premises, proceeding instead to *apply a purposive solution at the level at which we recognize the problem.* If there is too much acid in the lakes, we add lime to adjust the pH balance. The more effective this practice is in restoring a *semblance* of balance at the level of the particular, the more it will contribute to an inclusive addictive imbalance.

Shortcuts create short-circuits when they cross-cut contextual layers, when they breach or confuse what Bateson refers to as levels of logical type:

> In a large variety of cases, perhaps in all cases in which the shortcut generates trouble—the root of the matter is an error in logical typing. Somewhere in the sequence of actions and ideas, we can expect to find a class treated as though it were one of its members; or a member treated as though it were identical with the class; a uniqueness treated as a generality or a generality treated as a uniqueness. It is legitimate (and usual) to think of a process or change as an ordered class of states, but a mistake to think of any one of these states as if it were the class of which it is only a member. [21]

As contractions of the long-circuited solutions of cybernetic Mind, short-circuits are mistyped as completions and thus are condemned to repeat themselves over and over again. They are enacted as if they were a *class of solution* (i.e., a long-term adaptation) when in fact they are just *ad hoc* measures that leave uncorrected the deeper causes of the trouble and, worse, usually permit those causes to grow stronger and become compounded. In medicine, to relieve the symptoms without curing the disease is wise and sufficient *if and only if* either the disease is surely terminal *or* will cure itself.[22]

In their failure to account for inclusive patterns of relationship, *ad hoc* responses remain disjunctively separate, isolated and apart from the contexts of which they are a part.

Inebriation can be understood as an alcoholic's *ad hoc* adaptation—a short-term, and therefore dichotomous, solution applied at the same level of organization as problems in his or her sobriety. Bateson points out that if a drinker's

style of sobriety drives him to drink, then that style must contain error or pathology; and intoxication must provide some—at least subjective—correction of this error. In other words, compared with his sobriety, which is in some way "wrong," his intoxication must be in some way "right."[23]

Drinking can be considered purposeful to the extent that it is an expedient and single-leveled solution. And the more immediately "right" it is, and the more often the solution is invoked, the greater the later and more enveloping "wrong" it creates. The premises that give rise to addictive solutions are not undermined by failure; the person is simply challenged to do a better job of enacting them the next time around. As Bateson explains, "The premises of 'purpose' are simply not of the same logical type as the material facts of life, and therefore cannot easily be contradicted by them."[24]

Problem and attempted solution thus circle and become one, continually evoking the contractions of conscious knowing: that is, that there can be connection without separation and separation without connection, good without bad, unlimited growth without unlimited consequences, shortcuts without short-circuits, and so on. Further, and more important, the contextual bungling of addictive solutions reveals a fundamental mistyping of the relationship between whole and part. In order to trace this error, we must first distinguish the nature of complementary and symmetrical relationships.[25]

Complementary relationships are characterized by *co-operative difference,* where the behaviors of A and B mutually fit each other by virtue of their distinctiveness (e.g., dominance-submission, exhibitionism-spectatorship, nurturance-dependency, and so on). Symmetry, on the other hand, is a pattern of *competitive sameness*—opposition between participants is a kind of mirror reflection, such that the more A acts in a particular way, the more B symmetrically responds in kind (e.g., the fighting of boxers or the sprinting of racers). Note how the difference necessary for complementarity—

COMPLEMENTARITY / (COOPERATION/difference)

—is a cooperative connection that echoes COMPLETION / (CONNECTION/separation), whereas the sameness of symmetry is a function of an oppositional separation that mirrors CONTRACTION \ [SEPARATION\connection]:

SYMMETRY \ [OPPOSITION\sameness]

The mirrored opposition of symmetrical relationships ensures that both A and B will confront each other at the same logical level (as in the hegelian dialectic described in the last chapter). Similarly, the competition between opponents in a tennis match, as embodied in the rules for serving and hitting, scoring, winning, and so on, is between two "equal" participants. The game is *not* played between an individual and the tennis club to which he or she belongs; that is, it is not between a member and a class, not between a part and a whole, but between two members within the same context—in this case, two tennis players.

However, the situation is more complex with complementarity. While it is possible for the complementary differences between A and B to be of the same contextual order (as in the relationship between a teacher and a student, each of whom are members of a context called a school), it is also true that *any part of either a complementary or symmetrical relationship is always complementary to the relationship as a whole, to the context.* Thus the teacher and student are each complementary to the learning context they together define, just as the symmetrical tennis players are each complementary to the game they together play:

WHOLE/PART COMPLEMENTARITY /
  ((PART/PART COMPLEMENTARITY) / (part/part symmetry))

Another way of giving shape to this is to talk in terms of survival. For a relationship to endure, whether it be complementary or symmetrical, the participants must necessarily cooperate in its maintenance. Even competitive opposition is always nested within cooperation:

COOPERATION / (COMPLEMENTARITY/symmetry)

This is where conscious purpose makes its fatal error. Whereas competition is an either/or relationship organized to reap short-term gain, the both/and structure of cooperation is necessary if long-term survival is to obtain. Competition is not a problem if it is cooperatively contextualized (as in a friendly tennis match), but serious problems arise when the relationship between whole and part is mistyped as competitive. A member of a class simply cannot be symmetrically equal to the class of which it is a part; and if it acts as if it *is* possible, addictive disaster cannot help but ensue: "By living in opposition to nature," Berry argues, "we can *cause* natural calamities of which we would otherwise be free."[26] The analytic dichotomy of this is a pattern of addictive defection:

COMPETITION \ [SYMMETRY\complementarity]

Anthony Wilden clarifies that the unit of survival "is not *either* this organism (species, etc.) *or* that, nor *either* organism *or* environment, nor *either* this side of the line *or* that. *It is both-and.*"[27] It is not a matter of the survival of the fittest, but rather the *survival of the fit.* Berry continues: "Competitiveness cannot be the ruling principle, for the Great Economy is not a 'side' that we can join nor are there such 'sides' within it."[28] Wilden again:

> The dominant ideology has long been one which places mankind in a relationship of opposition to nature. Such a relationship of opposition is pathological, not just because it is exploitative (which does after all provide a simple ethical justification for calling it pathological), but rather because it substitutes short-range survival value (competition) for long-range survival value (cooperation).[29]

Out of ig-norance of connective long-term patterns of cooperative interaction, conscious purpose will always be tempted to maximize short-term gain for what it mistakes to be an isolated, independent component of a larger system. Violence and exploitation are "quick-fixes" that are "successful" in furthering the immediate goals of one side of a relationship, but only at the expense of the relationship as whole. Edward Sampson describes how winning can lose:

> In the single-minded pursuit of mastery, the pursuer becomes the pursued, trapped by the very lures and snares established to catch and dominate the presumed "enemy." The very tools and institutions established in the first place to achieve mastery become the source of the new problems that humanity confronts. . . . What is called for, therefore, is a different relationship between humanity and nature, one that partakes less of mastery and more of participation and receptivity.[30]

The alcoholic enacts participation and receptivity, but at the wrong contextual level. The symmetry (competitive separation) of conscious purpose is balanced by complementarity (cooperative connection), but the corrective is introduced as intoxication; as a "quick-fix," inebriation contributes to, and leaves unchallenged, the more encompassing competitive relationship between drinker and bottle.[31] The alcoholic is caught in the double bind of an analytic dichotomy—in order to *continue to win* the battle against the bottle, the drinker must repeatedly engage it in competition:

COMPETITION \
   [SYMMETRICAL BATTLE WITH BOTTLE \
    complementarity of intoxication]

The alcoholic is blind to the fact that this ongoing opposition is a contracted form of cooperation, that the symmetrical interaction with the bottle defines a complementarity between the drinker and the drinking relationship as a whole. As in all contractions, the competitive relationship between drinker and bottle can never complete; success of a particular battle ensures the continuation of the war. When a relationship is predicated on competition, winning (attempting to separate from the bottle by beating it) and losing (connecting to the bottle by continuing to drink) are each ways of maintaining the competition, of maintaining the relationship. Winning is not a way out of the relationship but a way back in.

COMPETITION \ [WINNING \ losing]

The reasons for this go back to the heart of knowing, to the way in which distinctions structure our experience. As George Kelly says, "Much of our language, as well as our everyday thinking, implies contrast which it does not explicitly state." [32] We are continually tripped up by the connections of our separations. The alcoholic's competitive opposition to the bottle is an attempt to get rid of his or her drinking problem by forcefully separating from it. But it is impossible to get to a place where drinking isn't an issue by taking issue with it. Desired separation forges a connection: *Not-drinking* only makes sense in relation to *drinking*. Bateson emphasizes the importance of such mutuality in the world of information (which is organized in terms of difference, or distinctions) by describing the functioning of the nervous system:

> From a systems-theoretic point of view, it is a misleading metaphor to say that what travels in an axon is an "impulse." It would be more correct to say that what travels is a difference, or a transform of a difference. The metaphor of "impulse" suggests a hard-science line of thought which will ramify only too easily into nonsense . . . and those who talk this kind of nonsense will disregard the information content of *quiescence*. The quiescence of an axon *differs* as much from activity as its activity does from quiescence. Therefore quiescence and activity have equal informational relevance. The message of activity can only be accepted as valid if the message of quiescence can also be trusted. . . .
>
> Always the fact that information is a transform of difference should be remembered, and we might better call the one message "activity—not quiescence" and the other "quiescence—not activity."
>
> Similar considerations apply to the repentant alcoholic. He cannot simply elect "sobriety." At best he could only elect "sobriety—not drunkenness," and his universe remains polarized, carrying always both alternatives. [33]

This doubleness of knowing renders change singularly difficult. The desire for absence exacts presence. This is the paradox of forgetting—it always occurs within the context of patterned mind.

CONSCIOUS MIND \
[FORGETTING \remembering]

How many times I've wanted
to forget you, forget

the things you told me in the dark
sweet scents of your body, the bouquet

of enchantment in each flower
we knew together

elusive and shortlived, overpowered
by the empty habits

that keep life
from flowering. Yet

each time I've tried
to forget you

groggy with sleep or too much drink,
there is the memory of wildflowers

and the faintest rueful scent of you
blossoms in the stalest air.

—Brian Fawcett

Henri Bergson argues that memory is not nearly as extraordinary a phenomenon as forgetting: "We no longer have to explain the preservation of the past, but rather its apparent abolition. We shall no longer have to account for remembering but for forgetting."[34] Something of this accounting is at least begun by Jon Elster, who, drawing from Kant, distinguishes between *active negation* and *passive negation*.[35] The following illustrations of Kant help distinguish the two modalities:

The passive negation of attention is indifference, the active negation is abstraction; in other words, the absence of consciousness of x is something other than the consciousness of the absence of x. . . . The passive negation of desire is again indifference, the active negation disgust; we could say that the absence of desire in x is something other than the desire for the absence of x.[36]

Elster goes on to explain the relevance of this for the act of forgetting.

The will to forget is an example of what has been called "to want what couldn't be wanted," an impossibility, since it relies on the confusion of active and passive negation. Forgetfulness, or indifference, is a passive negation—simply the absence of consciousness of x—while the will to forget requires the consciousness of the absence of x. Wanting to forget is like deciding to create obscurity from light.[37]

If memory is the patterning of information and information is composed of differences that make a difference,[38] then forgetting must have to do with differences that somehow *stop* making a difference. Thus the choice of the word *indifference* for passive negation is most appropriate. With *no-difference* there is no distinction drawn and thus no information: Knotted memories unravel and truly become *not* when they lose relevance.

The trouble is that differences make a difference *because we make them.* Thus, any attempt to *make* a difference *not make a difference* cannot help but make sure that it does. The purposeful effort to make something not matter is an act of what Elster calls *active indifference:*

Active indifference is . . . active negation hiding behind passive appearance. One could undoubtedly imagine an endless stream of such appearances, each more complex than the preceding one and capable of deceiving a great number of people; nevertheless, they would never be able to ignore their origin in active negation. By affecting indifference—from the first to the *n*th degree—one will never *become* indifferent.[39]

How then does one move from remembering to forgetting? As Elster points out, one cannot simply *feign* indifference and hope that it will catch hold in due course, as this simply underscores the memory.

A husband and wife who decide to stay married after one of them has had a serious affair are faced with precisely this dilemma. They are reminded again and again of the betrayal by the very particularities of their life together—comments, letters, dates, smells, notes, friends, thoughts, books, facial expressions, places, sounds, times of day, tones of voice, films, foods, gifts, arguments, pieces of music, clothes, and so on—and everything they do to put it behind them brings it to the fore. Unable to return to a context of

TRUST / (ASSURANCE/forgetfulness)

the partners continually find themselves braced in the chill of

DISTRUST \ [ACTIVE INDIFFERENCE \ reassurances]

Within a context of distrust, efforts to relegate an infidelity to the past will continually configure it in the present. The forced negations of active indifference can never add up to the relaxed negations of forgetfulness, and reassurances that "it will never happen again" fail to dispel uncertainty, fail to assure.

We are condemned to remember what we contrive to forget; the attempt to detach secures the attachment:

TRYING TO FORGET \
    [CONTRIVED DETACHMENT FROM MEMORY \
      condemned attachment to memory]

What are the implications of this for a couple caught in such a bind? If forgetting isn't possible, what is?

Some primary conceptual tools for understanding the relational organization of such entanglements can be found in G. Spencer-Brown's *Laws of Form*. The arithmetic forms he generates spill forth from two general axioms having to do with the nature of distinctions. Axiom 1, "the law of calling," says:

> *The value of a call made again is the value of a call.*
> That is to say, if a name is called and then is called again, the value indicated by the two calls taken together is the value indicated by one of them.
> That is to say, for any name, to recall is to call.[40]

Calling a name inscribes a boundary which distinguishes it from what it is not. This *difference* between inside (the named) and outside (not the name) creates and constitutes the information (what Spencer-Brown calls the *value*) indicated by the name. Floyd Merrell, commenting on this axiom, points out that by "evoking a name or a word, you automatically cross the boundary *differentiating* that which is inside from that which is outside."[41] A named presence on one side of a distinction is always *made present* by virtue its absence on the other side. D. T. Suzuki traces the recursiveness of the mutuality.

> "A" cannot be itself unless it stands against what is not "A"; "not-A" is needed to make "A" "A," which means that "not-A" is in "A." When "A" wants to be itself, it is already outside itself, that is, "not-A." If "A" did not contain in itself what is not itself, "not-A" could not come out of "A" so as to make "A" what it is. "A" is "A" because of this contradiction.[42]

The first axiom states that to recall is to call: If a name is called again, the same boundary is marked. The same difference recalled indicates the same information value as it did with the first calling—nothing new is added. Because information is a function of the *difference* between the two sides of a distinction, a function of the *separation* between the name and not-the-name (e.g., between "A" and "not-A"), anything that maintains the boundary will retain the information value of the call.

This explains, then, why the desire to forget always evokes the unwanted memory. A person who mistakenly believes a thought ("A") to be somehow self-contained will try to banish it from his or her mind. But such action only re-inscribes the boundary between the thought ("A") and its absence ("not-A"); and it is *there,* in the separated connection between the two, that the memory lives:

> each time I've tried
> to forget you
>
> groggy with sleep or too much drink,
> there is the memory of wildflowers
>
> and the faintest rueful scent of you
> blossoms in the stalest air.[43]

It thus begins to make sense how the memory of a significant separation between a husband and wife (such as an affair) can be kept painfully alive for years and even decades, despite (indeed, in large part, because of) the couple's best attempts to bury it.

The pattern

TRYING TO FORGET \
    [CONTRIVED DETACHMENT FROM MEMORY \
        condemned attachment to memory]

is an expression of the analytic matrix

CONTRACTION \ [SEPARATION \ connection]

and as such offers a convenient metaphor for characterizing people's defective relationships to their own and/or other people's symptoms. Requests for therapeutic help almost always reflect a desire on the part of clients to have some "piece" of themselves (or of other people) eradicated. Whether the issue concerns a torn relationship, distressing emotion, unacceptable behavior, nagging uncertainty, unrelenting pain, inappropriate attitude, annoying habit, or aggravating thought, the request for intervention invariably contains, however implicitly, the assumption that the problem, once isolated, can be banished and forgotten.

It should be obvious at this point that any move on the part of a therapist to directly answer such queries—that is, to accept the invitation to more deeply entrench the separation between the client and the symptom he or she desires to forget—will only help spin the vicious circles in which the person is caught that much faster and tighter. The next chapter will discuss how therapists can avoid getting whisked up in such swirls; it describes the means by which one can encounter the short-circuits of contraction with the long-circuits of completion. But first it is necessary to return to the work of Spencer-Brown.

Mind (memory) is composed not of things or even of ideas of things, but of distinctions, of relationships between. As has been discussed, anything that sharpens the *separation* between the two sides of a distinction highlights the difference that defines it and more clearly outlines the edges of the memory constituted by it. It follows, then, that in confirming the *connection* between the two sides of a distinction, a correspondence is established that takes the edge off the differentiation composing the memory. An image carved in bas-relief vanishes when the difference in height between it and its surroundings is sanded smooth. It is to the possibility of such disappearance of information that Spencer-Brown's second axiom, "the law of crossing," alludes:

> *The value of a crossing made again is not the value of the crossing.*
> That is to say, if it is intended to cross a boundary and then it is intended to cross it again, the value indicated by the two intentions taken together is the value indicated by none of them.
> That is to say, for any boundary, to recross is not to cross.[44]

When one of the two sides of a distinction is crossed into, its distinctiveness is underscored (as in calling or recalling) and it becomes foreground to the background of the other:[45] for example, **A**/not-A. But when the boundary is *recrossed*, each side (A *and* not-A) becomes foreground *and* background:

(**A/not-A**) / (A/not-A)

Foreground — **A/not-A** — and background — A/not-A —are now *identical,* which means that there is no longer a distinction marking them as different or separate. With no difference there is no information. To paraphrase the second axiom: "The information value indicated by the identity of the two sides is the information value indicated by neither of them."

Recrossing *connects* the two sides of a distinction such that the difference becomes *not.* When A and not-A are fully joined, there is neither A nor not-A; unified, with nothing to distinguish one from the other, relata and relationship dissolve. However, the noting (calling) of this unity differentiates *it* from what it is not, and thus puts it on one side (as foreground) of a still more encompassing distinction. The ongoing interplay between recrossing and recalling can thus be arrayed as a pattern of completion. Whereas recrossing reiter-

ates the connection between the two sides of a distinction, re-calling renews the separation:

COMPLETION / (RECROSSING/recalling)

Bateson notes that going beyond the vicious circles of ad-diction, "beyond the double bind," has something to do with the "*completion* of tasks."[46] The issue, then, is not how best to forget a memory or a symptom, but how to gather its pres-ence and absence in such a way as to allow it to complete. An affair cannot be forcefully forgotten, cannot be banished from the history of a relationship, but it *can* be connected to in a different way. Instead of continually recalling distrust (or trying not to recall it, which, as has been explained above, comes to the same end), a couple might find ways of recrossing the distinction between trust and distrust in all aspects—in both the foreground and background—of their relationship.

The notion of how to move from the tight circles of con-traction to the relaxed circling of completion is developed, in the final chapter, primarily within the context of therapy. However, the ability to "go beyond the double bind," to com-plete distinctions, is an art that transcends the formal rela-tionship between client and therapist. It has much to do with being fully and completely alive.

4

From
CONTRACTION \

(CONNECTION /separation)

to
COMPLETION /

[SEPARATION \connection]

夫　聖
唯　人
病　不
病　病
是　以
以　其
不　病
病　病
　　是
　　以
　　不
　　病

Only one defecting from defection is thereby
    not defective
The sage is not defective—
    defects from defection and is thereby
    not defective
                —*Lao Tzu*

To live by expert advice is to abandon one's life.
                —*Wendell Berry*

Every explicit duality is an implicit unity.
                —*Alan Watts*

Well, what I really said was that I don't know
anybody who could really work Taoism.
                —*Gregory Bateson*

Only by restoring the broken connections can
we be healed. Connection *is* health.
                —*Wendell Berry*

In executing Taoist principles, a therapist risks doing just that—executing them. The Greek root of the word *therapy* means "to heal" (make whole), but as a profession invented by and situated within a fractionated society, therapy cannot escape the hairline fissures of purpose that radiate through that world. In this it cannot fail but to be defective, to fall short of completion.

A systemic or relational approach to therapy is distinguished by its commitment to contextual understanding. Taken seriously, this stance prescribes a double focus. Before we can look at the importance of context *within* the domain of therapy, we must first turn and look without, at the context of which it is a part and to which it contributes:

CONTEXTUAL UNDERSTANDING /
>   (CONTEXT IN THERAPY / therapy in context)

THERAPY IN CONTEXT \
[SPECIALIZATION \ health]

The modern self-seeker becomes a tourist of cures, submitting his quest to the guidance of one guru after another. The "cure" thus preserves the disease.

—*Wendell Berry*

Therapy sets up shop in the schisms of our culture, and, as a business, profits by collecting rent on the rents. Wendell Berry bewails the way experts step into the breach, only to further widen the gap:

The modern urban-industrial society is based on a series of radical disconnections between body and soul, husband and wife, marriage and community, community and the earth. At each of these points of disconnection the collaboration of corporation, government, and expert sets up a profit-making enterprise that results in the further dismemberment and impoverishment of the Creation.[1]

To what extent, then, is therapy itself not just another symptom, a business whose very existence *demands* a continual supply of problems, a solution that by virtue of being a "solution," fails to escape the dichotomous premises of the ills it seeks to cure?

SOCIETAL ADDICTION \
    [DICHOTOMY EMBODIED IN "SOLVING PROBLEMS" \
        existential demand for problems to solve]

A therapy business, whether in the form of a private practice, a clinic, or an institute, is an enterprise and, even if run as a nonprofit organization, has a bottom line to meet. It is therefore organized by what Bateson refers to as the monotone values of money: "Money is always transitively valued. More money is supposedly always better than less money. For example, $1,001 is to be preferred to $1,000."[2] The economics of therapy are thus a *corruption* (from the Latin *cor-*, "together," "altogether," and *rumpere,* "to break," "violate": "to altogether violate") of the principles of its practice. This cannot be taken lightly; the logic of money is *contra naturam* as Ezra Pound would say, and it exacts its toll:

> with usura the line grows thick
> with usura is no clear demarcation[3]

Demarcations have indeed become unclear when practitioners who profess a relational orientation and denounce the dangers of labeling fall back on the insular categories described in the *Diagnostic and Statistical Manual of Mental Disorders,* 3rd Ed. Rev. (DSM-III-R) when it comes time for third-party billing. Instead of lobbying government officials with regard to who should or should not be allowed to diagnose with the DSM-III-R (i.e., who should or should not be allowed to collect third-party payments), why are we not convincing the officials and the insurance companies that there are better ways to organize treatment?

Are there better ways? Or is all treatment defective? Therapy is a profession, and therapists, as professionals, are specialists. Berry considers such expertise the bane of health.

> The disease of the modern character is specialization. Looked at from the standpoint of the social *system,* the aim of specialization may seem desirable enough. . . . The difficulties do not appear until we look at specialization from the opposite standpoint—that of individual persons.[4]

In giving our lives over to the dictates of specialists, we forgo our responsibility for our own health and the health of our world. And in losing our responsibility we lose our freedom. By separating problems into different domains—individual, familial, economic, environmental, political, societal, spiritual, biological, historical, and so on—specialists engender the schisms they study and strive to heal. This gives new, painful meaning to the Heisenberg hook. Berry elaborates:

> The problems thus become the stock in trade of specialists. The so-called professions survive by endlessly "processing" and talking about problems that they have neither the will nor the competence to solve. The doctor who is interested in disease but not in health is clearly in the same category with the conservationist who invests in the destruction of what he otherwise intends to preserve. They both have the comfort of "job security," but at the cost of ultimate futility.[5]

As *specialists of wholeness,* systemically oriented therapists are a living oxymoron: when our knowing of health is particular, we particulate the health of the known. Ignorance of such contracted double binds is a defection (不 知 知 病 *ignorant knowing: defective*) that, like an infection, can spread through the connected patterns of Mind:

ADDICTION TO SPECIALISTS \
  [IGNORANCE OF THE PARTICULATION OF HEALTH \
    particular knowledge of health]

For farmer, farm, and food in the following passage of Berry's, substitute therapist, therapy, and mind:

> If a farmer fails to understand what health is, his farm becomes unhealthy; it produces unhealthy food, which damages the health of the community. . . . The farmer is a part of the community, and so it is as impossible to say exactly where the trouble began as to say where it will end. The influences go backward and forward, up and down, round and round, compounding and branching as they go. All that is certain is that an error introduced anywhere in the network ramifies beyond the scope of prediction.[6]

Such recognition can occasion despair and give rise to efforts to contain or escape the ramiform influence of the errors.[7] But attempts to defect are themselves defective—there is no escape, there are no insular boundaries in a world of recursive connections. Whereas one cannot defect from defects, it *is* possible to defect from defection, to run away from running away—that is, to *stop running,* turn around, and find imaginative ways to *bring defect to effect* (i.e., *effect* in the sense of "accomplishment" or "fulfillment").[8] This is the beginning of making whole, of recrossing distinctions, and it can serve as a guide not only for therapy in context, but context in therapy.

CONTEXT IN THERAPY /
(COMPLETION/contraction)

Healing . . . complicates the system by opening and restoring connections among the various parts—in this way restoring the ultimate simplicity of their union. . . . The parts are healthy insofar as they are joined harmoniously to the whole.
—*Wendell Berry*

What is a therapist that a client may consult her, and a client that he may consult a therapist? Clients are clients because they ask therapists for help. But the person asked is the wrong person, and the question posed is the wrong question. Therapy is a process wherein the client learns how to stop being a client by discovering how not to ask the wrong person the wrong question. At the same time, the therapist must learn how to stop being the therapist by not answering the wrong question right away and discovering how to not-answer the wrong question in a right way.

Both the person queried and the question posed are wrong because the act of asking a specialist for help and the nature of the help requested each contribute to the contraction:

THERAPY AS SOLUTION \
   [ATTEMPTING TO ERADICATE (SEPARATE FROM) PROBLEM \
      asking help of (connecting to) specialist]

The therapist responds to such analytic dichotomies by completing distinctions:

THERAPY AS COMPLETING DISTINCTIONS /
   (BRINGING DEFECT TO EFFECT /
      not-answering dichotomous questions)

Con-versation (turning together) within this latter matrix creates a context in which the *chasmal* can become *chiasmal*.[9]

Bradford Keeney and Jeffrey Ross describe how to listen cybernetically to client requests in terms of the complementarity *change/stability:*

> A cybernetic view of multiple communication in systemic therapy begins with the assumption that troubled systems present multiple communications, sometimes taken as contradictory, to a therapist. These communications include: "change us" and "stabilize us." These two communications, when viewed as a double description, mark the recursive complementarity of a cybernetic system. In effect, dual requests for stability and change are a way of indicating that the system is exploring the possibility of altering the way it changes in order to remain stable.[10]

They then go on to suggest the implications of this for structuring interventions:

> A cybernetic view of therapeutic intervention suggests that a therapist mirror the multiple communications a troubled family presents. Accordingly, therapists may inform families to change *and* stabilize. . . . These messages are not contradictory, nor do they involve a logic of negation, but are connected through a logic of complementarity.[11]

Therapeutic conversation is interpreted slightly differently if it is considered a contrapuntal interaction of contraction and completion. Because clients' connections are contextualized by separation, their requests for change can be expected to be similarly divisive—change will be thought separable from stability. In asking for help to "change this symptom or that family member, while leaving everything and/or everyone else as is," they are expecting a dichotomous solution to a schismatic dilemma. And indeed, any direct re-

sponse to such a request will be contextualized by the premises of the question and thus will necessarily remain chasmal
in form.[12] A chiasmal response—in which change and stability are recursively *connected* within a context of completion—requires, in the not-acting spirit of *wu wei*, that the
question be *not-answered*.

Alan Watts affirms that "there is no direct answer to an
irrational question" and "As we say, 'Anyone who goes to
a psychiatrist ought to have his head examined!' In other
words, his problem is his question, his belief that the question
he is asking makes sense."[13] To be healing, the therapist must
turn people back to their questions in a way that is not merely
a recalling (for to recall is to call again and to stay stuck in
contraction) but a recrossing. The resulting completion will
be formally related to long-circuited *inversions* of contraction—to what Bateson refers to as "adaptations of high logical type, transcending . . . double-binds."[14]

LONG-CIRCUITS / (DISCIPLINE / *wu wei*)

Not-answering is a form of not-acting, a not-giving-in to requests for immediate (and thus potentially addictive) comfort.
Bateson describes the curious behavior of mountain climbers
who struggle to the top of a mountain despite heavy packs,
growing blisters, and exhaustion.[15] Whereas the commonsense
thing to do would be to stop, eat lunch, and turn back (as
when addicts give themselves another fix upon suffering the
first pangs of withdrawal), they instead press on until reaching the summit. Why do they do this? They obviously have
not done away with conscious purpose—they indeed set out
to get to the *top* of the mountain—but have properly embedded it as *discipline* in a relationship which includes the mountain itself as part of a long-circuited Mind. Similarly, as Watts

illustrates, desire has its place as one moves in the direction of no-desire:

> STUDENT How do I get rid of desire?
> TEACHER Do you really want to get rid of it?
> STUDENT Yes and no. I want to get rid of the desire that causes anguish; but I do not want to get rid of the desire to get rid of it.[16]

The *wu wei* of the climber's discipline includes a knowing ignoring (知 不 知) of the pleas and aches of their bodies for quick relief, thus allowing them to complete their ascent and to repair a rift between self and environment, recrossing a distinction that Berry says is usually conceived of as pure separation:

> Once we see our place, our part of the world, as *surrounding* us, we have already made a profound division between it and ourselves. We have given up the understanding—dropped it out of our language and so out of our thought—that . . . our land passes in and out of our bodies just as our bodies pass in and out of our land.[17]

Bateson equates the climber's discipline of not-answering the screams of the body with the discipline required of the Zen monk:

> Why does the Zen monk sit through hours of agony in the lotus position, his legs getting more and more paralyzed and his head getting more and more addled? And while he does this, why does he contemplate or wrestle with a koan, a traditional paradox, a sort of conceptual double bind?[18]

Watts explains *za-zen* (sitting meditation) as follows:

> It is simply a quiet awareness, without comment, of whatever happens to be here and now. This awareness is attended by the most vivid sensation of "nondifference" between oneself and

the external world, between the mind and its contents—the various sounds, sights, and other impressions of the surrounding environment. Naturally, this sensation does not arise by trying to acquire it; it just comes by itself when one is sitting and watching without any purpose in mind—even the purpose of getting rid of purpose.[19]

Common to both climbing and sitting meditation is the chiasmal discipline of recrossing severed distinctions, of making whole. Long-circuits replace short-circuits. This is the same relentless discipline that Berry deems essential in the maintenance of a working farm:

It's like having a milk cow. Having a milk cow is a very strict discipline and a very trying circumstance. It means you've got to be home twice a day to milk whether you want to or not, or else the cow will be ruined. Some days you'd rather do anything than go down to that barn and maybe some days you go and you're kind of bored with it. But other days it's a most rewarding thing and you realize that you get the reward and happiness of it because you stuck to it when it *wasn't* rewarding. There's some kind of wisdom in that fidelity.[20]

The wisdom is that of completion. The tightly coiled double binds of contraction are unknotted and relaxed (completed) by inverting the contextual layering of separation and connection. This movement—from

CONTRACTION \ [SEPARATION \ connection]

to

COMPLETION / (CONNECTION/separation)

—defines the nature of reversal in therapeutic process.

The chiasmal discipline of the therapist finds expression in the two complementary ways of not-acting mentioned earlier.

1. In *not answering a wrong question right away,* the therapist takes care not to act with haste or unmediated purpose. As in the practice of the Taoist martial art T'ai Chi Ch'üan, most can be learned by staying relaxed, most can be accomplished by acting at the right time, and balance is maintained by not *having* to learn or accomplish anything. As Watts suggests,

> it is a great disadvantage to any therapist to have an ax to grind, because this gives him a personal interest in winning. . . . But we saw, in reference to the Zen master, that he can play the game effectively just because winning or losing makes no difference to him.[21]

Bateson similarly discusses how purposeful manipulation precludes completion:

> If the therapist is trying to take a patient, give him exercises, play various propagandas on him, try to make him come over to our world for the wrong reasons, to manipulate him—then there arises a problem, a temptation to confuse the idea of manipulation with the idea of a cure. . . .
> This is, I think, really what these disciplines of meditation are about. They're about the problem of how to get there without getting there by the manipulative path, because the manipulative path can never get there. So, in a way one can never know quite what one is doing.[22]

2. In *not-answering a wrong question in a right way,* the therapist responds at a more encompassing level than the query and thus avoids being organized by its dichotomous premises. Such participation is a *connected separation,* an absorbed detachment that is not engineered by an oppositional pushing away but is inhered in the contextual gap between whole and part. The focus of attention and involvement is not on the level of the particular but on the *relations between,* on the context.

By embracing both sides of all distinctions, chasms are met with chiasms, the recalled is recrossed, and defects are brought to effect. Each of these three contextual responses are simply variations on the same pattern of therapeutic practice, on the discipline of completing distinctions.

COMPLETING DISTINCTIONS /
(CHIASM/chasm)
(RECROSSING/recalling)
(EFFECT/defect)

Now, I can't tell you the right answers—in fact, I'm not sure I would if I could, because, you see, to tell you the real answers, to know the real answers, is always to switch them over to that left brain, to the manipulative side. And once they're switched over, no matter how right they were poetically and aesthetically, they go dead, and become manipulative techniques.

—*Gregory Bateson*

To go in the dark with a light is to know the light.
To know the dark, go dark. Go without sight,
and find that the dark, too, blooms and sings,
and is traveled by dark feet and dark wings.

—*Wendell Berry*

As has been pointed out a number of times, there are important limits to what can and should be said about patterns of completion. When a constellated relationship—be it wildflower, sonata, idea, poem, or conversation—is encountered in context as a composed whole, it comes alive. Analytically explicated, the connections are severed and it dies.

It is with this understanding that the following case is presented. Not intended as an exhaustive illustration of the ideas developed in the book, it can be more appropriately thought of as a kind of melodic variation on some of the themes. The commentary will serve as program notes, providing background material and suggestions for how to listen.[23]

A woman in her mid-forties asked me (who, as a therapist, was the wrong person) the following wrong (divisive) question: "How can I get the panic-depressions [her term] that have been plaguing me under control?" Not-answering her right away took one meeting, not-answering her in a right way took three months. That is, the necessary context for completion was able to be established in the initial session; however, the process itself, always unpredictable, took place in its own time.[24]

At the time of her first appointment, Lynn had been divorced from Edward, her husband of twenty-four years, for two years, and she was living with her twenty-year-old daughter. Her son, Brian, sixteen, had headed up the coast a month earlier to live with his father in a different state. Although inconvenienced by, and embarrassed about, crying unexpectedly at work, Lynn was most concerned about the three recent panic-depressions that had occurred without warning when she was alone at home. Each one lasted about two hours and left her feeling frightened and drained. She had had somewhat similar "anxiety attacks" when she was married, but they had stopped after her divorce.

THERAPIST   When they happen, what do you think about? What goes through your mind?
CLIENT   Oh God, what do I think about? [pause] I think about killing myself.
THERAPIST   Mm-hmm.
CLIENT   And I talk myself out of it.
THERAPIST   And when you're thinking about killing yourself,

you said earlier—like thoughts of not having
friends—what . . .

CLIENT   But I do have friends.

THERAPIST Okay, but just, what sorts of . . . Do you think
about Brian? Or do you think about your hus-
band, or any person in particular?

CLIENT   No, I don't. I think that it's, um, it's just too big a
bitch to live. It isn't really hinged on anybody else.

THERAPIST So you go . . .

CLIENT   I just, uh, that's all it is. And then I feel, I'm real
good at guilt so I think "oh God" you know. The
guilt of how I might, what I might do to my children is my saving, my, you know, is what I hinge
it on.

THERAPIST With Brian gone, does that make that safety net
less safe?

CLIENT   No, no. Because I don't think of them, how if I
kill myself, they won't see me or anything on that
basis. I think of the psychological impact on their
lives.

Suicide, the ultimate separation, is a logical chasmal solution within a world of CONTRACTION \ [SEPARATION \
connection], and guilt can at best be an attenuated connection within such a context:

PANIC-DEPRESSION \ [SUICIDE \ guilt]

It could have been that talking about—or even the implicit
suggestion of—the potential of committing suicide was serving as its own connection to her daughter, ex-husband, or son:

PANIC-DEPRESSION \
    [SUICIDE \ messages about potential suicide]

But this avenue of exploration turned out to be a blind alley:
Her contact with her son and husband was minimal and per-

functory, and her relationship with her daughter was cordial but uninvolved—they were, as she put it, like roommates.

Asked about her creative interests, Lynn spoke of her work as an interior designer, a profession she had begun before marrying Edward; during their time together she had planned and helped build two of their homes. She also liked to write, but had stopped of late. The following was offered as an explanation:

CLIENT It's just when I'm thinking and speaking, I think there's perhaps covering up and denial going on.[25] It's not as authentic. When I write I read it back and I go "oh that's too, that is too close! I didn't mean to get that close to that. I'm not doing this anymore!"

THERAPIST When did you stop?

CLIENT Uh, well I, actually I think something, what you're talking about may be, with these panic attacks, they might have been somewhat triggered by my writing. I'm not, there may be a correlation, I can't quite remember, but I'm thinking that that might have something to do with it.

THERAPIST And you said they happen with the [unclear], is that what you said?

CLIENT Yah.

THERAPIST And so you've just in the last couple of days stopped writing, or . . . ?

CLIENT Yah, I mean I'm just, I'm working and sleeping and working and sleeping, I just try not to do anything but that. I'm avoiding myself [laugh]. I mean I know that I'm doing that, I mean I'm not. It's not anything, you know. It's no great shock to me that I'm doing that. But that, but I can't afford to write right now.

THERAPIST Can't afford . . .

CLIENT To write.

THERAPIST Because it's too close?

CLIENT Yah, yah.

THERAPIST When you write, is there a particular thing that you write about?

CLIENT No. Sometimes I just start to write a letter to a friend and the next thing I know I'm writing all this crap down, you know, and I don't really [unclear]. Or I'll write lists, or I try to say "okay, this is what I need to do tomorrow, and this, what I need to do, now what do I, okay, do . . ."

Lynn used separation as an attempt to keep in check something that was beyond her control, something that scared her deeply: "Oh that's too, that is too close! I didn't mean to get that close to that. I'm not doing this anymore!" Not writing and "avoiding" herself were contractions, divisive solutions that had the potential for schismogenic runaway: If even the writing of a list was enough to set the panic off, how long before the picking up of a pencil would become a dangerous act?

The term *panic-depression* is itself indicative of a short-circuit. The simultaneity of panic and depression suggests a tight spinning between the two, each feeding off the other. One way to stop their mutual escalation and to mark the beginning of a long-circuit is to separate them, both conceptually and in time:

THERAPIST I've got a couple of hunches that I want to check out with you. Because I think that it's significant that you think of what's been happening as panic-depressions. And you're not quite sure how you came up with that name but [unclear]. And, and I think your intuitive sense has been very good, from what you've told me. And in fact that's a very appropriate term, but I think maybe you weren't quite sure why the two were connected.

CLIENT Yah.

THERAPIST	And I had a couple of hunches. One, I think that the panic, that there is a panic component, and what you've panicked about is the depression.
CLIENT	Makes sense.
THERAPIST	You, you start, when you talk about, with the writing, you start off with something that's organized. It's either organized around writing a letter or writing a list.
CLIENT	Mm-hmm.
THERAPIST	It's very, it's left brain, it's very analytical, and you're an analytical person.
CLIENT	Mm-hmm.
THERAPIST	And what happens is ideas and feelings and thoughts start flowing out of that and it breaks away from the structure, . . .
CLIENT	Mm-hmm.
THERAPIST	. . . and it's free flowing and then you look at that and you say "oh shit!"
CLIENT	Yah, exactly.

The differentiation of panic and depression allows the vicious circle of Lynn's contraction to be more clearly layered as:

DEPRESSION \ [PANIC \ flow of thoughts and feelings]

Her panic was a function of a chasmal separation, a pushing away that *actively negated* her connected flow of depressing thoughts and feelings. This same pattern of solution was then applied to the panic itself, as she attempted to control *it* through distance (not-writing, avoidance). Doomed to failure, this could only lead to panic about the panic.

There is but a slight difference between contraction and completion, a small shift whereby the tight composition of the former becomes the relaxed composure of the latter: Chasm becomes chiasm when the imbrication of separation and connection is inverted:

CONTRACTION \ [SEPARATION \ connection]

becomes

COMPLETION / (CONNECTION/separation)

Of course it makes just as much sense to note that separation and connection invert when a contraction is completed. There is no beginning to a circle; a difference can be introduced anywhere.

The shift in this case came when the short-circuit of depression was recontextualized as a long-circuit of mourning. Having experienced a number of significant losses—most notably the demise of her marriage and, more recently, the departure of her son—it made sense to Lynn that the sadness she was feeling was part of a mourning cycle. Drawing on the traditions and rituals of her religion, it was possible to weave a context in which periods of deep sadness were seen as *natural* and *necessary,* as part of an encompassing healing. This then allowed for a defection from defection; rather than running away from painful thoughts and feelings, she could turn around and embrace them.[26] Separation within mourning is a *passive negation,* a letting go that happens when it doesn't have to, when memories are gathered up rather than pushed away:

DEPRESSION (VICIOUS CIRCLE) \
    [PANIC \ connected flow *of* thoughts and feelings]

becomes

MOURNING (COMPLETE CIRCUIT) /
    (CONNECTION *TO* THOUGHTS AND FEELINGS / letting go)

THERAPIST   It's a little bit like sleeping. If you say "I don't want to sleep, I'm just going to be organized and I'm going to work twenty-four hours a day," at some point in time you're going to fall asleep.

CLIENT   Yes, that makes sense, yes.

THERAPIST   Okay, so if you say "I'm not going to have these panic-depressions and I'm just going to control myself and make sure I don't have them" and you get tight and tight, they're going to happen. Because they're important and necessary. So, obviously, the thing to do is: You plan your sleep time; you also plan sad time. Plan mourning time. 'Cause see if you have them, if you have them for half an hour a day . . .

CLIENT   You're saying have them on my terms, and not on their terms, is what you're saying.

THERAPIST   Yah, mm-hmm.

This is an example of answering a wrong question in a wrong way. Having panic-depressions on *her* terms maintains the notion of control and thus oppositional distance. It would have been more appropriate to have said: "Plan them to *ensure* they happen. Protect time for them."

Defect was brought to effect through Lynn's writing, the activity she had identified as triggering her panic-depressions. The spiral runaway she described began with something structured—a list or a letter. At some point memories and ideas would begin to pour forth, she would get "too close" and, frightened, push them away. The pattern of this sequence—structure, flow, panic—was slightly modified and given back to her as an activity of mourning. Lynn was asked to begin her grieving time by writing something structured, to wait for it to break off into a flow of thoughts and feelings, and when she had enough material with which to work, to structure the flow into a poem. By folding the process back on itself—structure, flow, structure—the writing provided its own calibration, and control via separation was no longer necessary.

CLIENT I'm not going to have any problem with the flow. Read, reading what I've written is going to be what knocks me for a loop. I mean I know that, I mean because that's what always happens.

THERAPIST Okay.

CLIENT And then having to deal with that and condense it, um . . .

THERAPIST So what you might want to do, what you might want to do is only allow yourself to write for five minutes.

CLIENT Okay.

THERAPIST And then that will give you twenty-five minutes to form it into a poem, it won't give you as much to work with.

CLIENT Because there's always redundancy in it anyway.

THERAPIST So, however, but there has to be both.

CLIENT Okay.

THERAPIST There has to be both. Then, and *this* is mourning. See what I want you to do, what I, I want the flow to be centered on loss.

CLIENT Okay.

THERAPIST I don't want you to say "what a bastard the guy I had at work today was." Okay? And it can be the loss of your marriage, or of Brian, or of your cat when you were seven.

By the end of this first session a context had been established in which the dichotomous distinction between Lynn's *self* and her *heart's reasons*[27] could be recrossed, and her short-circuited responses could be relaxed and extended in time. Subsequent meetings and suggestions served to reiterate these chiasms.

The panic-depressions ceased after the first meeting, and Lynn began to notice some changes. For one, the black-and-white nightmares she had been having had diminished significantly, and in their stead came colorful dreams which were, for her, "positive signs of hope." Nevertheless, a number of weeks later she plummeted into some dark times which scared her, and she began the fifth session describing a recent nightmare, one she had had many times before.

CLIENT   All my life I've had one reoccurring dream, which is, apparently is not a dream, but something that happened when I was very, very, very young and in an air-raid shelter. But you know what "Bird's Eye Custard" is if you're from Canada, probably.

THERAPIST   [shakes head; no]

CLIENT   It's sort of a, it's a warm vanilla pudding, it's like a sauce.

THERAPIST   Oh yah.

CLIENT   Okay. And I remember, I don't remember this but I've always had this reoccurring nightmare where they're dishing it out and and and it's and it's in this sort of damp wet place and I'm in a highchair. And they ladle it out, and you know how when you were children you get to the bottom and you ladle it and you give, you know, two ladles, two ladles, and then half a ladle, half a ladle, half a ladle, and then quarter of a ladle, quarter of a ladle, it, you know what I'm talking about. Well get it all ladled out and there's this enormous explosion, and there's all this noise and the ceiling shakes and dirt falls down into *my* [unclear] pudding. . . . But, it after a long time, I must have been eleven or twelve, before my grandfather died, I woke up one time and he finally said, "You have these reoccurring 'bout time, nightmares, you 'bout time you told me about them." And I said, "It's always the same one." He said, "It happened to you when you were about seven months old." Okay? I still have those.

Connected to her mourning, Lynn's recent experiences of despair could be contextualized as necessary excursions into the darkness of her loss. Her task when they happened next would be to once again defect from defection and run *toward* that which she had previously run *from*.

THERAPIST So in terms of giving you "coming attractions" . . .

CLIENT [laughs]

THERAPIST . . . uh, it would be that . . .

CLIENT [sighs deeply, and then whispers] Do you know how *scared* that I get?

THERAPIST And and it's, and I understand feeling scared, because you're experiencing things that you don't understand. But the piece that you must add to that is an appreciation that not understanding and being afraid is an important and healthy part of what's going on.

CLIENT [emphatically] That's all right, I just don't want to wake up dead in the morning!

THERAPIST You won't.

CLIENT By mistake!

THERAPIST You won't.

CLIENT Okay [nods].

THERAPIST If, if, if you, if you deal with what's happening now by trying to climb out of it . . .

CLIENT [sighs]

THERAPIST . . . then it will feel like quicksand. But if you turn around—and you've been doing this—and you walk toward it and you dive into it, and you jump into it, and you work to make the uncontrolled happen, then you're going to start the momentum of that circular turning.

CLIENT   [nods, pause, nods]

THERAPIST   Now I don't know, I don't know where you are in terms of how much deeper you're going to go. It could be the next time you go down, it, it could be further than you went the last time.

CLIENT   I know it will be.

THERAPIST   And, and so when you go into there—there's a quote that I'd like to remember for you . . .

CLIENT   [quietly] I just want to be able to trust myself that [unclear] I am going to surface. I'm willing to do it.

THERAPIST   If you go in with a flashlight, you'll be robbing yourself of the, of the full benefits that you can bring out. It's like going into a deep cave, if you go in with a flashlight you can see some of the things better, but that's the analytical part, the the ordering part wanting to make sense of . . .

CLIENT   I'm trying not to do that.

THERAPIST   So when you go down, you might bring your flashlight for a little ways, but at some point what I'd like you to do is take the flashlight and say "what the hell" and throw the flashlight away.

CLIENT   [nods]

THERAPIST   And take down with you, as a guide, not light—'cause the light will come up once you start back up—so you don't need to take the . . .

CLIENT   So it *is* like drowning . . . kind of.

THERAPIST   Except that when you're drowning what, what you do to stop drowning is you, you have to make this incredible effort to come up. And what you're doing is here is making an incredible effort to go down.

CLIENT   Okay.

THERAPIST   So if you get, if you get scared, the place to go running is further down.

CLIENT   What do I do when I can't breathe?
THERAPIST Go further down.
CLIENT   Okay.
THERAPIST Because, you see it's not like this [moves hand straight down], it's never like that. It's like this [hand inscribes the bottom half of a circle, going down and then back up]. And the further you go down, the further you go up.

With this understanding, the contraction of her continually recalled nightmare could be recrossed, its defect brought to effect by two small, but significant, shifts in the pattern.

THERAPIST But I'd also like you to have a dream. [pause] I'd like you to have a dream of being in the shelter— in the bomb shelter. As a young child. And when the pudding has been spooned out, I want you to quick!, quick, quick as a bunny, *take a little dirt and pour it on your pudding*. [turns cupped hand over, miming a pouring motion, holds the over-turned hand in mid-air, and waits]
CLIENT   [eyes go wide, face muscles slacken, and says in a small voice] Okay. [pause, breathes out heavily, nods, and then says softly] I'll try.
THERAPIST [long pause] My guess is *that* dream will be in color.
CLIENT   [breathes out sharply two times and inclines her head to the side]

In the following week, Lynn followed through on a plan she had long nurtured. She flew to a city she particularly loved, found a job and a house to rent, and made inquiries about enrolling in the university there. She returned for two subsequent appointments, each of which elaborated the long-circuit already described. A month later she moved, presumably having learned how to not-ask the right question of the right person—herself.

COMPLETION /
(CONNECTION/separation)

The differences must be expressed directly, with no vagueness or ambiguity. The unity, on the other hand, must never be expressed: it must be overheard, seen in a glass darkly, felt like a breath of wandering air. So it is well said,

> The unity is to be seen: afterwards, all the
> differences. This is the function of the poet.
> —*R. H. Blyth*

What, then, is a complete action? It is, I think, an action which one takes on one's own behalf, which is particular and complex, real not symbolic, which one can both accomplish on one's own and take full responsibility for. There are perhaps many such actions.

> —*Wendell Berry*

For the writing of this book to be a complete action it was essential that it not be organized as a response to Gregory Bateson's criticisms of family therapy. Regardless of whether the critique was supporting or the field defending (or whether there was a shuffling back and forth between in an attempt to be "objective"), this work could not have moved outside the context established by the initial questions raised.

And yet Bateson's concerns *were* voiced and the questions *were* asked—so how could the writing *not* have been contextualized by them? *This* was the question, the challenge, posed by chapter 1—the question that has taken so many pages to not-answer. And it is the very same issue faced and embraced by Taoists, Zen Buddhists, and therapists. To wit: The knowing act of marking a distinction is a distinct act of marked knowing. Given that to mark is to be marked, how can we mark without being marked? How can we remember to forget? Find loss? Desire to not-desire? Hate hate? Act to not-act? Grasp how to let go? Not get caught trying not to get caught?

As a defection from defection, not-answering is a strategy of con-volution, a recrossing of the distinction created by the question, a response that is neither and both an answer and not-an-answer. The discipline of such completion is a discipline of un-discipline. Ma-tsu, a teacher who lived in the early part of the Tang dynasty (618–906 C.E.), chides:

> The Tao has nothing to do with discipline. If you say that it is attained by discipline, finishing the discipline turns out to be losing the Tao. . . . If you say there is no discipline, this is to be the same as ordinary [unliberated] people.[28]

This discipline of freedom is, in Gary Snyder's terms, the "real work" of living:

> What is the real work? . . . It's good to work—I love work, work and play are one. . . . The real work is what we really do. And what our lives are. . . .
>
> [The real work is] to take the struggle on without the *least* hope of doing any good. To check the destruction of the interesting and necessary diversity of life on the planet so the dance can go on a little better for a little longer.[29]

The real work, the disciplined play of not-acting connects separations and separates connections with the indifferent commitment of an imaginative rigor and the committed indifference of a rigorous imagination. Mind—living—resides in *the relation between.*

NOTES

Chapter 1. The Relation Between

1. Gregory Bateson, *Steps to an Ecology of Mind,* p. 1.
2. See, for example, a number of essays reprinted in Bateson, ibid. (including "Style, Grace, and Information in Primitive Art," pp. 128–52; "Social Planning and the Concept of Deutero-Learning," pp. 159–76; and "Toward a Theory of Schizophrenia," pp. 201–77); Gregory Bateson, *Mind and Nature;* and Gregory Bateson and Mary Catherine Bateson, *Angels Fear.*
3. Mary Catherine Bateson, *With a Daughter's Eye,* p. 113.
4. See Alan Watts, *In My Own Way,* p. 387. Steve Heims ("Gregory Bateson and the Mathematicians," p. 150) views Bateson's relationship in the early 1950s with Watts as an important influence: "Typically for Bateson, he was drawing his ideas from a mathematician [Norbert Wiener] on the one hand, and from a student of oriental mysticism [Watts], on the other."
5. See M. C. Bateson, *With a Daughter's Eye,* and David Lipset, *Gregory Bateson: The Legacy of a Scientist.*
6. Gregory Bateson, "Intelligence, Experience, and Evolution," p. 50. Bateson's initial statement refers to the correspondence in form between processes of learning and processes of evolution.
7. Bateson, *Mind and Nature,* p. 97.
8. Heinz von Foerster relates that the participants came from the disciplines of psychiatry, engineering, physiology, anthropology, computer science, neurophysiology, zoology, psychology, sociology, philosophy, mathematics, biophysics, electronics,

and anatomy (quoted in Lynn Segal, *The Dream of Reality,* p. 160).

9. Bateson ("The Birth of a Matrix or Double Bind and Epistemology," in Milton M. Berger, ed., *Beyond the Double Bind,* p. 52) uses the term "'cybernetic' to describe complete circuiting systems."

10. Gregory Bateson, "From Versailles to Cybernetics," in *Steps,* p. 476.

11. See Steve J. Heims, "Gregory Bateson and the Mathematicians." As Jay Haley comments ("Plenary Session Dialogue," in Berger, *Beyond the Double Bind,* p. 192): "Looking back, I think Bateson introduced the idea of levels of communication into human and animal behavior. He keeps giving other people credit for it, but I don't know anybody else who introduced it before him. He also introduced the idea that when you do communicate on levels, these levels can conflict."

12. Bateson, *Mind and Nature,* p. 210.

13. Gregory Bateson, "Effects of Conscious Purpose on Human Adaptation," in *Steps,* p. 245.

14. Gregory Bateson, Don D. Jackson, Jay Haley, and John H. Weakland, "Toward a Theory of Schizophrenia," reprinted in *Steps,* pp. 201–27.

15. See Gregory Bateson, "Minimal Requirements for a Theory of Schizophrenia," in *Steps,* pp. 244–70; "Double Bind, 1969," in *Steps,* pp. 271–78; "The Birth of a Matrix," in Berger, *Beyond the Double Bind,* pp. 39–64; "Theory versus Empiricism," in Berger, *Beyond the Double Bind,* pp. 234–37.

16. Gregory Bateson and Jurgen Ruesch, *Communication,* p. 179. Bateson gives credit to Warren McCulloch for first proposing that messages can be seen in terms of report and command (Bradford P. Keeney and Frank N. Thomas, "Cybernetic Foundations of Family Therapy," in Fred P. Piercy and Douglas H. Sprenkle, eds., *Family Therapy Sourcebook,* p. 263).

17. Jay Haley ("Development of a Theory," in *Reflections on Therapy and Other Essays,* p. 43) dates the change to 1958.

18. Gregory Bateson, "A System's Approach," p. 242. Family ther-

apy arose not only in the Bateson project. Psychiatrists such as Ackerman, Bowen and Wynne, Boszormenyi-Nagy, Lidz, and Whitaker were, in the same time period, each initiating family sessions at their various locations around the United States.

19. Lipset, *Gregory Bateson*, p. 215.

20. Ibid., p. 237. Letter from Gregory Bateson to E. G. Mishler, 22 May 1964.

21. Bateson, "Theory versus Empiricism," in Berger, *Beyond the Double Bind*, p. 237.

22. Bateson, "Minimal Requirements for a Theory of Schizophrenia," in *Steps*, p. 269.

23. Bradford P. Keeney, "Gregory Bateson: A Final Metaphor," p. 1.

24. Bateson and Bateson, *Angels Fear*, p. 204.

25. Bateson, "Social Planning and the Concept of Deutero-Learning," in *Steps*, p. 163.

26. See Gregory Bateson, "A Re-examination of 'Bateson's Rule,'" in *Steps*, pp. 379—95.

27. Bateson and Bateson, *Angels Fear*, pp. 204—5.

28. Bateson, "Double Bind, 1969," in *Steps*, p. 273.

29. Stewart Brand, "Both Sides of the Necessary Paradox," p. 28.

30. Gregory Bateson, "Pathologies of Epistemology," in *Steps*, p. 479.

31. In Gyomay M. Kubose, *Zen Koans*, pp. 156, 69, 31, and 30 respectively.

32. See, for example, Alan Watts, *The Way of Zen*, and Arthur F. Wright, *Buddhism in Chinese History*.

33. Yu-lan Fung, *A History of Chinese Philosophy: Volume 1*, p. 175.

34. Opinions vary as to dates. See John Blofeld, trans., *I Ching*; Yu-lan Fung, *A History of Chinese Philosophy*; Iulian K. Shchutskii, *Researches on the I Ching*; Alan Watts, *Tao: The Watercourse Way*; Hellmut Wilhelm, *Change: Eight Lectures on the I Ching*; Richard Wilhelm, trans., *The I Ching or Book of Changes*.

35. John C. H. Wu, trans., *Lao Tzu: Tao Te Ching*; Burton Wat-

son, trans., *The Complete Works of Chuang Tzu;* Titus Yü and Douglas Flemons, trans., *I Ching: A New Translation.*

36. L. Wieger, *Chinese Characters,* p. 789.
37. Ibid., p. 326.
38. Watts, *Tao: The Watercourse Way,* p. 40.
39. Bateson, "A Systems Approach," p. 244.

Chapter 2. COMPLETION

1. Gregory Bateson, *Mind and Nature,* p. 147.
2. Francisco J. Varela, *Principles of Biological Autonomy,* p. 84.
3. Bateson, *Mind and Nature,* pp. 7–8.
4. Gregory Bateson, "Form, Substance, and Difference," in *Steps to an Ecology of Mind,* p. 457.
5. Ibid.
6. Varela, *Principles of Biological Autonomy,* p. 84.
7. Morris Berman, *The Reenchantment of the World,* p. 355.
8. Abraham H. Maslow, *The Psychology of Science,* p. 119.
9. Floyd Merrell, *Semiotic Foundations,* p. 11.
10. Benjamin Lee Whorf, "Language, Mind, and Reality," in J. B. Carroll, ed., *Language, Thought, and Reality,* p. 262.
11. Gregory Bateson, "Afterword," in John Brockman, ed., *About Bateson,* p. 244.
12. See especially: Gregory Bateson, *Steps to an Ecology of Mind;* Wendell Berry, *Home Economics;* Morris Berman, *The Reenchantment of the World;* Abraham Maslow, *The Psychology of Science;* Alan Watts, *Psychotherapy East and West;* Anthony Wilden, *System and Structure.*
13. Maslow, *The Psychology of Science,* p. 119.
14. Bateson, "Form, Substance, and Difference," in *Steps,* p. 462.
15. Berry, *Home Economics,* p. 9.
16. Watts, *Psychotherapy East and West,* pp. 19–20.
17. Berman, *The Reenchantment of the World,* p. 108.
18. Ibid., p. 125.
19. Gregory Bateson, "The Cybernetics of 'Self': A Theory of Alcoholism," in *Steps,* p. 313.

20. Ibid., p. 310.
21. Wilden, *System and Structure,* p. 210.
22. Berry, *Home Economics,* pp. 69–70.
23. Gregory Bateson, "The Roots of Ecological Crisis," in *Steps,* p. 493.
24. Kenneth Burke calls the shifting between "a part of" and "apart from" an "unassuming miracle-worker": "It can so readily function as a tiny difference that can make a world of difference. . . . Its susceptibilities admonish us to recall that while we are all 'a part of' our natural environment, there is also a notable respect in which each of us is 'apart from' it, and even apart from the others of our own kind" ("Addendum on Bateson," in Carol Wilder and John H. Weakland, eds., *Rigor and Imagination,* p. 342). The interplay is between separation and connection.
25. Francisco J. Varela, "Not One, Not Two"; and *Principles of Biological Autonomy.* In keeping with Varela's usage, *hegelian* is left uncapitalized.
26. Ibid.
27. Varela, "Not One, Not Two," p. 63.
28. The notion of logical types is discussed in chap. 1.
29. Bateson, "Minimal Requirements for a Theory of Schizophrenia," in *Steps,* p. 267.
30. Varela, *Principles of Biological Autonomy,* p. 102.
31. Varela, "Not One, Not Two," p. 64.
32. Ibid.
33. Quoted in Lynn Segal, *The Dream of Reality,* p. 164.
34. Bateson, *Mind and Nature,* p. 222.
35. This characterization of whole/part distinctions has obviously been significantly influenced by Varela ("Not One, Not Two"; *Principles of Biological Autonomy*) and owes much to the work of Bradford Keeney (*Aesthetics of Change*); however, I make a departure in explicitly contextualizing whole/part complementaries as an expression of the relationship between connection and separation. I have also developed somewhat

different conventions for representing and discussing the layered patterns of complementary relationships (see below).

36. See Douglas R. Hofstadter, *Gödel, Escher, Bach,* pp. 310–36, for a unique and engaging presentation of much the same idea.

37. "Not One, Not Two" is the title of Varela's 1976 article.

38. R. H. Blyth, *Haiku,* p. ix.

39. Quoted in Milton M. Berger, ed., *Beyond the Double Bind,* p. 82.

40. Bateson, *Mind and Nature,* p. 242.

41. Berry, *Home Economics,* p. 10.

42. Ibid., pp. 11–12.

43. Wendell Berry, "The Cold," in *Collected Poems,* p. 59.

44. See Bateson, *Mind and Nature,* pp. 88–90.

45. See Bateson, *Mind and Nature.*

46. Ibid., pp. 157–58.

47. Adapted from John C. H. Wu, trans., *Lao Tzu: Tao Teh Ching,* p. 3; Wing-Tsit Chan, trans., *The Way of Lao Tzu,* p. 101; and Titus Yü, personal communication, spring 1981. I have omitted the semicolons that usually grace the end of each line, as the parallel structure and paratactic juxtaposition of the phrases are adequately indicated by their placement on separate lines. The words *presence* and *absence* render *yu* 有 and *wu* 無 respectively.

48. Adapted from Wu, *Lao Tzu,* chap. 40, p. 59. The word *fan* 反, translated here as "returning," was originally written as 𠬝. According to L. Wieger (*Chinese Characters,* p. 120), it depicts the motion ⌐ of a hand 彐 turning over. He says it means "to turn over, inversion."

49. Lionel Kearns, postcard to author, 21 April 1985.

50. Bateson, *Mind and Nature,* p. 104.

51. Bateson, "The Cybernetics of 'Self,'" in *Steps,* p. 315.

52. Bateson, *Mind and Nature,* p. 104.

53. Bateson, "Form, Substance, and Difference," in *Steps,* p. 459.

54. Alan Watts, *Tao: The Watercourse Way,* p. 40.

55. Wu, *Lao Tzu*, p. 7. The words "within you" render *chung* 中, or "center."
56. Chung-yuan Chang, *Creativity and Taoism*, p. 19.
57. Lao Tzu says elsewhere (chap. 47) that one can know all under heaven without ever leaving one's door.
58. Watts, *Psychotherapy East and West*, p. 11.
59. Bateson, "Form, Substance, and Difference," in *Steps*, p. 461.
60. Varela, *Principles of Biological Autonomy*, pp. 270–71.
61. Cited in Gregory Bateson and Mary Catherine Bateson, *Angels Fear*, p. 25. The authors actually slightly misquote and mispunctuate the question as: "What is a number that a man may know it: and what is a man that he may know a number?"
62. Bateson, *Mind and Nature*, p. 9.
63. Ibid., p. 12.
64. Bateson, "The Cybernetics of 'Self,'" in *Steps*, p. 313.
65. Ibid.
66. Alasdair MacIntyre, "Ontology," in P. Edwards, ed., *The Encyclopedia of Philosophy: Volume 5*, pp. 542–43.
67. Bateson and Bateson, *Angels Fear*, p. 19.
68. Bateson, *Mind and Nature*, p. 110.
69. Ibid., page 108, footnote.
70. Werner Heisenberg's Uncertainty Principle, formulated in 1927, generalizes the realization that the light needed to observe an electron will itself possess enough energy to knock the electron out of position; the conducting of an experiment alters its own results (Berman, *The Reenchantment of the World*, p. 137).
71. Watts, *Psychotherapy East and West*, p. 88.
72. Berman, *The Reenchantment of the World*, p. 137.
73. Varela, *Principles of Biological Autonomy*, p. 275.
74. Ernst von Glasersfeld, "An Introduction to Radical Constructivism," in Paul Watzlawick, ed., *The Invented Reality*, p. 24.
75. Bateson, *Mind and Nature*, p. 108, footnote.
76. Bateson and Bateson, *Angels Fear*, p. 24.
77. Bateson, *Mind and Nature*, pp. 31–32.

78. Bateson ("Afterword," in Brockman, ed., *About Bateson*, p. 244) himself equates his idea of "difference" with Spencer-Brown's notions of "distinction" and "indication."

79. Bateson, *Mind and Nature*, p. 12.

80. Bateson, "Form, Substance, and Difference," in *Steps*, p. 459.

81. Bateson, *Mind and Nature*, p. 107.

82. Varela, *Principles of Biological Autonomy*, p. 275.

83. Bateson and Bateson, *Angels Fear*, p. 207. G. Bateson (*Mind and Nature*, p. 97, footnote) also uses the term *consciousness* to refer to "that strange experience whereby we (and perhaps other mammals) are sometimes conscious of the products of our perception and thought but unconscious of the greater part of the process."

84. Koans are knotted stories or questions that do not make "conventional" sense. They are given to students in the Zen tradition as part of their practice in breaking out of habits of dichotomous thinking and acting.

85. A play on his phrase, "not one, not two" (see Varela, "Not One, Not Two").

86. Francisco J. Varela, "The Creative Circle," in Watzlawick, *The Invented Reality*, p. 322.

87. See especially Bateson, *Mind and Nature*.

88. G. Spencer-Brown, *Laws of Form*, p. 105.

89. Bateson, "Style, Grace, and Information in Primitive Art," in *Steps*, p. 145.

90. Bateson and Bateson, *Angels Fear*, p. 188.

91. Chan, *The Way of Lao Tzu*, p. 97.

92. Gregory Bateson, "Ecology of Mind: The Sacred," in Rick Fields, ed., *Loka*, p. 24.

93. Chan, *The Way of Lao Tzu*, p. 97.

94. *Tao Te Ching*, chap. 1.

95. *Tao Te Ching*, chap. 14.

96. Bateson, *Mind and Nature*, p. 107.

97. As we shall see later, this question resounds with implications for memory and for therapy.

Notes | 147

98. The words *holy, health,* and *whole* share a common etymological root—the Old English word *hal.*
99. Bateson, "Ecology of Mind," in Fields, *Loka,* p. 24.
100. Adapted from Chang (*Creativity and Taosim,* p. 30) and R. H. Blyth (*Zen in English Literature and Oriental Classics,* p. 141).
101. Wu, *Lao Tzu,* chap. 27, p. 37.
102. Bateson, "Afterword," in Brockman, ed., *About Bateson,* p. 244.
103. Bateson and Bateson, *Angels Fear,* p. 28.
104. Gregory Bateson, *Metaphors and Butterflies.* Audio cassette of lecture given at Esalen Institute, 1975.
105. Octavio Paz, *Children of the Mire,* pp. 72–73.
106. Bateson, *Metaphors and Butterflies.*
107. Gregory Bateson, *What Is Epistemology?* Audio cassette of lecture given at Esalen Institute, 1979.
108. Bateson maintains that "poetry is not a sort of distorted or decorated prose, but rather prose is poetry which has been stripped down and pinned to a Procrustean bed of logic" ("Style, Grace, and Information in Primitive Art," in *Steps,* p. 136).
109. From William Carlos Williams, "To Daphne and Virginia," in *Pictures from Brueghel and Other Poems,* pp. 75–76.
110. Bateson, *Mind and Nature,* p. 14.
111. Bateson, "Style, Grace, and Information in Primitive Art," *Steps,* p. 133.
112. It is not surprising that it was a poet who brought a relational understanding to the field of botany, given how exquisitely aware poets must be of the shape of their descriptions.
113. Bateson, *Mind and Nature,* p. 17.
114. Bateson and Bateson, *Angels Fear,* p. 154.
115. Bradford P. Keeney, *On Paradigmatic Change,* p. 16.
116. From William Carlos Williams, "The Desert Music," in *Pictures from Brueghel,* pp. 108–9.
117. *Tao Te Ching,* chap. 64. Wu's *Lao Tzu* (p. 93) served as a

crib, but much verbiage has been eliminated, the form has been streamlined, and the inappropriate male pronouns have been removed. "Doesn't fuss" renders *wu wei* 無 為 (see below).

118. *Tao Te Ching*, chap. 5.

119. *Tao Te Ching*, chap. 4.

120. Adapted from Wu, *Lao Tzu*, chap. 48, p. 69. The words translated here as "accumulating" 益 and "diminishing" 損 are the respective titles of chapters 42 and 41 of the *I Ching*. In that context they were rendered as "Giving To" and "Taking Away" (Titus Yü and Douglas Flemons, trans., *I Ching*, pp. 153, 150).

121. Bateson and Bateson, *Angels Fear*, p. 81.

122. Blyth, *Haiku*, p. 192. Blyth (p. 28) relates that Ryota (1707–1787) studied Zen under Rito and Ransetsu.

123. John Cage, "Lecture on Nothing," in *Silence*, p. 109.

124. Varela, *Principles of Biological Autonomy*, p. 104.

125. Chan, *The Way of Lao Tzu*, p. 97.

126. This character means both "continuum" and "continuation." The English word *forever* almost contains a "river," an image which Lao Tzu relies on frequently as a metaphor for Tao (e.g., chaps. 8, 28, 32).

127. To appreciate the pun it is necessary to know that *Tao* is pronounced "dow."

128. Berry, *Home Economics*, pp. 4–5.

129. Heinz von Foerster, *Observing Systems*, p. 308.

130. Richard Wilhelm, *Lectures on the I Ching*, p. 7.

131. Titus Yü, personal communication, January 1981.

132. In Ernest Fenollosa, *The Chinese Written Character as a Medium for Poetry*, ed., Ezra Pound, p. 45.

133. Benjamin Hoff, *The Tao of Pooh*, p. 68.

134. Wu's actual rendering of the phrase *wei wu wei* is, in my opinion, a little less compelling: "Do the Non-Ado" (*Lao Tzu*, p. 91).

135. Wu, *Lao Tzu*, p. 53.

136. John Grinder and Richard Bandler, *Trance-formations*, ed., Connirae Andreas, p. 67.

137. Berman, *The Reenchantment of the World*, p. 17.

138. Watson, *The Complete Works of Chuang Tzu*, chap. 19, pp. 204–05.

139. Gary Snyder, *The Real Work*, p. 67.

140. Yü and Flemons, *I Ching*, p. 26.

141. See particularly Bateson, *Mind and Nature*. The story of this puzzle and its interpretative solution is based on the research and analysis conducted by Yü and Flemons in preparing our translation of the *I Ching*.

142. Iulian K. Shchutskii, *Researches on the I Ching*, p. 143.

143. Ibid.

144. Richard Wilhelm, trans., *I Ching or Book of Changes*, p. 369.

145. Shchutskii, *Researches on the I Ching*, p. 136.

146. In contrast, the hypotactic structure of English is hierarchical. In Wilhelm's sentence, *sublime* modifies *success* and is thus subordinate to it.

147. An archaic form of the word *inflame*.

148. Bateson, *Mind and Nature*, pp. 193–94.

149. Ibid., p. 52.

150. Ibid., p. 53.

151. Watson, *The Complete Works of Chuang Tzu*, chap. 22, p. 235.

152. In this sense, *threshold* becomes virtually synonymous with *structure*. See Bateson and Bateson, *Angels Fear*.

153. Bateson, *Mind and Nature*, pp. 114–15.

154. Snyder, *The Real Work*, p. 116.

155. Bateson, *Mind and Nature*, p. 59.

156. Bateson, "Style, Grace, and Information in Primitive Art," in *Steps*, p. 146.

157. *Tao Te Ching*, chap. 22. Adapted from D. C. Lau, trans., *Lao Tzu: Tao Te Ching*, p. 79; and Richard Wilhelm, trans., *Tao Te Ching*, pp. 35–36.

158. Ariane Rump and Wing-Tsit Chan, trans., *Commentary on the Lao Tzu by Wang Pi*, p. 68.

159. Berry, *Home Economics,* p. 15. The artist Harold Towne says precisely the same thing of Picasso: "His genius lay in his timing—he always knew when to stop." (Interview by Peter Gzowski, 22 August 1986. "Morningside" [radio program]. Canadian Broadcasting Corporation.)
160. Wu, *Lao Tzu,* chap. 29, p. 41.

Chapter 3. CONTRACTION

1. *O. E. D.,* 1971, *s.v.* "defection."
2. Ibid., *s.v.* "defect."
3. The double bind is discussed briefly in chap. 1. See Gregory Bateson, *Steps to an Ecology of Mind,* especially pp. 201–78.
4. Gregory Bateson ("Style, Grace, and Information in Primitive Art," in *Steps,* pp. 128–52) considers feelings to be patterns of relationship, algorithms of the heart or unconscious (see especially p. 140).
5. Roy A. Rappaport, "Sanctity and Adaptation," p. 54.
6. Gregory Bateson, "Effects of Conscious Purpose on Human Adaptation," in *Steps,* p. 445.
7. Gregory Bateson, "Conscious Purpose versus Nature," in *Steps,* pp. 433–34.
8. See Stewart Brand, "Both Sides of the Necessary Paradox."
9. *Tao Te Ching,* chap. 42.
10. Gary Snyder, *The Real Work,* p. 109.
11. Gregory Bateson, "The Cybernetics of 'Self': A Theory of Alcoholism," in *Steps,* p. 335. A Taoist would be more likely to characterize nature in terms of no purpose rather than multi-purposes, but the point is much the same. Cf. also Francisco J. Varela, *Principles of Biological Autonomy,* p. 67, who says that living systems are purposeless.
12. E. E. Cummings, "whatever's merely wilful," in *Complete Poems 1913–1962,* p. 742.
13. Gregory Bateson, "Minimal Requirements for a Theory of Schizophrenia," in *Steps,* p. 265.

14. Gregory Bateson, "A Conversation with Gregory Bateson," in Rick Fields, ed., *Loka,* p. 31.
15. The quote—"Knowing ignorance: tiptop / Ignorant knowing: defective"—is from chap. 71 of the *Tao Te Ching.* The Chinese is read top down and right to left. The words *ignorance* and *ignorant* (from the Latin *in-,* "not" and *gnoscere,* "to know") render the characters *pu chih*—literally "not 不 know 知." The term *tiptop* translates *shang* 上, which means "above" or "up."
16. Bateson, "Style, Grace, and Information in Primitive Art," in *Steps,* p. 146.
17. Paul Watzlawick, John H. Weakland, and Richard Fisch specifically discuss solutions as problems in their book *Change.*
18. Gregory Bateson, "The Birth of a Matrix or Double Bind and Epistemology," in Milton M. Berger, ed., *Beyond the Double Bind,* p. 62.
19. Gregory Bateson and Mary Catherine Bateson, *Angels Fear,* p. 133.
20. Wendell Berry, *Home Economics,* p. 69.
21. Bateson and Bateson, *Angels Fear,* p. 91. The notion of logical types was also discussed briefly in chap. 1.
22. Gregory Bateson, "The Roots of Ecological Crisis," in *Steps,* pp. 488–89.
23. Bateson, "The Cybernetics of 'Self,'" in *Steps,* pp. 310–11.
24. Gregory Bateson, "The Logical Categories of Learning and Communication," in *Steps,* p. 301.
25. See Bateson, *Steps,* and *Mind and Nature.*
26. Berry, *Home Economics,* p. 71.
27. Anthony Wilden, *System and Structure,* p. 222.
28. Berry, *Home Economics,* p. 72.
29. Wilden, *System and Structure,* p. 116.
30. Edward E. Sampson, "The Inversion of Mastery," pp. 35–36.
31. See Bateson, "The Cybernetics of 'Self,'" in *Steps,* especially pp. 320–29.
32. George A. Kelly, *A Theory of Personality,* pp. 62–63.

33. Bateson, "The Cybernetics of 'Self,'" in *Steps*, 318–19.
34. Henri Bergson, *An Introduction to Metaphysics*, p. 153.
35. Jon Elster, "Active and Passive Negation," in Paul Watzlawick, ed., *The Invented Reality*, pp. 175–205.
36. Ibid., p. 182.
37. Ibid., p. 185.
38. Bateson, *Steps; Mind and Nature*.
39. Elster, "Active and Passive Negation," in Watzlawick, *The Invented Reality*, p. 195.
40. G. Spencer-Brown, *Laws of Form*, p. 1.
41. Floyd Merrell, *Semiotic Foundations*, p. 11.
42. D. T. Suzuki, "Existentialism, Pragmatism and Zen," in William Barrett, ed., *Zen Buddhism*, p. 269.
43. Brian Fawcett, "How many times I've wanted," in *Tristram's Book*, p. 52.
44. G. Spencer-Brown, *Laws of Form*, p. 2.
45. In Spencer-Brown's terms, the marking of a distinction creates an *indication*, where one of the two sides becomes primary. Bradford Keeney (in *Aesthetics of Change*) equates indication with the notion of punctuation.
46. Bateson, "The Birth of a Matrix," in Berger, *Beyond the Double Bind*, p. 64.

Chapter 4. From CONTRACTION to COMPLETION

1. Wendell Berry, *The Unsettling of America*, p. 137.
2. Gregory Bateson, *Mind and Nature*, p. 59.
3. Ezra Pound, "Canto XLV," in *The Cantos of Ezra Pound*, p. 229.
4. Berry, *The Unsettling of America*, p. 19.
5. Ibid., p. 22.
6. Ibid., p. 110.
7. Alan Watts (*Psychotherapy East and West*, p. 98) advises that any system of therapy "which leaves the individual upon one horn of the dualistic dilemma is at best the achievement of courageous despair."

8. Cf. the *O.E.D.* (1971), *s.v.* "effect": "*To bring to effect, carry into effect:* to accomplish, bring to a successful issue." Note that in the epigraph by Lao Tzu at the beginning of this chapter, the words *defecting, defection,* and *defective* all render *ping* 病. As explained earlier, *defect* means "the lack or absence of something essential to completeness" (*O.E.D.,* 1971).

9. The *O.E.D.* (1971) defines *chasmal* as being "of the nature of or belonging to a chasm." It is used here to denote a dichotomous orientation to distinctions. A *chiasm* is an intercrossing or a decussation (*O.E.D.,* 1971). Recalling Spencer-Brown's notion of *recrossing* (*Laws of Form*), the term *chiasmal* can be understood as referring to the recrossing or the completion of distinctions.

10. Bradford P. Keeney and Jeffrey M. Ross, *Mind in Therapy,* p. 53.

11. Ibid.

12. For example, Carl Whitaker (John R. Neill and David P. Kniskern, eds., *From Psyche to System,* p. 205) notes that "the ordinary medical system of replying affirmatively to a request for help by one person in a marriage, excluding the other, may in effect be an intervention favoring divorce."

13. Alan Watts, *Psychotherapy East and West.* The first quote is from page 125, the second from page 129.

14. Gregory Bateson, "The Birth of a Matrix or Double Bind and Epistemology," in Milton M. Berger, ed., *Beyond the Double Bind,* pp. 62–63.

15. Ibid., pp. 62–64.

16. Adapted from Watts, *Psychotherapy East and West,* p. 135.

17. Berry, *The Unsettling of America,* p. 22.

18. Bateson, "The Birth of a Matrix," in Berger, *Beyond the Double Bind,* p. 64. Gary Snyder speculates that the origins of meditation lie in hunting: "Our earlier traditions of life prior to agriculture required literally thousands of years of great attention and awareness, and long hours of stillness" (*The Real Work,* p. 107).

19. Alan Watts, *The Way of Zen,* pp. 152–153.

20. Wendell Berry, "The Plowboy Interview: Wendell Berry," p. 8.

21. Watts, *Psychotherapy East and West,* p. 158.

22. Gregory Bateson, "Ecology of Mind: The Sacred," in Rick Fields, ed., *Loka,* p. 26.

23. The particularities of the case and the general orientation of the approach are necessarily entwined; the commentary will, at times, attempt to point out the differences.

24. The client, Lynn, was seen a total of seven times. The following excerpts are from two of the meetings: the first and the fifth. Names and extraneous details have been changed to protect anonymity. Working relationally with one person is, in many respects, the most demanding of therapeutic situations, but circumstances dictated that she be seen alone.

25. Lynn freely used psychological terminology, and it was thus incorporated into the talk. She had been to a number of therapists in the past.

26. The notion of mourning was an appropriate fit given the specifics of the situation; however, the stacking of Lynn's double bind could have been inverted in other ways as well.

27. Pascal via Bateson (see *Steps*).

28. Cited in Watts, *Psychotherapy East and West,* p. 128.

29. Snyder, *The Real Work,* pp. 81–82.

BIBLIOGRAPHY

Bateson, Gregory. "Social Planning and the Concept of Deutero-Learning" (1942). Reprinted in *Steps to an Ecology of Mind,* 159–76. New York: Ballantine Books, 1972 (cited hereafter as *Steps*).

———. *Naven: A Survey of the Problems Suggested by a Composite Picture of the Culture of a New Guinea Tribe Drawn from Three Points of View.* 2nd ed. Stanford, Calif.: Stanford University Press, 1958.

———. "Minimal Requirements for a Theory of Schizophrenia" (1959). Reprinted in *Steps,* 244–70.

———. "From Versailles to Cybernetics" (1966). Reprinted in *Steps,* 469–77.

———. "Style, Grace, and Information in Primitive Art" (1967). Reprinted in *Steps,* 128–52.

———. "Conscious Purpose versus Nature" (1968). Reprinted in *Steps,* 426–39.

———. "Effects of Conscious Purpose on Human Adaptation" (1968). Reprinted in *Steps,* 440–47.

———. "Double Bind, 1969" (1969). Reprinted in *Steps,* 271–78.

———. "Pathologies of Epistemology" (1969). Reprinted in *Steps,* 478–87.

———. "Form, Substance, and Difference" (1970). Reprinted in *Steps,* 448–65.

———. "The Roots of Ecological Crisis" (1970). Reprinted in *Steps,* 488–93.

———. "The Cybernetics of 'Self': A Theory of Alcoholism" (1971). Reprinted in *Steps,* 309–37.

———. "The Logical Categories of Learning and Communication" (1971). Reprinted in *Steps,* 279–308.

———. "A Re-examination of 'Bateson's Rule'" (1971). Reprinted in *Steps*, 379–95.

———. "A Systems Approach." *International Journal of Psychiatry* 9 (1971): 242–44.

———. *Steps to an Ecology of Mind.* New York: Ballantine Books, 1972.

———. "A Conversation with Gregory Bateson." In *Loka: A Journal from Naropa Institute*, edited by Rick Fields, 28–34. Garden City, N.Y.: Anchor Books, 1975.

———. "Ecology of Mind: The Sacred." In *Loka: A Journal from Naropa Institute*, edited by Rick Fields, 24–27. Garden City, N.Y.: Anchor Books, 1975.

———. *Metaphors and Butterflies.* Big Sur, Calif.: Esalen Institute, 1975. Speaker. Audio cassette.

———. "Afterword." In *About Bateson: Essays on Gregory Bateson*, edited by John Brockman, 235–47. New York: E. P. Dutton, 1977.

———. "The Birth of a Matrix or Double Bind and Epistemology." In *Beyond the Double Bind: Communication and Family Systems, Theories, and Techniques with Schizophrenics*, edited by Milton M. Berger, 41–64. New York: Brunner/Mazel, 1978.

———. "Intelligence, Experience, and Evolution." *Revision* 1 (Spring 1978): 50–55.

———. "Theory versus Empiricism." In *Beyond the Double Bind: Communication and Family Systems, Theories, and Techniques with Schizophrenics*, edited by Milton M. Berger, 234–37. New York: Brunner/Mazel, 1978.

———. *Mind and Nature: A Necessary Unity.* Toronto: Bantam Books, 1979.

———. *What Is Epistemology?* Big Sur, Cal.: Esalen Institute, 1979. Speaker. Audio cassette.

Bateson, Gregory, and Mary Catherine Bateson. *Angels Fear: Towards an Epistemology of the Sacred.* New York: Macmillan, 1987.

Bateson, Gregory, Don D. Jackson, Jay Haley, and John H. Weakland. "Toward a Theory of Schizophrenia" (1956). Reprinted in *Steps*, 201–27.

Bateson, Gregory, and Jurgen Reusch. *Communication: The Social Matrix of Psychiatry*, 3rd ed. New York: W. W. Norton, 1987.

Bateson, Mary Catherine. *With a Daughter's Eye: A Memoir of Margaret Mead and Gregory Bateson*. New York: Washington Square Press, 1984.

Berger, Milton M., ed. *Beyond the Double Bind: Communication and Family Systems, Theories, and Techniques with Schizophrenics*. New York: Brunner/Mazel, 1978.

Bergson, Henri. *An Introduction to Metaphysics: The Creative Mind*. Translated by Mabelle L. Andison. Totowa, N.J.: Rowman and Allanheld, 1946.

Berman, Morris. *The Reenchantment of the World*. New York: Bantam Books, 1984.

Berry, Wendell. "The Plowboy Interview: Wendell Berry." *Plowboy*, March 1973, 7–12.

———. *The Unsettling of America: Culture and Agriculture*. San Francisco: Sierra Club Books, 1977.

———. *Collected Poems*. San Francisco: North Point Press, 1985.

———. *Home Economics*. San Francisco: North Point Press, 1987.

Blofeld, John, trans. *I Ching*. New York: E. P. Dutton, 1965.

Blyth, R. H. *Haiku*. Tokyo: Hokuseido Press, 1949.

———. *Zen in English Literature and Oriental Classics*. New York: E. P. Dutton, 1960.

Brand, Stewart. "Both Sides of the Necessary Paradox." *Harper's*, November 1973.

Burke, Kenneth. "Addendum on Bateson." In *Rigor and Imagination: Essays from the Legacy of Gregory Bateson*, edited by Carol Wilder and John H. Weakland, 341–46. New York: Praeger, 1981.

Cage, John. *Silence*. Cambridge: MIT Press, 1961.

Chan, Wing-Tsit, trans. *The Way of Lao Tzu*. Indianapolis: Bobbs-Merrill, 1963.

Chang, Chung-Yuan. *Creativity and Taoism*. New York: Harper Colophon, 1963.

Cummings, E. E. *Complete Poems 1913–1962*. New York: Liveright Publishing Corp., forthcoming.

Elster, Jon. "Active and Passive Negation: An Essay in Ibanskian Sociology," translated by Ronald Garwood. In *The Invented Reality: How Do We Know What We Believe We Know? (Contributions to Constructivism)*, edited by Paul Watzlawick, 175–205. New York: W. W. Norton, 1984.

Fawcett, Brian. *Tristram's Book*. Vancouver: *The Capilano Review*, no. 19 (1981).

Fenollosa, Ernest. *The Chinese Written Character as a Medium for Poetry*. Edited by Ezra Pound. San Francisco: City Lights, 1936.

Foucault, Michel. *Language, Counter-Memory, Practice: Selected Essays and Interviews by Michel Foucault*. Edited by Donald F. Bouchard and translated by Donald F. Bouchard and Sherry Simon. Ithaca, N.Y.: Cornell University Press.

Fung, Yu-Lan. *A History of Chinese Philosophy: Volume 1 (The Period of the Philosophers)*. 2nd ed. Translated by Derk Bodde. Princeton: Princeton University Press, 1952.

Grinder, John, and Richard Bandler. *Trance-formations*. Edited by Connirae Andreas. Moab, Utah: Real People Press, 1981.

Haley, Jay. "Plenary Session Dialogue." In *Beyond the Double Bind: Communication and Family Systems, Theories, and Techniques with Schizophrenics*, edited by Milton M. Berger, 191–96. New York: Brunner/Mazel, 1978.

———. "Development of a Theory: A History of a Research Project." In *Reflections on Therapy and Other Essays*, 1–63. Rockville, Md.: Family Therapy Institute, 1981.

Heims, Steve. "Gregory Bateson and the Mathematicians: From Interdisciplinary Interaction to Societal Functions." *Journal of the History of the Behavioral Sciences* 13 (1977): 141–59.

Hoff, Benjamin. *The Tao of Pooh*. Middlesex: Penguin Books, 1982.

Hofstadter, Douglas R. *Gödel, Escher, Bach: An Eternal Golden Braid*. New York: Basic Books, 1979.

Keeney, Bradford P. *On Paradigmatic Change: Conversations with Gregory Bateson.* Typescript, 1977.
————. "Gregory Bateson: A Final Metaphor." *Family Process* 20 (1981): 1.
————. *Aesthetics of Change.* New York: Guilford Press, 1983.
Keeney, Bradford P., and Jeffrey M. Ross. *Mind in Therapy.* New York: Basic Books, 1985.
Keeney, Bradford P., and Frank N. Thomas. "Cybernetic Foundations of Family Therapy." In *Family Therapy Sourcebook,* edited by Fred P. Piercy and Douglas H. Sprenkle, 262–87. New York: Guilford Press, 1986.
Kelly, George A. *A Theory of Personality.* New York: W. W. Norton, 1963.
Kubose, Gyomay M. *Zen Koans.* Chicago: Henry Regnery, 1973.
Lau, D. C., trans. *Lao Tzu: Tao Te Ching.* Middlesex: Penguin Books, 1963.
Lipset, David. *Gregory Bateson: The Legacy of a Scientist.* Boston: Beacon Press, 1982.
MacIntyre, Alasdair. "Ontology." In *The Encyclopedia of Philosophy, vol. 5,* edited by Paul Edwards, 542–43. New York: Macmillan and The Free Press, 1967.
Maslow, Abraham H. *The Psychology of Science.* New York: Harper and Row, 1966.
Merrell, Floyd. *Semiotic Foundations: Steps Toward an Epistemology of Written Texts.* Bloomington: Indiana University Press, 1982.
Neill, John R., and David P. Kniskern, eds. *From Psyche to System: The Evolving Therapy of Carl Whitaker.* New York: Guilford Press, 1982.
Paz, Octavio. *Children of the Mire: Modern Poetry from Romanticism to the Avant-Garde.* Translated by Rachel Phillips. Cambridge: Harvard University Press, 1974.
————. *The Collected Poems of Octavio Paz: 1957–1987.* Edited and translated by Eliot Weinberger. New York: New Directions, 1987.

Pound, Ezra. "Canto XLV." In *The Cantos of Ezra Pound*, 229–30. New York: New Directions, 1972.

Rappaport, Roy A. "Sanctity and Adaptation." *CoEvolutionary Quarterly*, Summer 1974, 54–68.

Rump, Ariane, and Wing-Tsit Chan. *Commentary on the Lao Tzu by Wang Pi*. Hawaii: University of Hawaii Press, 1979.

Sampson, Edward E. "The Inversion of Mastery." *Cybernetic* 2 (1986): 26–39.

Segal, Lynn. *The Dream of Reality: Heinz von Foerster's Constructivism*. New York: W. W. Norton, 1986.

Shchutskii, Iulian K. *Researches on the I Ching*. Translated by William L. MacDonald, Tsuyoshi Hasegawa, and Hellmut Wilhelm. Princeton: Princeton University Press, 1979.

Snyder, Gary. *The Real Work: Interview & Talks, 1964–1979*. Edited by William Scott McLean. New York: New Directions, 1980.

Spencer-Brown, G. *Laws of Form*. New York: E. P. Dutton, 1979.

Suzuki, D. T. *Zen Buddhism: Selected Writings of D. T. Suzuki*. Edited by William Barrett. Garden City, N.Y.: Doubleday Anchor Books, 1956.

Varela, Francisco J. "Not One, Not Two." *Coevolutionary Quarterly*, Fall 1976, 62–67.

———. *Principles of Biological Autonomy*. New York: Elsevier North Holland, 1979.

———. "The Creative Circle: Sketches on the Natural History of Circularity." In *The Invented Reality: How Do We Know What We Believe We Know? (Contributions to Constructivism)*, edited by Paul Watzlawick, 309–23. New York: W. W. Norton, 1984.

Von Foerster, Heinz. *Observing Systems*. Seaside, Calif.: Intersystems Publications, 1984.

Von Glasersfeld, Ernst. "An Introduction to Radical Constructivism." In *The Invented Reality: How Do We Know What We Believe We Know? (Contributions to Constructivism)*, edited by Paul Watzlawick, 17–40. New York: W. W. Norton, 1984.

Watson, Burton, trans. *The Complete Works of Chuang Tzu*. New York: Columbia University Press, 1968.

Watts, Alan. *The Way of Zen*. New York: Mentor Books, 1957.

———. *Psychotherapy East and West*. New York: Vintage Books, 1961.

———. *In My Own Way*. New York: Vintage Books, 1972.

———. *Tao: The Watercourse Way*. New York: Pantheon Books, 1975.

Watzlawick, Paul, John H. Weakland, and Richard Fisch. *Change: Principles of Problem Formation and Problem Resolution*. New York: W. W. Norton, 1974.

Whorf, Benjamin Lee. *Language, Thought, and Reality: Selected Writings of Benjamin Lee Whorf*. Edited by J. B. Carroll. Cambridge: MIT Press, 1956.

Wieger, L. *Chinese Characters: Their Origin, Etymology, History, Classification and Signification. A Thorough Study from Chinese Documents*. 2d ed. Translated into English by L. Davrout. 1927. Reprint. New York: Paragon and Dover, 1965.

Wilden, Anthony. *System and Structure*. London: Tavistock, 1972.

Wilhelm, Hellmut. *Change: Eight Lectures on the I Ching*. Translated by Cary F. Baynes. Princeton: Princeton University Press, 1960.

Wilhelm, Richard, trans. *The I Ching or Book of Changes*. 3rd ed. Translated from German by Cary F. Baynes. Princeton: Princeton University Press, 1967.

Wilhelm, Richard. *Lectures on the I Ching: Constancy and Change*. Translated by Irene Eber. Princeton: Princeton University Press, 1979.

———, trans. *Tao Te Ching: The Book of Meaning and Life*. Translated from German by H. G. Ostwald. London: Arkana, 1985.

Williams, William Carlos. "To Daphne and Virginia." In *Pictures from Brueghel and Other Poems*, 75–79. Norfolk, Conn.: New Directions, 1962.

———. "The Desert Music." In *Pictures from Brueghel and Other Poems*, 108–20. Norfolk, Conn.: New Directions.

Wright, Arthur F. *Buddhism in Chinese History.* Stanford, Calif.: Stanford University Press, 1959.

Wu, John C. H., trans. *Lao Tzu: Tao Teh Ching.* New York: St. John's University Press, 1961.

Yü, Titus, and Douglas Flemons, trans. *I Ching: A New Translation.* Simon Fraser University, Faculty of Interdisciplinary Studies, Burnaby, B.C. Typescript, 1983.

CREDITS

ISBN: 0-9965720-8-2
ISBN-13: 978-0-9965720-8-8 (PAPERBACK)

Cover Design: T.M. Cromer and Heather Neal Designs

This is a work of fiction. Names, characters, businesses, places, events and incidents are either the products of the author's imagination or used in a fictitious manner. Any resemblance to actual persons, living or dead, or actual events is purely coincidental.

DEDICATION

There are people in this world who, without anything to gain other than the good feeling it gives them, will go out of their way for you. They'll help you learn the ropes, so to speak. Just knowing these type of people makes me a better person. So it's with that, that I dedicate this to the individual who has influenced me the most while writing this story.

Thank you Cynthia St. Aubin!

Your generous spirit and willingness to help a "newbie" to the industry warms my heart. You are a rockstar!

Chapter One

She showed up late with rainbow colored hair and a nose ring. And although she was dressed semi-professionally, Ty Jensen mentally crossed her off his list of nanny candidates. What the hell was he going to do now? In dire straits, he needed someone to start immediately, and all the applicants to date had been unsatisfactory.

He half listened as Lana Martell stumbled through her apologies and excuses. Ah yes, the old "my car wouldn't start" excuse. It would be impossible to count the number of times he'd heard that little gem, or something similar, from his employees.

As Ty held his screaming daughter, helplessness gripped him. Maybe he should have allowed his brother Quinn to retain custody. Maybe he wasn't qualified to be a dad. But Ty knew he didn't want his daughter growing up in the limelight. Any child of his famous brother was bound to be hounded by paparazzi throughout her life. Also, Ty fancied that he'd felt a special something when he first found out about her. A shifting in his chest. *A baby.* He hadn't even realized he wanted to be a dad until his brother had informed Ty of his intention to fight him for custody. Nevertheless, in the here and now, his infant daughter had him seriously rethinking parenthood.

Serena Jensen was proving to be a handful, and not quite as serene as her name implied. Talk about misnaming a child. Ty thought they should have selected a major hurricane to name her after. The kid had blown into his life and left considerable collateral damage. She'd come early and spent the first month of her life in an incubator.

Four days ago she'd been ready to come home from the hospital. Since Ty picked her up, her non-stop crying had him exhausted from lack of sleep. Hearing loss was a distinct possibility, because the only sounds he registered were a baby's shriek, ringing in his ears, and the excuses his rainbow-haired interviewee babbled on about. Serena kicked it up another two decibels, and Ty was ready to pull his damn hair out.

"May I?" Little Miss Rainbow Bright asked, holding out her arms.

While Serena wailed in his ear making it difficult to hear himself think, misgivings churned about in his stomach. The idea of turning his daughter over to a complete stranger created unease. Yet a certain something in her eyes, an understanding of sorts, had him reluctantly handing over the baby.

"Hey there, sweet girl. No need to carry on so. What's up with all that? Hmmm?" she spoke in soothing tones, rubbing the baby's back and bouncing like he'd seen the nurses at the hospital do when they'd held Serena. "Are you hungry, darling?"

Ty was transfixed by her voice. It appeared that Serena was too, if the abrupt cessation of her crying was any indication.

"When did she eat last?"

"Umm, I just prepared her bottle. I can't get her to take it," he replied a bit defensively. He was a good dad and didn't want her thinking he was negligent.

"May I?"

Leading the way to the kitchen, Ty wondered what the hell he was doing. This crazy-haired sprite would get the impression she would be the new nanny if he didn't set her straight soon. Perhaps seeing her in action would allay his misgivings. He didn't want to be too hasty. After all, she did get Serena to go from raising holy hell to a coo in under a minute.

Ty handed her the bottle as he watched a frown form on her face.

"What?"

"Did anyone teach you how to warm the formula up first?"

He eyed her to be sure she wasn't being judgmental. He didn't need a critical influence in his house. There was enough of that in his family.

"To be honest, it's possible it went in one ear and out the other. There was a lot to take in," he acknowledged.

She shot him an understanding glance. "No worries, we've got this. I'll walk you through it. You can do this one of two ways - the stove or the microwave. Right now the microwave will be fastest. For future reference though, I'm not a big advocate of heating things that way."

She went on to explain the process and how to test the temperature of the liquid on the inside of his wrist. Then she showed him how to feed the baby and hold her to force out any air Serena had taken in during the process of guzzling down her meal.

"You should always have a towel or cloth for your shoulder and another soft cloth to wipe the spit. I've not met a baby who doesn't spit up a little bit. How are you on diaper duty? Need some pointers?"

Ty blushed and admitted he did.

"Not a problem. She's made us a nice mess to practice with."

"I wondered what that smell was," he said, sick with dread. That kid produced what must be the nastiest poop on the planet. "Should it be that green-ish? Does that mean something is wrong with her?"

The laughter from his soon-to-be nanny rang out like tinkling bells. After seeing her handle this crisis, and it had been a crisis to Ty's way of thinking, his decision to hire her had been cemented.

"No, I'm afraid that's par for the course. Green goo is the norm," she grinned.

"Oh dear God!" he grimaced.

"You'll get used to it."

"Never!"

Lana Martell liked her new employer. She didn't doubt for a second she'd get the job. The man was drowning and reaching out to her for a lifeline. However she did debate accepting the position because of her concern about his looks. Even with rumpled dirty-blond hair and those frantic green eyes, he exuded a sex appeal that forced her to concentrate so as not to forget to breathe. Added to that was his deep, rumbly voice with a hint of a Southern accent. That could be the one thing that prevented her from taking the job when he eventually offered it. Being a nanny to a good looking, wealthy man was always trouble. It invariably turned a working woman's head when he paid attention to her. And the men always paid attention to the nanny at some point, a few with more sinister intent than others.

Professionalism was not an issue for Lana. Although it tended to be a little more of a dilemma for her past employers. Men and women alike came on to her. She didn't know why. Over the years, she worked hard to make herself as unattractive as possible. It didn't help. Lana was a magnet for unwanted sexual advances. She hoped Ty Jensen would control himself. If she didn't find employment soon, she didn't know what she'd do. The medical bills for her mother were piling up. God, she hated being a poor struggling artist. Even though she loved caring for children, art was her first love. The problem was that being an unknown in the art world didn't produce enough income to pay the bills.

It didn't take long to bathe Serena, get her bundled up, and then tucked into her crib. Ty and Lana made their way to the kitchen to discuss terms of employment over a cup of coffee.

"Tell me your terms. I don't care what they are. You're hired," Ty gushed. He took a sip of the piping hot coffee and sighed. "This is my first moment to relax in four days."

Lana had to laugh. She understood better than most the never ending care of another. If it wasn't for her brother Liam splitting shifts to help with their mother, Lana was convinced she would have committed murder/suicide years ago. Liam would tease her out of her gloomy mood when she became dark and brooding. While it may be true that Lana would never go so far as to hurt another, she wasn't opposed to fantasizing about it on occasion. Especially when her mother became ugly and nagged her half to death.

"My one sticking point is being a live-in nanny. I have a sick mother. My brother and I share responsibilities, so I need to be home no later than seven p.m. three nights a week to prepare her meals and bathe her. My brother Liam works third shift so it's no trouble during the day. I could be here by six-thirty in the morning and work-"

He held up a hand to cut her off. "That isn't going to work for me, at least not at first. I need help round the clock until Serena starts sleeping through the night. I may not know a lot, however I do know newborns are up all hours."

"I understand. Thank you for your time."

To say Lana was disappointed would be stating it mildly. She blinked in rapid succession to disperse the tears starting to build. Damn it! She really needed this job. Trying to paste a smile on her face, she stood to gather her belongings.

"Wait! I didn't mean I wasn't going to hire you!"

Lana noted the frantic tone in his voice. Ah, here was a man on edge. Maybe she did have some bargaining power. She decided to see how this played out. "I don't understand."

"Yes, well…I…That is…" Ty paused to clear his throat. "I have a small guesthouse out back. It's empty, and if your mother wouldn't mind living there, rent free of course, we could work something out. The cottage is two bedrooms, two baths. The kitchen there is probably too small for any real cooking. You can prepare her meals here and take them to her throughout the day if that works for you. Your brother can live there too, provided you and your family are okay with a background check. I hope you understand my precautions."

"Of course."

Ty watched Lana as she stood there trying to take in everything he'd just offered up. He hadn't meant to suggest his guest house to her family, but the thought of her leaving when he so desperately needed her sent him into panic mode. A frown marred her forehead, and she chewed her lip as she deliberated. Ty took the time to study her. It surprised him to discover how attractive she was underneath all the curly, colored hair and thick eyeliner. Her pale complexion was kept from being too light by the soft natural blush tingeing her cheeks and the smatter of freckles across the bridge of her upturned nose. He'd detected a dimple in her left cheek when she laughed earlier. Rosebud lips completed the picture, giving her an overall sexy pixie appearance. However, it was her large golden-amber eyes which held him transfixed. When she had started to tear up, he scrambled his brain trying to figure a solution to the live-in predicament.

"Okay. But we pay rent."

It seemed Lana decided letting go of their current residence would be no great loss. Ty suspected the location wasn't in the greatest neighborhood anyway. If her brother was smart, he would be thrilled to get his sister and mother removed from a less than safe area.

Seeing how earnest she was about the rent made Ty want to laugh. He didn't need the money, however he suspected her pride wouldn't let her accept the place for free.

"I'll tell you what, since there is no mortgage on the house, and I don't need the money, you can pay for utilities on the place; cable, water, and electric. Fair enough?"

"Can I discuss it with my brother? He won't want to feel like a charity case," she explained.

"That's fine. Please be sure to stress to him you will be doing me a great service in caring for Serena night and day."

As if on cue, the baby started to scream. Ty closed his eyes, fatigued at the thought of dealing with her.

"I can start now, if you need me to," she offered. "You can

go and take a nap or catch up on work."

He could have kissed her. Instead he offered up a wide grin and headed for his office.

"Lana Martell, you are an angel," he called over his shoulder.

***

Lana rocked the baby as she walked around the house. She noticed the room off to the left of the nursery and assumed that would be her bedroom. The decor appealed to her. The lovely plum sheets with the white comforter and the deep amethyst drapes made her smile. Next to red, purple was her favorite color. A general sense of rightness struck her as she took in each of the beautiful knick knacks that brought all the elements of the room together. While she wandered around, touching this or that, she showed Serena the different items and described everything in great detail to her. It fascinated the baby, who gurgled in response.

"What are you doing in my room?"

Ty's deep voice scared a squeak out of Lana and set the baby fussing. Working to soothe the infant once more, Lana spoke to her and showed her another object. After Serena was calm, she turned to Ty.

"I'm sorry. I didn't realize. I thought to tour the nursery and assumed this was the nanny's room. It never occurred to me you would exchange the master suite to sleep close to her," Lana felt like she was babbling, and she hated it. The sick feeling of starting off on the wrong foot with her employer started to take root in her gut.

The twinkle in his beautiful green eyes gave him away. "Nah, I'm just messing with you. It's the designated nanny's room."

"Jerk." It was out before she could stop it. Her eyes went wide with horror.

His bark of laughter had the baby jumping. Luckily enough, it didn't upset her.

"Nice professionalism you've got going on there," he teased.

"Yeah, you're one to talk, buddy." Lana leaned her head closer to Serena and lowered her voice, "Daddy's being a brat. Yes, he is."

Lana couldn't stop her impulse to kiss the baby's forehead. She was just that precious. When she glanced up, the tenderness in Ty's eyes surprised her. Their gazes locked. She stood hypnotized by his very presence, not unlike a rabbit being frozen by a snake poised to strike. Why she made a comparison of that nature, she wasn't sure. Lana thought it must have been the initial surge of fear she felt in attracting the attention of another man. A dangerous one to her emotional well-being at that. Breathing became difficult and the hair on the back of her neck stood at attention.

Ty took a step forward before a voice brought them crashing back to reality.

"Get that little slut away from my baby!"

Chapter Two

Oh, hell. Lana cringed when her nemesis started shouting.

"I mean it Tyler! You get rid of her this instant!"

The strident tones of the newcomer set Serena to wailing. Lana tried to soothe her as best she could. Unfortunately, she wanted to cry too. Of all the damn places to encounter Jeri Newberry. God, she hated that woman! She'd made Lana's life a living hell all through high school, and then did her best to destroy Lana's professional credibility as a nanny through her elite social channels. So much for the perfect job with Ty and Serena. It had been a great dream, for all of the ninety minutes it lasted.

Lana silently berated herself for not putting it all together sooner. Jeri Newberry was sister to Hailey Newberry, the actress who recently died as a result of a plane crashing into an airport terminal. Hailey had been the girlfriend of the famous movie screen actor, Quinn Jensen. Based on the name, resemblance, and a few newspaper articles she'd read, Lana had a strong suspicion that Ty was the twin of Quinn. She thought she'd read, or seen recently, that the brothers were estranged due to a paternity fight over Hailey's baby girl. Oh what a tangled web we weave, and all that bullshit.

"I don't know what your deal is Jeri, but you *will not* just walk into my home and make demands," Ty ground out.

"Number one, Serena is *my* child. Where do you get off saying she's yours? Number two, *I* decide who will or will not care for her. If I want to hire a stripper from a gentlemen's club, then that's what I'll do. And num…"

"That's exactly what you did!" Jeri retorted, cutting him off and getting in his face. "Was that not on her resume, Ty? Or did you just happen to catch her show and think 'Hey, she'd be a good babysitter for my kid. Why don't I hire her?'"

By Ty's reaction, Lana could see Jeri, aka the bane of her existence, had stupefied him. Dread balled up in her belly, making her glad she hadn't eaten much at lunch. Real fear that she would lose the contents of her stomach here and now had her swallowing convulsively in an effort to keep the vomit at bay.

The writing was on the wall. Or on Ty's face would be more accurate. Lana peered down at the red faced infant in her arms. Odd that she felt more for this child in a few hours than she'd felt for all her other charges combined. Maybe it was having a boss she liked for a change. Her heart was heavy at having it all ripped away so soon.

Jeri's ugly words shocked Ty. He hadn't really thought Lana worked at a strip club when he lit into Jeri. His accusatory gaze met Lana's guilty light brown eyes. He shook his head in stunned disbelief. Jesus, he was a shitty judge of women. That he'd just hired a woman who took her clothes off as a profession to be a nanny to his innocent daughter was almost laughable.

Dropping his head back, Ty cast his eyes toward the ceiling, hoping for divine intervention. He supposed he had no choice other than to take back the job offer. Fuck. He really thought she'd be a good fit. The sick mother bit must have been a lie to make him feel sorry for her. She probably needed the three nights off a week for the club.

He felt her presence next to him before he saw her. She offered up the baby, blinking furiously to dispel the tears in her eyes. If he didn't know better, he would have said she was contrite.

"I'm sorry. You should know it's not what I do anymore. I..." She swallowed, inhaled deeply and raised her chin before continuing, "I did it to pay for college. That's what you do to raise money when you're from the wrong side of the tracks. You strip for all the rich frat boys."

Reaching out a hand, she started to touch the baby's cheek in goodbye. Ty stepped back not allowing her hand to connect. Seeing Lana's shame had him experiencing embarrassment of his own. Although he opened his mouth, the words to make it right wouldn't come. Why was he the one feeling guilty here? Wasn't she in the wrong for not disclosing on her resume that she was a stripper?

When Ty pulled Serena away, Lana felt the gesture like a slap to the face. Refusing to look at the adults in the room, she made her way down the hall to where she'd left her purse in the kitchen. She heard Jeri mutter, "Good riddance, whore. Ty, give me the baby. You should make sure she doesn't help herself to anything on her way out. She did that at Carter and Ashley Nichols' house."

Lana wanted desperately to defend herself against that accusation. But the truth was she *had* helped herself to money from Carter's wallet. That cheap prick stiffed her on her salary after she refused to sleep with him. It didn't matter. Lana didn't care if she had to wait tables. She'd never work for these upper-crust snobs again. It had been nine years since she'd worked at The Dancing Dolls strip club, yet the stigma would follow her around this shitty town for life. It was past time she talked to Liam about packing up and getting the hell out of this place.

Footsteps followed Lana down the hall. Two sets. She snorted her disbelief. Wow, those two were made for each other. She didn't want to think how hurt she was that Ty believed the worst of her. Why should she care? She just met him less than two hours ago.

"Lana, wait," Ty demanded.

However, Lana wasn't in the mood to be ordered about just then. It wasn't like he was her boss or anything. She scooped up her messenger bag and slung it over her shoulder.

"Good grief, Tyler. Let her go already," Jeri's nasally voice directed.

"How about you shut the hell up, Jeri." Two pairs of stunned eyes stared at her. Lana didn't care. She was tired of

Jeri Newberry making her life miserable. "Yeah, I said it, you twat! I am sick to death of you popping up, insulting me, and doing your damnedest to get me fired from every job I've ever worked. By my count, this is the sixth position you've cost me. For what? Because some stupid jock in high school asked me out once upon a time? Get a fucking life and stay out of mine!"

If Lana had a camera, she would have taken a picture of Jeri's fish-like expression. The opening and closing of her pie-hole almost caused Lana to giggle. Instead, she started to beat a hasty retreat to the front door. Because she couldn't help herself, she shot one last glance at Ty Jensen. He gaped at her in delight. Not what she expected to see on his face at all. In that moment, Lana almost paused in her escape.

Wrenching open the door, she made her way to the bus stop. Thirty seconds too late. Shit! As she watched the tail lights of the bus pull away, Lana contemplated her life. Was it always going to be so sucky? What had she done to deserve the crap hand the universe had dealt her? Honestly, she couldn't figure it out. She rustled through her purse to see if she had enough for cab fare. She came up short. Typical. Next, she thought to call Liam for a ride, only her phone was dead. Great. Out of options, she started to walk. The sky chose that moment to open up and pour down upon her. Big fat raindrops, mixed with hail. The chunks of ice stung where they struck. Going back to the shelter of the bus stop was her best option.

Lana ran and skidded her way back to the plexiglass enclosure, twisting her ankle in the process. This fucking day was getting better and better. She limped the last few feet before plopping down on the bench. A very wet bench. Whatever. At this point, it was a damn joke. She'd question if it could get worse, but she feared the powers that be would take that as a challenge and maybe throw a tornado her way.

A dark figure in a rain slicker strolled up to the bus stop as if he were impervious to the inclement weather. Lana knew a small quiver of fear when he stood just out of the line of her vision, staring at her. She could tell he was focused on her because she felt the intensity of his eyes. After stripping on and off for the better part of three years, she had a good idea when someone was watching her. Even though her phone was dead, she decided to use it as a prop and make it seem like she was communicating with someone. Quite possibly the ruse would deter an attack.

"Are you done being a stubborn, independent woman determined to show the world your middle finger?"

The sound of Ty's deep voice startled her into dropping her phone. Of course it had to be in a puddle at her feet.

"Goddammit!"

"Should I take that as a no?"

Lana snatched her phone up and dropped it into her purse with another curse.

Still he stood there.

"What do you want, Mr. Jensen?" she asked wearily.

"I want you to come back to my house to discuss what happened earlier. I still need a nanny, and Serena seems to have taken to you. So much so, that we haven't been able to get her to stop crying since you left," he said.

"I can't."

"Look, I'm not going to stand here and beg you. I-"

She interrupted him. "No, I mean I literally can't. I sprained my ankle."

Without another word, Ty stepped up to her, shoved an umbrella into her hands, and scooped her up.

"What the hell do you think you're doing?" Lana demanded.

Ty paused in his trek to his SUV to study her indignant face. Her pointy little chin jutting up and out in her anger amused him.

"Rescuing a damsel in distress," he explained.

Confusion flashed in her eyes and some of her irritation faded away. Ty felt a pang that she hadn't had anyone to care for her. Her every action to this point said as much.

"I can't go back there. I...well, I was mean to Jeri. This isn't a good idea. I should probably go home," Lana babbled.

"She deserved it. For what it's worth, I said a few choice words to her myself." Ty's voice was gruff. He tore his eyes away from her wounded amber gaze and moved toward his vehicle again.

"You made it seem like I'd tainted your baby by touching

her. You jerked her away when I was going to say goodbye."

Ty tried not to think how sick that one gesture had made him. He embarrassed her, and himself, with his physical response to the news.

"You judged me wi-without stopping to find out the facts," she said in a small voice, sounding broken.

"I know. It was a knee-jerk reaction, and I'm not proud of it. But something you said hit me. You said you did it to pay for college. I'm assuming that was some time ago. Am I wrong?"

"No. You're not wrong. I did it for three years. From the time I was seventeen until I was twenty. It really was to pay for my college tuition."

Ty noted the catch in her voice. It told him Lana was ashamed of that point in her life. Seventeen? God! What was it like to need money so badly at such a young age that it would drive an underage girl to have to work in a place like that? Ty clicked open the lock of his Suburban and gently settled Lana in the passenger's seat. He reached over and behind her for a blanket from the back. Her quick intake of air had him fighting a grin. Little Lana wasn't immune to him. Exactly why it pleased him, he refused to question.

After tucking her in and fastening the seatbelt, Ty ran around to his side of the SUV. He cranked the engine and directed all the vents toward her so the heat pumping through the cab would warm her. It bothered him that her lips were turning blue. When he was satisfied he'd done what he could to ward off a chill, he answered her unspoken question. "I'm not going to hold something against you that you did when you were a kid, Lana. However, I do need someone I can trust. What I am finding difficult to deal with is you stealing money from Carter Nichols. Care to elaborate on that one?"

He watched as her lips compressed in anger. For a few moments she said nothing, and he figured she might be working up a lie. Disappointment gripped him. Still, he waited. Ty wanted an answer.

"I had worked for the Nichols' for about four months. His harassment of me started about two months in. Whenever his wife wasn't around, Mr. Nichols would make suggestive comments. Because I needed the job I ignored them, acting as if he never said anything. Then came the little touches here or there. I tried to make sure I was never alone with him. It worked for a while. My last day there, he cornered me in the nursery," Lana stopped and shivered. Taking a deep breath, she continued with her tale, "He knew I couldn't scream without waking the baby. It was a game to him, ya know? He got off on putting me in awkward situations. Sometimes when his drinking buddies were there, he would make a game of it, and they would all laugh."

"You don't need to tell me any more," Ty ground out, enraged on her behalf. He could see it all happening. Carter was an ass of epic proportions. Ty had known him since college. Lana's words held a ring of truth. Knowing what he did of Carter's proclivities, Ty suspected she hadn't fabricated the story.

"No, you asked why I stole from him. I had to set the background. Mr. Nichols hadn't paid me in weeks. He said I had to meet him in his study if I wanted my check. There was no way I intended do that. When I went to his wife demanding to be paid, she took his side. She told me she'd talked to Jeri Newberry and knew what kind of person I was. Mrs. Nichols told me her husband would escort me to get my things from the nursery and see me out. Then she went back to her room with her bottle of wine." Lana shifted in her seat, clearly uncomfortable with the topic, yet still determined to continue. "He got ugly in the nursery. Started pushing me and ripping at my shirt. I kneed him in the balls, grabbed my few things, and ran for the door. In the hallway, I noticed his wallet sitting in a dish next to his keys. I didn't think twice. I took part of what he owed me.

"My brother happened to be home when I arrived at the apartment that night. He was livid after seeing the bruises. Liam drove me back to the Nichols' house and demanded they pay me what they owed me. They threatened us with the cops. Both my brother and I had been in trouble with the law when we were younger. I begged Liam to let it go because I didn't want trouble again."

Lana finished her story and met his stormy green eyes. Her heart stuttered.

"How much does he owe you, Lana?"

She didn't even dream of prevaricating. His forbidding expression and matching tone had her blurting the amount in nothing flat, "Two thousand three hundred dollars."

"Fuck. That rat bastard," Ty swore. "How long ago did this all happen?"

"Three weeks."

"Okay, first things first. We need to get you settled at my house. Tomorrow, I'll pay Carter a visit. You'll get your money. I promise you that."

Ty was putting the car in gear when he paused. She could see something she said struck him. He shifted into park and faced her.

"You said you and your brother were in trouble at some point. Is there something else you need to tell me?"

Dread flooded through her. Lana knew the next words she uttered would have him shoving her out the door on her ass.

"Lana."

That one word was issued as a warning. She couldn't ignore it. Couldn't not tell him of the ugliness in her past.

"I shot my father."

Chapter Three

The air whooshed out of Ty's lungs. Whatever he had been expecting, it hadn't been *that*.

"Jesus Christ," he whispered, trying to suck in air, staring at her with something akin to shock.

"I didn't kill him!" Lana was quick to assure him. "He came home drunk one night. He'd brought some man with him. Apparently, he owed the guy money. His intent was to tr- trade me for the money he owed."

The story was an ugly one and far from original. Ty knew that much. Just because he and his siblings were lucky enough to have exceptional parents didn't mean the rest of the world did. He listened in silence as Lana described the night in question. How her brother had attacked their father in an effort to save her. Liam had received the beating of his life according to his sister. Lana, knowing where their father kept his handgun, retrieved it and threatened to shoot him if he didn't leave. Their mother, weak-willed woman that she was, attempted to snatch the gun from Lana's hands. During the struggle for the weapon, it went off. The bullet tore through Dan Martell's thigh.

Both children were taken away for aggravated battery and assault. Oddly enough, the stranger came forward with the truth. He hadn't been aware Dan intended to trade his daughter for his debt and wanted to clear the air. The reason he went home with Dan Martell was because Dan had promised to pay what he owed. After the court date, their father had taken off to parts unknown, leaving a bitter wife and two teenage children who were grateful for his disappearance. It meant the abuse would stop.

Ty dragged his hands over his face in an effort to erase the image of a young Lana being abused. It didn't sit well with him that her father never paid for his actions.

"You've had a tough life, haven't you?"

The question was rhetorical. Even if Lana had wanted to play it down, he knew she couldn't. Her life *had* been tough until now. Adjusting to the trials fate threw her way had been essential. If she hadn't rolled with the punches, she wouldn't have gotten back up. He imagined Lana learned a long time ago complaining wasn't an option. Lying down and dying wasn't one either. Ty had been there. There were days when it was tough to accept the shitty hand that life had dealt out. On the whole, pushing through was the only way to keep moving forward. To take life one day at a time, one hour at a time if need be, to find a better way. Deep down she was an optimist. He recognized that just in the short time he'd been around her.

"Now you know everything. I understand if you don't want me around your daughter."

Ty contemplated her earnest pixie face. What he saw there made his heart speed up. He had never seen a more beautiful visage. Now the strength could be recognized there. The frown marring his face deepened. Should he reconsider hiring her? The worry he couldn't keep his hands to himself, that he would be no better than Carter Nichols, was real. This woman had a certain something that drew men in, made them ache for one taste of those pouty, cherry red lips. Yet, the need to offer her a way out, a better situation, nearly suffocated him in its intensity. God, he'd only known her for the better part of three hours. What the hell was she doing to him?

As Lana unbuckled the seatbelt and reached for the handle to let herself out of his SUV, Ty caught her arm to stop her. "No. The job is yours if you want it."

The surprise on her face mirrored his own surprise at offering her the job. The feeling gave way to a rightness, especially when she beamed her joy at him. Fuck! He wanted to kiss her so badly he could taste it. Clearing his throat, Ty turned and fastened his seatbelt. Removing the unwelcome sexual thoughts would be paramount. He had one thing to concentrate on, and that was providing Serena with the best childcare he could.

"Thank you!"

He nodded, not trusting himself to speak.

***

"Oh hell no! Are you seriously bringing her back into this house? After what she said to me?"

Jeri's tone resembled nothing if not fingers dragging down a chalkboard. Ty ignored her and continued further into the kitchen with his burden. In his mind, he wanted to carry Lana forever. In reality, her one hundred fifteen pound frame winded him. He told himself he would punish himself later at the gym for being so out of shape. When he reached his destination, Ty hoisted Lana onto the counter and reached down to remove her soggy shoes. The sprained ankle was evident. As his fingers examined the puffy area, he registered her sharp hiss of pain.

"It's already developing a bruise. I'm wondering if I should take you to have an X-ray."

As Ty expressed his concern, he saw tears well in Lana's eyes. It clarified to him no one besides her brother Liam had ever cared whether she lived or died, much less sprained a joint.

She cleared her throat twice before she dared attempt speech. "I'm not sure. To be honest this is the worst injury I've ever had. Though I'm a klutz, I've been fairly lucky in the past. I don't normally sprain or break anything," she explained.

When she looked up at him with her brave face on, his heart stuttered in his chest. The air around them crackled. If she didn't need the job so badly, she would probably let her self-preservation keep her miles away from him. He knew that deep down. Yet, Ty couldn't help wanting to pull her into his arms and assure her that she could trust him to take care of her. God, what was it about this one small woman? She brought out his baser instincts on every level.

"Tyler! Are you listening to me? I refuse to allow this woman anywhere near Serena." For once Ty was grateful for Jeri's presence in his life, as her bitching distracted Lana, who had become uncomfortable under his unwavering stare.

"Jeri, in case you've forgotten, let me reiterate. This is *my* home. Serena's *my* daughter, and *I* make the decisions regarding who I do or do not hire to care for her. *Now back the hell off.*"

Ty knew it was well past time to lay down some ground rules about walking into his home unannounced and acting as if she owned the place. He wasn't sure when it had begun, probably when he brought the baby home this week. It stopped now.

Lana fell a little in love with her new employer. Three times today he had come to her rescue. First, with offering her the job, second with caring for her ankle, and now with telling Satan's Spawn Jeri off. Mostly, she loved him being able to shut Jeri up. Not wanting to create conflict, Lana kept her eyes downcast. Past experience had shown her people like Jeri didn't care to be rebuked in front of others. In the end, they would find a way to take it out on the hapless witness. She did raise her gaze to see the backside of Jeri storming out in a huff.

The silence became uncomfortable as it dragged on. Lana

refused to look directly at Ty. She sensed his regard, but she needed to prepare herself for the impact those eyes had on her system. When she pulled up the courage from the furthest recesses of herself, she met his steady gaze. The intensity made her decidedly uncomfortable.

"We should ice that ankle and get you something dry to put on." The husky timbre in his voice sparked a warmth low in her abdomen. All she could produce was a jerky nod of her head. Damn, she was in trouble. "And maybe remove some of the eyeliner running down your cheeks. The Alice Cooper imitation might scare the baby."

Horror was embarrassment's boon companion in that moment. Lana's hands flew to her face as Ty's wicked laugh rang out. There was little doubt in her mind that he knew the effect he had on her, and that he took delight in her predicament.

After she had changed into a pair of Ty's old sweats, her ankle was bound, raised, and a towel full of ice rested against it, Lana realized this was the most cared for she'd ever felt in her life. A wimpy, needy part of her wanted to cry in gratitude. The stronger part of her refused to let that happen.

"Do you need to call someone to let them know you're here? If I'm not mistaken, your phone took a swan dive into a puddle by the bus stop," Ty teased with a smirk.

"Didn't I already tell you I was a klutz?" she sassed in return.

"Please tell me you carry a boatload of insurance on everything you own."

"Shut it."

He grinned as he rocked Serena, who had finally quieted down. Lana suspected the baby sensed when S.S.J. aka Satan's Spawn Jeri had left.

"If you don't mind, I'd like to let my brother know I'm here and check on my mom."

Without missing a beat in his rocking motion, Ty handed her his cell phone and offered up the code to unlock it.

"Try to memorize it. That is also the code for the house alarm."

"Mr. Jensen, I-"

"Ty. My name is Ty."

Lana wondered if she shouldn't try to keep their working relationship on a more formal basis. "Mr. Jen-"

"Ty," His tone came out harder as he emphasized his name.

"It isn't professional for me to call you by your first name."

"Neither is it professional to tell me to shut it or to tell my daughter's aunt to go fuck herself, but you didn't have a problem with that."

He made a valid point. Lana chewed on her lip with indecision. If she allowed herself to become comfortable around him, she feared she could come to care for him. Bad idea. Men like him would never look at someone like her twice, except for a convenient lay. Then where would that leave her?

His deep sigh drew her attention back to his face. "What were you going to say, Lana?"

A frown marred her features as she forced herself to remember how their conversation started. Oh, right! She intended to thank him.

Ty watched as the gambit of emotions took turns flashing across her features. Every thought she had displayed for the world to see. He wondered if she knew how expressive her beautiful face was. If he was correct, she was about to gush in gratitude.

"I wanted to say thank you for…"

And there it was. He listened to her rattle on without ever registering her words. Her voice washed over him, waking feelings he hadn't experienced in a long while. If he were smart, he would send her packing. Nothing good would come from those desires. With no little difficulty, he tore his focus from her to glance down at Serena. Ty had to remember it was all for his baby girl. For whatever reason, Serena calmed in Lana's presence. He could do it. He could rein in his pervy thoughts for his daughter's nanny. Either that or end up embroiled in a lawsuit over sexual advances toward an employee. Ty wondered if that applied in cases like these where neither of them worked for a larger corporation. He mentally slapped himself. Cold showers would probably be plentiful in his future.

"You're not listening."

Caught! He bit back a smile at the disgust on her face. "Just call your brother and let him know where you're staying tonight. Unless this is the night you need to be home for your mother. I can run you home, in that case."

***

Lana could see that meeting Liam made Ty feel more comfortable about having her family move into the guesthouse. As they sat at the kitchen table, they discussed the transition for their mother.

"Are you sure you want us invading your space?" Liam asked, working on destroying the label of the beer bottle in front of him.

"It's not an issue for me personally. I like the idea of Lana being on hand for Serena. With you and your mother within walking distance, it makes it easier all around," Ty said matter of factly.

Liam tipped his beer in Ty's direction before taking a sip.

Lana observed the play between the two and wondered how men could get away with saying so little and yet conveying so much. Everything was said with a look, a gesture, or a nod. At times, a grunt. Men really were simple beasts she decided. Speaking of beasts, her eyes were drawn once again to her new boss. Her fascination for him grew by the minute. She watched as his throat worked to swallow a sip of beer. In her most private of thoughts, she daydreamed about licking the rough column of his throat. Of running her tongue along the dips and crevices of those muscles and biting his corded trap as she came under him.

Embarrassed by her own thoughts, Lana had to force her mind to jump track. The man was temptation personified. The beating of his pulse captured her attention next. Strong and steady, like the man himself. She'd gleaned that much from the day she'd spent in his company. Always a good judge of character because she needed to be, Lana was comfortable he would be an above-board boss. She wouldn't need to fend off advances at every turn as she'd been forced to do in the past. A comfort could be found in that. To know you could be yourself and not have to be on guard would take away about fifty percent of the stress of the job in caring for Serena.

As the thought popped into her head, the baby sounded off from her crib. Her tentative cry could be heard through the monitor. Forgetting about her ankle, Lana made to rise, only to be gently pushed back down by Ty's hand on her shoulder.

"I got this," he smiled down at her with a light squeeze of his fingers. Her breath caught, and for a moment, they stared into each other's eyes, unable to disconnect. A clearing of Liam's throat brought the two of them back to reality. Ty quickly removed his hand from her shoulder and strode off in the direction of the nursery.

"What the hell was that about?"

Liam's sharp tone had her head whipping in his direction. Disapproval radiated off him in waves.

"Lana, don't start something with this man. It won't end pretty. You'll be back in the unemployment line in a month, tops," he warned. "I'd have thought you'd be a little cautious of flirting based on the perverts you've dealt with in the past."

"Ty isn't a pervert!" she protested.

"I didn't say he was," he snapped back. "I happen to like him. But screwing the boss isn't a good idea, and you know it."

"I don't intend to screw him. Just shut up about it."

Exactly why she was irritated with her brother, Lana refused to examine. Everything he said was correct. Any type of relationship other than employee/employer would be a horrible mistake. If she could just make that little piece of her heart longing for a family of her own remember that, she'd have it made.

Chapter Four

The next evening Lana discovered Ty was as good as his word. After dinner he presented her with a check from Carter Nichols. Her stunned disbelief had him chuckling.

"How in the world did you manage to get him to pay up?"

"There is one thing the Carters of this world understand. That is the threat of exposure. I promised him I would run an ad in the paper to find any ex-employees willing to testify to his sexual assault. I also told him his behavior would become widely known in our mutual circle of friends. He couldn't get to his checkbook fast enough."

Lana wanted desperately to jump up and hug him. Curbing her desire took great willpower.

"I don't know how to thank you."

"No need."

"Yes. There is a need. No one, besides my brother, has ever done anything kind for me like that. You don't know how much it means to me. I won't forget it."

Ty was uncomfortable with her gratitude. Lana realized she'd taken what amounted to a simple gesture from him and blown it up to be more than it was. Funny how two people could view the same circumstance so differently. She made an excuse to check on the baby and hurried off as fast as her ankle allowed her. The whole way down the hall she berated herself for being an idiot. Why couldn't she have left it at thank you?

"Stupid, stupid, stupid Lana! Now he knows you are crushing on him," she muttered to herself.

Serena was awake when Lana leaned over the crib. The baby's cross-eyed concentration on the mobile above the bed had Lana smiling. Made of flowers, pearls, and shimmering crystals, she understood Serena's fascination with the swirling decoration. Instead of feeling envy that this child would be lavished with beautiful things growing up, Lana experienced a sense of happiness at the thought this darling little girl would never have to face the hardships she herself had suffered.

"Aren't you so precious? Are you ready to eat, sweet girl?"

Ty realized his daughter's nanny must have failed to remember the baby monitor she'd left in the living room. Her words had him grinning from ear to ear. Little Lana had a crush on him. He couldn't say he was disappointed. The feeling was mutual. It also warmed his heart to hear her treating Serena in such a wonderful manner. The micro cameras placed throughout the nursery, living room, and kitchen had shown him as much earlier today whenever he chose to check in throughout his work day. This further confirmation eased his mind for taking a chance on hiring her.

He hadn't heard from Jeri all day, a welcome relief to be

sure. Fending off her advances and ignoring her innuendoes was quickly getting old. Since her divorce from Austin Gentry, Jeri had stepped it up with the aggressive flirting. And because Austin was his best friend, Ty had honored the bro-code of hands off. Not that Austin would have cared at this point. Their divorce had gotten uglier and uglier as it had dragged on. Many a night his buddy had crashed in his spare room after drinking his woes away. They'd had that in common with the sisters. Only Austin knew the whole truth of what Ty had gone through with Hailey. How he'd betrayed his own brother to capture a piece of her light. Of course, that light was a glint of fool's gold. She had been as false as they come.

Lana's entrance to the living room pulled his thoughts from the past. Having her close brought a sense of peace he hadn't felt in a long while. That she already made a difference with Serena spoke to her kind spirit. He graced her with a warm smile, which froze her in her tracks.

"What?"

The smile on his face transformed into a full-blown grin.

"Why are you staring at me like that? Do I have something on my face?"

Ty's amusement shot up as she inspected herself, as much as holding a baby allowed. Her nervousness as he approached became pronounced. He reached out and tucked a wild curl behind her ear before taking Serena from her arms. Color blossomed in her cheeks. There was a distinct shift in his chest. An opening up of sorts. He'd gone so long closed off, never allowing himself to care. Funny how here in the span of only a week, he became a dad and had hired a nanny he was majorly attracted to.

Unease slipped across her features, dimming the pleasure he received from the brief contact. He shifted his attention to the babe. No reason to let the situation get more awkward. His brother was an actor. Surely Ty could pull off normal for a few minutes until his impulsive gesture was forgotten.

"I didn't realize you were bringing Serena back out. You shouldn't be carrying her around on a bum ankle. Go ahead and sit. Relax," he directed.

"How do you think I've been caring for her all day?" she asked with a half smile.

"Now I feel bad because I didn't think about it. Does that make me a terrible person?" he asked, chagrined.

"Oh, no. I didn't mean it that way. But I still need to make her a bottle. I-"

Ty cut her off by lifting Serena from her arms. "I'll prep her formula. Now sit, please. Prop that foot up, and I'll hand you the baby."

Once he'd settled his daughter with Lana, he headed off to heat a bottle the way she'd taught him.

As the water warmed, he thought about the attraction building for his new employee. Not good. The ink from her background check hadn't even dried yet. This instant magnetism he felt on his side had his head spinning and his heart making odd little leaps at intermittent intervals. The answer was simple, if he cared to accept it. A mild flirtation with absolutely no touching and no inappropriate suggestions. On the heels of that thought came a sense of dismay that he would never find out how smooth her skin could be. Never taste those pouty lips of hers. Never…No! Torturing himself with thoughts of making out with Lana wasn't going to change things. He needed to get his mind straight.

A quick glance over his shoulder assured him she wasn't looking his way. He took the opportunity to reach down and adjust himself. Damn! He was worse than a teenage boy with a Playboy magazine. Once the idea of seeing Lana naked entered his mind, it refused to leave him alone. Last night, knowing she rested in the bed a few feet down the hall, had him tossing and turning until the wee hours of the morning. Between her and the baby, he wondered if he would ever experience a full night's sleep again.

A hissing brought him back to the present. Shit! The water boiled over. He tamped down the urge to smack his own forehead.

"Can I help?"

"I can warm water, Lana," Ty snapped. Upon seeing her concern, the irritation left him. "I'm sorry. My mind was preoccupied. The anger was directed at myself."

Relief flashed in her eyes, followed by a tight smile. He hated that he'd caused that look. The formula making finished, he added an ice cube to the mix to help the liquid cool down. He started for the living room when an idea struck. Ty rifled through the cabinets to find his emergency store of candy. Grabbing a few pieces of chocolate, he headed back to the living area.

Plopping down next to her, he offered up the nectar of the baby gods. He followed that up with a magician-like move and opened his fist to reveal every woman's secret desire. Lana's delighted laugh calmed him, making him feel light and young again. When was the last time he'd felt that way? In college? Since then, his world had morphed into a jaded, jumbled mess. Yet, in two days of knowing her, a sense of renewal filled him. Here he sat, shoulder to shoulder with her, thigh resting against thigh. The want was there, sure, but the sensation bubbling up bordered on happiness.

Yep, he was definitely crushing on her too. A little devil in him prodded him to ask, "Is now a bad time to tell you the speaker for the baby monitor was on?"

She went white before turning a dark shade of red. Still, he had to admit the blush was becoming on her and worked well with her wild hair color. Chagrined, her head dropped back to rest against the sofa. Her lids lowered to conceal her turbulent emotions. The reaction tickled him. A better man wouldn't have teased her. He wasn't a better man.

"So, you have a crush on me, huh?"

"Crap! I'm sorry. I'm never going to learn to shut my mouth. Are you sure you want me as Serena's nanny? My bad habit of blurting whatever is on my mind might not be so cute on a toddler."

"Nah, I think it's adorable."

Lana's head whipped up and around to gauge his seriousness. A lifted brow and a roguish grin told her he did indeed find it funny. She had never wanted to kiss a man more than in that moment. A deep inhale to calm her nerves had the opposite effect. His scent filled her nostrils, sending heat to her lady bits. The attraction his lips held for her eyes was infinite. They refused to cease and desist. They observed his grin spreading wider, then tapering off. They saw his lips part and his tongue sneak out to moisten them. They watched that same tongue glide across his upper teeth as if testing for smoothness. In some people, it would be a gesture of apprehension. What did Ty have to be nervous about? That she might latch on to his mouth like a succubus? Taste all he had to offer and more?

Thankfully, Serena chose to make it known the bottle had been removed from her mouth in an absent motion. With great difficulty, Lana refocused on the baby to finish feeding her and shift her for a burp. She tucked her on the shoulder closest to Ty. The move afforded her the opportunity to hide her flaming face. Crikey, that had been a close call! If the little human hadn't burst her fantasy bubble, Lana would have been all over the kid's father like white on rice.

Racking her brain for any distraction, Lana chose to remind her boss her family was moving this week.

"Did you remember -"

"I wanted to remind yo-"

"You go-"

"You go-"

Laughter took them both. Finally, he held up his hand.

"I imagine we are both trying to discuss the move." At her quick nod, he continued, "I told your brother I would provide a moving van. He said something about not wanting to taint the guesthouse with your old crappy furniture. His words, not mine. So I imagine there are only going to be a few boxes of personal items per room. I'll go help him load those up tomorrow."

"No. I can do it. You shouldn't concern yourself with things like that."

She tucked her head. A blush stained her cheeks. Discomfort settled over her. The embarrassment of him seeing their current living conditions was great. She wasn't sure how he picked up on her desire to hide her past, but he was gracious enough to allow her to own her pride.

"I'd prefer you stay off that ankle and stay with Serena, Lana," he waited until she met his gaze, "But I understand if you don't want my help."

"You do?"

He offered up a half smile and a nod. "My family didn't always have money. My brother and I shared a wardrobe when we were younger. I also think the hand-me-downs my sister wore helped contribute to her being the tomboy she still is today. We got teased a lot growing up."

"When did it all change for you?"

"My dad got a job with one of the race teams in Charlotte. Then, about that time, someone approached my mother one day about using us boys for modeling. Surprisingly, we were successful. I hated it, and Quinn loved it. So he went into acting as a permanent career choice. You can see for yourself how well he's done."

"I never asked you. What do you do for a living?"

"Until five months ago, I was exclusively Quinn's PR rep. We've had a parting of the ways. Since then, I've picked up a few new clients. I'm good at it, and it's a living. Mostly I work from home. There is a satellite office in Charlotte where I have a few employees. I pop over there a few times a month to keep them honest."

"I think I read something about a custody battle between you and your brother. Was that what your 'parting of the ways' was about?"

Ty hated the conflict between him and Quinn had been found out. Even as a PR rep, he hadn't been able to cover it up or put a good spin on it. Bottom line was he cheated with his brother's almost fiancée, she'd gotten pregnant, and his relationship with his twin suffered for it. He was an idiot to be taken in by Hailey. The one thing he couldn't regret was Serena. She was the innocent in all of this.

He'd realized too much time had passed between her

question and what should have been his answer. Lana deserved to know the truth. She might be caught out and about unaware some day. She needed to have the ability to mask any reaction to whatever the paparazzi threw at her. Her expressive face would be pay-dirt for those vultures.

"I need to tell you what happened. I find it difficult because I don't want you to think poorly of me," he stated gruffly.

"I could never think that. Not after what you are doing for my family and me."

"You don't know what I've done, Lana."

Because the baby was finished eating and had dozed off again, Lana was able to use her free hand to clasp his. The spontaneity behind the gesture stunned Ty. He reveled in her touch, as innocent as it was. Fear gnawed his belly. She would think differently of him after his confession.

"We both met Hailey Newberry at the same party. I had gotten there first, and in hindsight, I think she must have initially thought I was Quinn. Dressed up we're almost identical. Unless you know us personally, it's difficult to tell. We seemed to connect, Hailey and me." Ty paused in an attempt to form the words to continue. "When he arrived, she accused me of playing games with her. Then she set out to catch his eye. And she definitely succeeded there."

"Over time, when we saw each other, she alternated between treating me like shit and ignoring me. It set something off in me. I became a bit obsessed with making her acknowledge our connection. It killed me that she was with him. Every time I saw them together, it was like a fist to my gut. One night Quinn called me to say he was stuck on a shoot. Apparently Hailey was tipsy and needed a ride home. He didn't like sending a car around with an unknown driver because you never know who sneaks shots to the press. I drove to pick her up and take her back to Quinn's place. She thought I was Quinn that night."

"You slept with her." It was a statement more than a question. Ty knew that, yet he confirmed it all the same.

"Yes. I didn't set out to take advantage of her. She came on to *me*. I never got the chance to tell her I wasn't him before she started undressing right there in the entryway of his penthouse. I wanted her more than I can remember wanting anyone. Trying to get her to go to bed while keeping my eyes averted wasn't an option. She kept slipping from me to dance around. Finally, I threw her over my shoulder and carried her up to their room. When I dumped her on the bed, she refused to let go of my neck."

"I don't need the intimate details."

Ty noted the primness in her voice. Maybe he'd gotten too graphic. He'd been trying to explain what led up to their sleeping together.

"Yeah, sorry. Anyway, she came on to me thinking I was Quinn. I had wanted her so long, I thought why not? Essentially, I took advantage of her. Or so I thought. In reality, she had never been drunk and knew it was me. Hailey wanted a baby, and Quinn had said he wasn't ready to be married or start a family. She thought by getting pregnant by me she could trick him and there wouldn't be any issue of the baby not resembling him."

"Ohmygod, Ty! How awful!"

"Oh believe me, it gets better. This past Christmas they were planning on flying to his place on St. Maarten. A plane crashed into our local terminal. There had been another passenger, a psychic chick, who'd tried to warn them beforehand. As it was happening, she tried to save Hailey. Later, after she developed feelings for Quinn, she felt it was her duty to rat out the two of us. Annie, that was her name, told Quinn she didn't believe the baby was his."

Ty sighed and went on to explain, "My brother thought maybe she was being spiteful or trying to come between him and Hailey. Then he thought she leaked the story to the press. Later, it came out that one of the nurses overheard her telling him about her premonition, or feelings, or vision. I'm not sure what it's called. Anyway, that's when the shitstorm happened."

He studied the hand still gripping his and trailed his fingers over the veins on the back.

"What happened?"

"Quinn confronted me, kicked my ass. I let him. I don't know, I guess I felt I deserved it." Ty didn't acknowledge her indrawn breath. "A reporter for a major tabloid had been there trying to bribe a nurse for information on Hailey's condition.

He caught the whole thing on his camera phone. I was a bloody mess, and Quinn was hauled away for assault. When I refused to press charges, they released him. However, I did have him legally served papers so I could get care of Hailey and the unborn baby. He didn't take it well. We found ourselves standing across the courtroom from each other, fighting for the right to be Serena's dad.

"In the end, the judge sided in Quinn's favor. He had co-guardianship of Hailey's care with her parents until the baby was born and a DNA test could rule one of us out. Annie, the psychic woman I told you about earlier, helped with that too. I don't think Quinn has forgiven her for it."

"How did she do that?"

"I'm not sure. Another feeling? A premonition? She told the doctor she suspected someone in the lab had mixed up the samples. Being identical twins, the DNA is almost impossible to tell apart. We had to have a specialized test. So the tech didn't intentionally screw up. We were tested a second time. Sure enough, I was Serena's father. I think deep down Quinn knew it. He wouldn't have let her go otherwise."

"So the custody battle is over?"

"Yes."

"Have you been able to start repairing things with your brother?"

Trust her to hit at the heart of the matter. The one wound that probably would never heal.

"He won't talk to me."

They sat in silence after his last statement, neither knowing where to go from there. Their hands were still locked together. Ty broke the silence first.

"Thank you."

"For what?"

"For listening. For reserving judgement."

"It's not my place to judge you, Ty. You're talking to the queen of dysfunctional family life, remember? I shot my father."

"He deserved it," he said, his tone hard, pissed on her behalf. "What father does something like that to his daughter? Fucking scum."

"I won't argue."

"Give me the baby. I'll put her to bed." He reached over to take his daughter. "I'm going to get a beer and watch some tv. Want to join me? I could pour you a glass of wine."

"I probably shouldn't."

"Why?"

"It wouldn't be professional."

"I think we long passed professional, Sweetheart."

Ty watched the indecision war with the want on her face.

"Okay. Sweet wine if you have it."

"Be right back."

Lana couldn't believe what was happening here. She and Ty had connected on some strange level over the events of the last two days. And still she wondered, in what universe would they ever be a couple? Maybe she was putting the cart before the horse, and he only wanted company to chase away the loneliness. Quite possibly he wasn't seeking more than friendship. It was impossible to tell. However, she refused to deny herself the simple pleasure of his companionship.

The sounds of him putting the baby to bed made her smile. His words coming through the monitor had her heart thudding in her chest and butterflies swirling in her belly.

"I'm crushing on you too, Lana."

Chapter Five

Neither of them mentioned his confession. They opted for a movie instead of a standard television show. After plenty of friendly debate, they settled on a suspense thriller that had Lana on the edge of her seat, pillow clutched in her lap.

The film failed to hold any attraction for Ty. Lana had bewitched him. He had more fun watching her than what was happening on screen. During one suspenseful scene, as she leaned forward enthralled, he inched his arm behind her to grab her shoulder. Her yelp made him laugh until she reminded him the baby was sleeping, then elbowed him in the ribs in retaliation.

"You asshole! You almost scared me to death."

"Language, Ms. Martell," he joked.

"Yeah, suck it."

"Let's not talk about sucking. It's too early in our relationship. Or is it?"

His hopeful expression had her smacking him in the face with the throw pillow.

"Should I take that as a no?"

"I don't make out until at least the third date. And since we're not dating..."

"We could be. I don't mind mixing business with pleasure," came his low-voiced response. "For you."

His tone started a fire low in her belly. Instant desire wrapped around her. She could see the matching flame in his green eyes.

"Kiss me."

His words were a command. One she couldn't ignore. She shifted to her knees until they were face to face and ran her palm along his rough jawline. The texture of his stubble pleased her. Of their own accord, her fingers traced the outline of his mouth, dipping in to steal moisture to smooth on his full lower lip. Jealous of her own fingers, Lana leaned in and nipped that dampened lip, giving it a small tug with her teeth. She rained little clinging kisses upon his mouth. All the while he sat still as stone, chest heaving with his rapid inhales and exhales.

"Was that what you had in mind?" she purred as she pulled back.

She never had a chance to retreat fully before he tackled her back on the sectional. He rested an elbow on either side of her head, balancing himself above her. She felt him shift to nestle between her thighs, his sex pressed to hers, separated only by their jeans.

"It's technically our fourth date."

"What?" Lana was clueless as to what he was referring to.

"After you showed up here, we had coffee. That's one. I picked you up at the bus stop, brought you back here, and heated up soup for you. That's two. For lunch we had takeout. That's three. Tonight's dinner and a movie were four."

"You never clarified any of those were dates," she argued laughingly.

"Didn't I? Hmmm, how curious," he murmured, before claiming her lips in a kiss that had them ripping at each other's clothes to experience flesh on flesh.

Being swept away by a man brushing his fingers across her skin had never happened to Lana. Sure, she'd dated and had the occasional sexual encounter. But Ty brought to life something in her which caused her to abandon all reason. His lips against her neck, his teeth nipping her breast, these were all things he alone could do that made her burn solely for him.

She reached down and unsnapped his pants, sliding her hand between the waistband of his boxers and jeans to feel the length of him.

"Fucking the nanny? How cliché."

The words were like a bucket of cold water thrown on the two of them. Lana was the first to pull back in confusion. She shoved at Ty's chest and jerked her discarded shirt across her breasts in an attempt to cover her wares.

"What the..." Ty frowned down into her face, slow to come back to reality. He closed his eyes and dropped his head to her chest. Her strangled cry had him lifting up to see her horror. Ty almost laughed. Six months ago he might have. Quinn might have too, rather than standing there glaring at him.

He forced himself to leave the comfort of her arms. In jerking movements, he pulled his t-shirt back over his head and closed the button on his jeans. With a quick twist of his wrist, he flung the throw blanket over Lana.

"Kitchen," he barked at his twin.

Quinn cast a glare in his direction before he spun on his heel and headed away.

"What is he doing here? I thought you said you two didn't speak anymore?"

"Believe me. It's a surprise to me too, Sweetheart," he sighed in frustration as he watched her shove her arms and head through the various holes in her shirt. God, it was such a shame she had to cover that magnificent chest of hers. "I have the feeling this conversation is going to drag on. Come on, I'll help you to bed."

"Ty, I can walk," she assured him.

"I like carrying you," he grinned down into her pixie face. With that, he scooped her up and headed to her room off the nursery.

When he'd settled her on the mattress, he leaned in for a quick kiss. "I'll see you in the morning."

"Oh! The monitor!"

"I'll take care of Serena tonight. I'm not kidding when I say I want you off that ankle. I'm worried you've overdone it today."

Lana loved the stern voice that indicated his caring. She hugged it to her long after he left.

"I'd ask why you're here, but I have the feeling I already

know. Let me take a stab at it. Jeri called you. She's concerned that I hired Lana. How am I doing so far?" Ty stalked past his brother to the fridge. He needed another beer to deal with the argument about to go down. "Don't you think a call would have sufficed?"

"She's concerned, and from what I can see, with good reason."

"I'll tell you what I told her. It's my house and my child. Butt out!"

Ty watched a pulse throb in Quinn's cheek as his brother clenched his jaw shut, a sure indication of his anger.

"My money paid for this house or have you forgotten?" Quinn taunted.

"As if you would let anyone forget what you've done for them. And no, you didn't pay for this house. You paid for my services to keep your name clean in the media world. You've paid for me to be a middleman between you and real life. I was damn good at it too. *My salary* paid for this house."

Quinn let out a sigh and ran a hand over his face. The face that matched his almost identically. Ty noticed his brother appeared exhausted. Loneliness hit him. He missed their old camaraderie. There was no one to blame, only himself.

"You're right."

Ty paused with the beer halfway to his lips to stare at him. A wry smile formed on Quinn's lips.

"Don't look so shocked. I can admit I'm wrong when need be."

"Right," Ty snorted without heat. He took a long pull of his drink. "Why are you really here, Quinn?"

"I miss her. Serena. I spent so many days in that hospital. At first waiting for her to develop, then be born, and finally, in that little box, to grow enough to go home. I thought she was my daughter. Wanted her to be," he paused to take a ragged breath. "I don't know how to let go. I need her to be part of my life."

Ty closed his eyes against his brother's pain. He couldn't stand to see Quinn hurt. None of it was his brother's fault. All that lay on Ty's own shoulders.

"Okay."

"Okay?" Hope filled Quinn's voice.

"I can't see why we can't work something out. Dual parenting or some shit."

"What like Three Men and A Baby style? You and I can't live in the same house, Ty. We'd kill each other." After a thoughtful moment, he continued, "I could always stay in the guesthouse on occasion."

"Yeah, about that. You can't. Lana's family is going to be staying there. I was thinking you can have a room here in the house when you're in town."

Quinn was silent for a moment, as if assessing the best way to address an issue. Ty suspected he knew what it would be. His twin didn't disappoint.

"What do you know about these people, Ty? I mean really?"

"Admittedly, not much. But it feels right, Quinn. Have you ever met a person and had that instant connection? Everything just falls into place? I have that with Lana. It's not anything I've ever experienced before."

Ty watched his brother struggle with some inner demon.

"I get it. I can't say I'm happy about the situation, or that your judgement shouldn't be called into question based on past actions. However, I do get it. I've felt that exact way."

"Annie, the psychic woman?"

"She's an empath, but yeah, that's her."

"Should I be worried with how bad you've fucked that up? Speaking of... anything you want me to help clean up?" Ty surprised himself by offering. Surprised his brother too, if the raised brows were an indication.

"Not much you can do. I made the mistake of trusting the wrong woman, again. Of thinking she was my friend. I should know better in my business."

That his twin's voice contained such a bitter quality bothered Ty. He had to acknowledge his part in jading his brother. However, if he could help clear up the mess the paparazzi had made of Quinn's life, he would.

"You don't really believe it was her setting you up with those photos, do you? Annie seems a little more straightforward than that."

"I know. Still, I can't see who else it could have been, Ty. No one else knew I'd be there with her. It doesn't matter now. She hates me," Quinn said with a shrug.

"Quinn," Ty paused, unsure what to say. How could he make right the sins of the past or ease his brother's pain with the present?

"You don't have to apologize again. I spoke to Dad. He filled me in on the truth of your relationship with Hailey."

"I don't feel as if I can tell you enough how sorry I am," Ty said hoarsely. "To make right what I took from you. I miss you."

One second the brothers were on opposite sides of the kitchen island, and the next they were embracing. Tears flowed over the barrier of Ty's bottom lids. The dam broke, and he sobbed in Quinn's arms. The fear of things never being right between them started to dissipate.

"I forgive you, Ty."

After a short time, Quinn pulled back, clasped the back of Ty's skull and shifted to put forehead against forehead. Ty's hand came up to duplicate the gesture. It was an old stance they perfected as children. A way to show they were united as one against the world. Brother to brother.

"Can I peek in on Serena?"

"Of course. She's grown like a weed in the last five days."

Ty led the way to the nursery. He studied the room through Quinn's eyes. Other than the crib, a fancy mobile, and the pink walls, there wasn't a lot to recommend the room. The time had come to get serious about the decor. Maybe Lana would have some ideas on that. Speaking of, he walked to the connecting door and leaned his weight against it while his brother stared down at Serena. Ty liked to think he could feel a connection to Lana even while she lay sleeping on the other side.

What he hadn't expected was the door to be flung open. He just about landed on his ass.

"Crap! You might want to warn someone when you do that. I almost busted my butt."

"Shhhh!" Lana scolded quietly. "How was I to know you were in here? I thought I heard something and decided to check on the baby."

"I told you I had it handled tonight. Speaking of which, why the hell can't you follow directions and stay off that ankle?" Ty argued back in a whisper, careful to keep his voice low so as not to wake his sleeping infant.

Without warning, he scooped her up to deposit her back on her bed.

"Will you stop! You keep going all caveman on me. I am perfectly capable of walking on my own," she groused.

"Lana, I'm not playing around. You need to heal. What happens if you are holding Serena and your ankle gives out? It's foolish to be so stubborn."

Lana slapped her hands on the comforter in frustration. He had a point. Still, she was loathe to admit it.

"I'm pretty sure you wrote the book on stubborn," she retorted. Once she heard her own words and the tone she used to deliver them, Lana had to acknowledge she was indeed stubborn. Perhaps they could co-author a book on it.

"If you two are done staring each other down in your battle of wills, would one of you mind showing me where to find the diapers and formula? Our little princess is awake and starting to fuss," Quinn said dryly, as he stood cradling the babe.

Lana moved to pop up only to have Ty's large hand connect with her chest and shove her back on the bed.

"Dude! Seriously?!" She offered up her best glare.

"Park it. You aren't going anywhere."

Ty's tone thrilled and pissed her off at the same time. The whole alpha male thing was hot. She had to get this infatuation under control. Next thing she'd be simpering and batting her eyelashes at him. Then where would she be?

A deliberate clearing of Quinn's throat interrupted their second stare-off. A blush worked its way up from her chest to her hairline. It annoyed her to be caught ogling her boss twice in as many minutes. She noticed Ty trying to suppress a grin. Jerk.

When both men laughed, she realized her filter malfunctioned again and she'd muttered the insult aloud. Closing her eyes, she shook her head. Maybe therapy would help. She'd have to check into that. Upon opening her eyes, she saw Quinn frowning at her. Lana figured he disapproved on the familiarity with Ty. It shouldn't surprise her. In most instances of comparison, she was found wanting.

"Have we met?" Quinn asked walking further into her

room. "I can't help thinking you seem familiar to me somehow."

Fear lit her eyes and she sought Ty's calming green gaze. Wrong move. Lana could tell her gesture sparked his distrust. He probably thought she had something to hide.

"I don't think so. I'm sure I would remember if we had," she finally spoke up.

Quinn nodded in a distracted manner as if he didn't believe her and would eventually place where he knew her from. She decided to be bold and come out with it.

"If you've ever visited the Dancing Doll strip club nine years or so ago, chances are you would have caught my act."

Confessing her past got easier every time she owned up to it. Trying to be brave, she lifted her chin and met the gaze so similar to Ty's. Those same eyes made a cursory scan of her pajama clad body, taking in the tank top and baggy bottoms. On the return trip up her body, they paused on her full breasts in appreciation.

"No. I would have remembered that," he grinned.

Lana folded her arms across her chest. She was sure that if Ty had uttered those words she'd be a liquid pool of lust. Quinn left her feeling nothing. Odd.

"You remind me of someone…"

She tilted her head in question and waited for Quinn to finish his sentence. Instead, he shook his head as if to dispel the thought.

"Do you know a woman by the name of Annie Holt?"

"No. Should I?"

"Never mind." His smile was rueful. "I seem to be mistaken. But if I didn't know better, I would say you were related. Same build. Same mannerisms. Except for your brown eyes…"

"Amber," Ty injected. His comment drew their attention.

"Pardon?"

He cleared his throat. "Lana's eyes are amber."

Those same gemstone colored eyes lit up as they focused on Ty. Lana was sure the heat surging to his face matched the blush dusting hers. The idea that he might really feel the same way as she did, enough to notice the color of her eyes and flush with the embarrassment of being caught at it, thrilled her.

"Amber. Right. Okay, back to diaper duty. Point me in the direction of the essentials. I'm smelling something rank."

Lana moved to leap off the bed a second time, only to be shoved back by Ty.

"Dammit!"

"Stay."

"I'm not a dog."

"For the love of God you two, give it a rest already," Quinn sighed in exasperation. "Ty the stink is making me nauseous. Get me a damn diaper, man."

Lana had to laugh. Two gorgeous men, one an A-List movie star at that, trying to hold a squalling infant while trying not to gag as they changed her was hilarious from

Lana's vantage point. Ty seemed to possess the weaker stomach of the brothers. He was as green as some of the gunk that came out of Serena's pipes. Watching him turn away to breathe through his mouth or dry heave had her giggling behind her pillow. Diaper duty was not for the faint of heart.

The glare she earned for her hilarity set her off even more. She paused in an attempt to try and remember when she'd last laughed that hard. Never. Her life hadn't allowed for frivolity and fun. The best part being that she knew Ty wouldn't hold it against her. She couldn't say how she was so sure, but she was. The knowledge warmed her from the inside out.

As she listened to the low tones of their voices soothing the babe, Lana allowed her lids to drift shut. She fantasized about one day building a family of her own. Remarkably, Ty played into that daydream. If only!

Chapter Six

A few days later, as Lana finished putting the baby down for a nap, Quinn confronted her. The menacing body language made her nervous. The fact that he shut the door behind him when he walked in ratcheted up her alarm. This couldn't be good.

"What do you want, Mr. Jensen?"

She was always careful not to call him Quinn. Professional barriers were key. The little voice in her head snickered because not only did she not have that wall between her and Ty, she'd helped him bust it down with a wrecking ball the second night she stayed in his house. Slowly, she'd needed to start replacing the bricks to that wall. It would take some time for her to get over her infatuation with him.

"Want? That's a loaded question, Lana," he purred.

Fuck. She recognized the tone. He intended to force his attentions on her. She quickly scanned the room for a weapon or, at the very least, a large item to block his direct path to her person. Finding nothing, she trained her wary gaze on him.

"It isn't intended to be. You came to the nursery for a reason. Knowing it's Serena's nap time and seeing that you've closed the door, I doubt it was to visit her," she said. "I'm not buying what you're selling, buddy. You need to turn your happy ass around and walk out of this room."

An unnamed emotion flared in his eyes before it was extinguished. A few more steps brought him within arm's reach. Fear tried to take hold. She tamped it down. If she allowed panic to rule her, he'd win. She had to keep her head on her shoulders for this confrontation.

"You haven't heard my proposition. Maybe you'll change your mind about what I'm…selling."

Quinn invaded her space further, stroking her neck with his fingers. Her pulse kicked up a notch. The last thing she needed was his interest in her.

"I won't."

"I think you will. How about a little wager?" he murmured against her neck as he started to nuzzle the spot under her ear.

"How about not?" she snapped with a shove to his chest.

Surprise showed briefly on his face. She noted his lips compress in what she assumed was irritation.

He sauntered off to peruse the yard outside Serena's window. Taking advantage of his distraction, Lana bolted to the door.

"Wait."

She spun back with her hand on the knob, ready to escape. Quinn perched on the window seat, legs outstretched in front of him and hands tucked in his pants pockets. The picture of non-threatening. She took her hand off the door and rested her back against the wall, arms crossed in front of her chest.

"Start talking. You desire me about as much as you desire that pillow next to you. What's with the sudden come on?"

He pressed his lips together again. This time she understood the gesture for what it was - amusement.

Lana couldn't help compare him to his twin. They were mostly identical, but where Quinn had a more GQ-esque quality about him, Ty put out a more down to earth, guy-next-door vibe. They both let their stubble go on occasion, so the difference wasn't there. Maybe it was the length of their hair. Ty's tended to be a bit shaggier in nature. Also, Quinn came across as more worldly. Again, odd because they were both in the same industry. She had to admit he probably had the harder job of the two. Dealing with the public day in and day out had to be unbearable at times.

She thought it strange that her sexual attraction for Ty was off the charts while Quinn did nothing for her. Chalk that one up to pheromones. Though if they had the same DNA, it would stand to reason Quinn's would set her off in a puddle of goo like Ty's did. She chucked all thoughts out the window. Brick wall. She had to remember she was a mason now.

"I'm waiting."

"I want to pay you to sleep with me."

Laughter burst from her throat, so loud and so fast, she woke the baby, who immediately started fussing.

"Oh sonofabitch! Now see what you've done! Well, get to rocking, mister. It's your fault," she ordered.

"Isn't Ty paying you good money to do your *job?*" he asked snidely.

Lana didn't miss the emphasis on the word job.

"If you have a complaint regarding how I care for that baby, you need to bring it to Ty's attention. On the other hand, if you are insinuating I am providing other favors in exchange for pay, I'm gonna throat punch you." Although she delivered the words calmly, he could be left with no doubt how insulted she was. Lana hung on to her patience with a thread. "How about I go get him for you? You can tell him you believe I'm horrible at my job."

"Stop the drama. I get enough of that in my line of work." He stood to pick up Serena. Tucking her in his arm, he relaxed into the overlarge rocker and started to hum.

"How about you stop the games? Obviously you have an agenda. Why don't you tell me what it is so I can prep for lunch?"

"Fair enough. What do you know about the situation with Hailey Newberry?"

"He told me everything."

Surprise showed in his visage, enough so that he paused in the motion of standing with the baby.

"Hmmm. I'm somewhat shocked he shared. He's usually a little more circumspect than that," he said softly. He circled the room, bouncing lightly and patting Serena's diapered bottom as he went.

"What are you saying? You want to pay me so that you can have revenge sex with someone he may or may not want?" her tone rose to barely shy of a shriek.

"Shhhh, the baby. You can look at it that way if you'd like. But no, I want to take a relationship with you off the table for him," he told her. "You're not good for him. Honestly? Over the last two and a half days, I've seen the way his eyes follow you around whenever you're in the room. I'm worried he could develop feelings for you. Ty tends to fall hard and fast."

Lana noted his pause. He wanted a reaction from her. She had no intention of giving him one.

Quinn nodded as if he expected her to behave that way. He continued his explanation, "He deserves better. Better than the Haileys and Lanas of the world. Better than someone who only wants him for what he can provide for her."

A chill chased its way down her spine. She was hot and cold all at once. Embarrassed and shocked.

"I can see by your face, you didn't expect me to catch on to your little plan. Moving the family into the guesthouse was a bit much right off the bat, wasn't it?" he asked in a taunting, snide tone as he paused in front of her. "What will it take to get rid of you? Three years salary?"

Had he not been holding the baby, she would have done him bodily harm, regardless of his size.

"I have work to do," she choked out.

She turned to go and before she could yank open the door, he leaned in to relay his final ultimatum. With a soft, steel-infused voice, he said, "Stay away from my brother, Lana. I promise, you won't like me for an enemy."

* * *

Ty found Lana preparing lunch in the kitchen. Remembering how jumpy she'd been the night they watched the horror flick, he decided against sneaking up to steal a kiss. Instead, he rested on his elbows against the island and waited for her to finish chopping vegetables for their salads. The dopey grin that had taken up residence on his face that night refused to dissipate.

The knife came to rest on the counter, and she moved to carry the fruits of her labor to the table. When she would have passed him, he snaked an arm out to catch her about the waist and drag her close. Burying his head in her cloud of crazy hair, he inhaled her scent.

"Ty. Don't."

"Don't what?" he murmured as his lips came to rest on the silky skin of her neck.

"You're my boss. This isn't going to lead to anywhere good," she told him firmly. With the bowl in her hand, he knew her struggling against his hold was futile. He hoped that perhaps a small piece of her didn't care to struggle.

His teeth grazed the spot he kissed the moment before. "The baby's napping. I checked."

"Oh-kaayyy."

Pulling back, he spun her around to observe her. Why was she being so distant today when she'd engaged in flirting with him over the last few days?

"I'd hoped we could pick up where we left off the other night," he said and took the bowl from her hands. That he knew the exact location of the counter from years of living in this house was good, because he slid it on the granite countertop without looking. Lana had all his attention.

"What about lunch? I'd hate for you to think I'm not doing my *job*."

The stress on the word job alerted him to a problem. She was mad. Offhand, he couldn't figure why, though he intended to. If he learned nothing else in his thirty-four years, he'd certainly learned when a woman was upset and how to maneuver a pissed-off woman's minefield. He played the last two and a half days through his mind.

Glancing down, he factored in her hands resting on his chest. They weren't pushing him away. That told him she wasn't angry with him directly. It had to be an outside source. Jeri? No, she hadn't been by since the first day. Liam? Possibly, but Ty would bet her brother would be smart enough not to anger his sister during working hours. That left only one possibility since, to the best of his knowledge, she hadn't been out to see her mother this morning. Quinn.

That he could get around. Ty pulled her to rest between his legs. He met with little resistance this time. One hand found its way into the back pocket of her jeans to hold her against him. The other lifted her chin. After dropping a quick kiss on her lips, he addressed the issue.

"Want to tell me why you're upset?"

He expected the denial.

"I'm not upset," she grumbled.

"Hmmm."

"What's that supposed to mean?" she asked, with a slight shove.

He grinned as he touched his nose to hers. With tiny back and forth movements, he teased her.

"Just that. Hmmm."

"Your brother's an asshole."

Bingo.

"You won't get an argument from me. What did he do?" The hand cupping her ass inside her pocket urged her closer. His right hand, previously resting on her hip, worked its way under her t-shirt and traced a swirling pattern against the skin above the waistband of her pants.

"It isn't important."

He felt her lips against his jawline. Score.

"You're sure?" Ty rounded first base.

"Mmhmmm."

"Want to go make out in your room?" He unfastened the top button on her jeans.

"What about lunch?" she gasped.

"I'm not hungry…for lunch."

His lips fastened against her pouty lower lip and sucked.

"Okay."

"Okay, what?"

"Okay, let's go make out in my room."

Lana was faster than he'd given her credit for. She whipped up the bowl containing their lunch, threw a lid on it, and shoved it in an unknown location in the recesses of his massive ass fridge. All before he could think to stand up.

She leaned back against the stainless door and inched her zipper down, centimeter by centimeter until she had his head twisted up and his penis on full alert.

"Fuck the bedroom. Counter. Now!"

Ty hauled Lana up and plunked her down on the counter. She leaned back and arched up to allow him the ability to draw her pants down over her hips. He didn't stop until they were in a heap on the floor. Because he had grabbed the lace underwear at the same time, she now sat bare-assed on the cool counter. With great deliberation he backed up a step, then two. Her confusion was adorable.

"Spread your legs."

"What?"

"Spread 'em," he ordered.

Slowly she inched her legs open, teasing him. The satisfaction in Ty's smile made Lana wet on the spot.

"Wider," he demanded. Seeing her thighs spread open further, exposing her fully to his gaze, made him inhale sharply. When he was able, he continued with his instruction. "Touch yourself."

She whimpered his name.

"I need to see you touch yourself, Lana," he growled in return.

Giving in to his demand, she slid her hand down to the juncture between her thighs.

His gaze was focused with laser precision on where her hand met her sex.

"Pleasure yourself," he said hoarsely.

"No."

His grunt told her he hadn't expected resistance at this point. She smiled at the realization she held the power to make him yield to her wishes from here on out.

"*You* touch me. I need to feel your hands on me."

The skin across his cheeks tightened with desire.

"Please, Ty. Touch me," she urged.

There was no need to ask a second time. Not when the first time was so effective. He stepped up, locked gazes and shoved her legs wider still.

Lana inhaled a lungful. Goddammit this man was hot. In form, and in deed.

When he plunged two fingers into her, she almost came. The pressure built as he used his thumb to rub the nub of her clit. In mere moments, she was panting and crying out with the orgasm rocking her body. The muscles surrounding the walls of her vagina spasmed around the fingers still inside.

"Nice," he said, a self-satisfied smile playing about his mouth.

That same mouth captured hers as he repeated the motions that brought her to orgasm the first time. Not exactly knowing where she gathered the strength, she stopped his hand and unlocked their lips.

"No, Ty. I want you in me this time."

The last time she'd seen a guy move that fast to shuck his jeans was high school. A giggle erupted.

"It's not good to laugh when you see a man's penis for the first time, Sweetheart. If I wasn't confident of my size and ability, you might give me a complex," he joked.

Reaching down, she wrapped him in both hands.

"I'd say you're spot on about that size comment. Let's see how you are with ability."

"Oh, fuck yeah," he moaned as she stroked the length of him.

He removed her hands and whipped them up against the dark wood of the cabinets above her head.

"If you touch me like that, I'm not going to make it," he growled low in his throat.

As his mouth devoured hers, he shifted to rub his cock against her drenched core. The ease in which he slid up and down had him groaning.

"Condom," she mouthed against him.

"Huh?"

"Where's the condom?"

"Do we *need* a condom?"

"We do if you plan to put that bad boy in me," she said as she clenched her knees on his hips to halt any forward progress.

"Oh, Sweetheart. Don't do this to me. Not now," he begged. "Tell me you're on birth control."

"That's not the issue."

It was a long time coming and finally the light bulb went off in Ty's head.

"Ah. That. Yeah, I'm clean. After...well, I was tested," he promised. "You?"

"Yep. We're good to go."

On that, she wrapped her legs around him and met him thrust for thrust. Their pelvises slammed and ground against each other, accompanied by their mingled moans of pleasure. They came together in an explosion of cries.

"Jesus!"

"Yeah, I concur," she laughed between gulps of air.

"I'm getting really tired of walking in on you two without your clothes on," Quinn said. His tone was as cold as Ty had ever heard. Maybe more than when he'd discovered the indiscretion with Hailey.

"Whose fucking house is it?" Ty roared over his shoulder. "Want to give us a damn second to get decent?"

"Take a few. And make sure you sanitize that counter while you're at it. Seems like you're not particular where you shove your dick or what you shove it into," Quinn snapped back.

Lana's sharp, indrawn breath told him she'd understood the barb. Rage flooded him like never before. All he wanted was to bask in the afterglow of sex with her. Now he had to deal with a second insult to her. He placed a palm on either side of her face, silently encouraging her to look at him. He ducked a few inches and tilted his head in an attempt to capture her gaze.

"Sweetheart," he said softly. "Look at me."

The chagrin in her amber eyes was more than he could stand. His arms encircled her and pulled her close. He cradled her against his heart.

"I swear, after I kill him and bury the body, we can resume this without worrying about any future embarrassment."

Those words had the desired effect. She snorted and relaxed into his chest.

"Your brother's an asshole."

"I'm pretty sure we already established that."

Chapter Seven

Quinn got a call to re-shoot a scene from his last movie. Because he stayed gone for the better part of a week and a half, Ty noticed Lana open up more and relax around the house. It was a fun time for both of them. During the day, he worked out of his home office while she took care of Serena and her mother. In the evenings, after the baby was put to bed, they were able to enjoy one-on-one time. Their evenings were filled will wine, old movies, and making love.

This night, Ty rested against the pillows on the sectional, baby on his chest and bare legs thrown over Lana's smooth, thighs. He took pleasure in the sensation of skin on skin. Maybe he would insist that shorts and a tank top would be the new nanny uniform. He also enjoyed the way she absently rubbed his feet while they talked.

"You have ugly feet," she stated.

He frowned at the appendages in question. "No, I don't."

"You do. Look at the hair on this big toe." She pinched said toe.

Squinting, Ty struggled to make out any hair. Okay, maybe one, but really? Who didn't have a stray toe hair?

"One hair? You are seriously making fun of my feet for one hair?"

"Well, it's a long one. And see the way this toe curls. Ty

Jensen, you have ugly-ass monkey feet."

"Shut up. I do *not!*"

She fought a smirk, her dimple winking at him. "Yep, you do. I'm glad. I mean, you needed something to detract from those good looks."

"You think I'm good looking?" he asked with a devilish grin.

She snorted and rolled her eyes. "Oh please! Stop fishing for compliments. As if you didn't already know you're hot. Pffft."

"You think I'm ho-otttt. You want my bod-eeee!" he sang tauntingly.

"Like I'm going to deny that. But you need to wear socks to cover those monster feet. I don't want to be doing the reverse cowgirl and accidentally catch a glimpse. It could ruin the mood."

"Jesus! You have a mean streak, you know that?" He shoved her over with the aforementioned foot. "To mention my sexual fantasy and then ruin it with a visual of my feet all in one shot is cruel."

"So you admit they're hideous?"

"I am not talking to you right now. You're fired. Pack your bags and go."

Lana's laughter rang out, triggering Ty's. For the longest while they were held captive by each other. They relished the moment, lost in each other and their shared merriment.

A sound behind him indicated another person had entered

the room. Even if Ty hadn't known to expect Quinn back that evening, Lana's distasteful glare in his direction would have given away his presence. She still hadn't warmed up to his twin, and Ty had yet to learn why. He suspected Quinn of insulting her more than once the day Ty had first made love to her in the kitchen. The trouble was neither of them were talking. It frustrated the hell out of him. More than anything, he wanted the people he loved most in the world to get along.

His last thought brought him up short. Love? He felt pole-axed. Could he possibly be in love with his daughter's nanny that fast? Yes. He had to acknowledge, if only to himself, he'd fallen hook, line, and sinker. This feeling was so much more intense in nature than what he'd felt for Hailey. This emotion transcended sex. Sure, he carried a permanent woody for Lana, and still the feelings overwhelming him were endless.

The struggle to come to grips with his revelation must have shown. Lana regarded him with concern. She gripped his leg to get his full attention, drawing his gaze to her beautiful pixie face.

"Ty? What's wrong?"

He shook his head twice as an indication he was fine. The half smile he offered up to circumvent additional questioning must have made him appear more sickly than convincing.

Quinn paused behind the sofa and studied him.

"What?" Ty demanded to know, as a grin burst across his brother's face.

"I'm trying to memorize your expression for when I

finally fall. I want to be able to recognize the look in case a mirror happens to be close at hand," Quinn teased.

"Fuck off."

"What look? What's going on?" Lana asked. Her questioning eyes were for Ty alone as she made a concerted effort to ignore his brother's presence.

"Well, what do you know," Quinn mocked. "The lovely, little Lana is sporting the same look. Must be an outbreak."

Ty sat upright and cast a sharp glance at her face. His sibling's words made him search her features, hoping to find the truth. All he saw was her apprehension as she shifted her gaze between the two of them.

As he opened his mouth to question her, Serena let out a soft mewl. The moment was lost as Lana chose that particular distraction to make a break for it and remove herself from the hot seat.

"I'll heat a bottle," she threw over her shoulder as she headed to the kitchen.

"You're an ass," Ty hissed at his sibling when she'd cleared the room.

Quinn's comeback was to sing, "Ty and Lana sitting in a tree, K I S S I N G..."

"That's real grown up, dickhead."

A snort from Quinn indicated he appreciated that he'd scored a hit. When all humor left his brother's face, Ty experienced a moment of unease. Quinn had it in for Lana, and Ty needed to find out why. As if his twin read his mind,

Quinn said, "Seriously, when she feeds the baby, you and I need to talk."

A sick sensation gripped Ty. He didn't want to hear what his brother had to say. Didn't want to have to rethink his budding relationship.

Lana coming back into the room caught his full attention. The limp from her ankle injury was gone now. In its place was a sexy, rolling walk that had her hips swaying from side to side. A temptation to every man on the planet. Just watching her walk was making his dick hard. Admittedly, he had it bad for her.

Ty waited until Lana was settled on the couch with a pillow propped under her arm before he handed over Serena. Reaching out, he caressed his baby's soft, fuzzy scalp. His daughter was his everything. He'd fallen madly in love with her in the short time since she'd entered his life. Now that he'd been able to get rest, he could enjoy her more as each day her personality emerged.

As he raised his head from studying his beautiful little girl, he met and held Lana's soft gaze. He didn't care what his brother had to say. She was special. Dropping a quick kiss on her lips, he hefted himself up from the sofa to follow his brother outside.

"What's going on?"

"I don't like that you two are playing house together so quickly," Quinn got right to the point.

"It's none of your business. I'll thank you to stay out of it," Ty said sharply.

"Wrong. I have no intention of standing by while you get hurt again," his brother returned. Sighing, Quinn went on to express his reservation, "You have a thing for slutty women, Ty, and you have a serious lack of self-preservation."

"Fucking insinuate, or call her a slut *one more time,* and I will knock your teeth out," Ty ground out, enraged.

"For God's sake, Ty. Listen to yourself! How long have you known her? All of two weeks? You're ready to strike me for telling you to be cautious?" Quinn asked incredulously.

"I have no issue with you telling me to be cautious. What I *do* take issue with is the nasty digs and insults," Ty said, a little more calmly than he felt. "I mean it. Knock it off. You don't know her."

"And you do?"

Ty turned his back on him and walked the few feet to study the lighted pool. Absently, he realized it was past time to pressure wash the pool and deck. Scanning the rest of the property, he noticed Lana's mother peeping out of the curtains of the cottage fifty yards away. She'd probably heard their raised voices and decided to investigate, he surmised.

Quinn came up to stand beside him, unconsciously mimicking his stance of hands in pockets and shoulders hunched.

"You have to admit you don't, Ty. Two weeks isn't enough time to know anyone."

"She's a sweet person, Quinn."

"Please, just think about slowing things down a little okay? Lana herself admitted to working at a strip club, and then she jumped right between the sheets with you only two days after meeting you. You're a handsome guy, bro, but any self-respecting woman doesn't move that fast." Quinn sighed heavily. "Also, Jeri said she's prone to stealing other women's men and that she had an affair with her last boss. Things don't add up with this chick. If you want to hit it and quit it, that's fine. Keep your heart out of it. That's all I'm saying."

His brother brought up questions Ty didn't care to think about. Had she lied in her version of the events with Carter Nichols? Ty didn't think so. Why would Carter have written the check so readily? Between the two, Ty would believe Lana over that waste of space any day of the year.

However, Quinn had a point. Ty was falling fast and hard. The brakes needed to be applied before he crashed and burned. If he figured in his past track record, this romance didn't stand a snowball's chance in hell.

"Fine, I'll go slow and be sure things are on the up and up. You need to back off and let me handle my own life, Kwee," Ty said, reverting to calling his brother by his childhood nickname. As a young child, Ty had been unable to pronounce his brother's name and as a result, Quinn became Kwee.

Quinn knew his brother was in over his head with Lana. The fact that Ty had used his childhood name said as much.

He only referred to Quinn as Kwee when he was feeling overly emotional.

The attraction the cute little nanny held for his brother was understandable. She was sexy as hell. Her curvy, hourglass figure and crazy colored hair made men fantasize about her wild side. Of course there was the whole taking care of Ty's child factor too. It made her more appealing to Ty on a more basic, primitive level. Quinn understood his brother's need for love and a family. It wasn't so very different from his own. He wanted it for both of them. Funny how they both picked women who weren't good for them. For him, it had been Sylvie and Hailey. He refused to think about Annie, because he wasn't ready for the emotional fallout from that one. If he thought too long about the past seven months, he might have to admit he misjudged her. All he knew was that he missed her.

Which brought him back around to thinking about Lana. Why did she remind him of Annie so much? What was it about her? Perhaps Ty was right and he had labeled her without getting to know her. That could be the nagging in the back of his mind. He pushed the feeling aside for now. His primary goal was to watch out for his twin, as he'd done the entirety of their lives. He didn't know how to be any other way. If Quinn had to step on a few toes or crush a few people in the process of protecting Ty, so be it. It's not like it would be the first time. Ty's and Serena's welfare came first. Anyone else was disposable as far as Quinn was concerned.

Chapter Eight

Days, then weeks, passed. Lana settled into a new routine. One without Ty. He'd pulled back from any display of affection after the night Quinn returned from filming. She supposed the attraction fizzled out for him once he'd gotten what he wanted. Having those two stolen weeks together had the opposite effect on her. It made her want more. She was sure the chemistry was real. Or at least it had been. Since then, he treated her like she was a plague carrier. All the old insecurities kicked in, making her feel not good enough.

She also figured his brother, or hers, must have warned him off, and being a smart, decent guy, he listened. Still, it hurt. Lana lectured herself it was for the best. Crossing professional barriers would surely find her out of a job, and her family out of a home. Having him put it all back on business-like footing could only benefit them both. Hell, she was surprised she still had employment. Although, he couldn't complain about her work ethic, or the way she cared for Serena. Never once had she failed in that capacity. Maybe it was why he kept her on. Perhaps added to the fact was Lana's lack of neediness. She hadn't wanted, nor demanded, an explanation as to why he pulled away. For her, it didn't matter. He called it quits. Begging wasn't in her to do.

Today she'd made herself scarce. The distraction of Ty

had been too great. Upon seeing Ty guzzling his coffee wrapped only in a towel this morning, Lana's mind was all aflutter. Right along with her heart and her sex drive. She'd stood and stared for such a length of time, he had to clear his throat and physically move her to pass by. Idiot woman. Luckily, she had been on her way out the door. Had she been forced to work in close proximity to him, she…well, there was no telling what she would have done. It didn't help that her hormones were whack and the desire to bang nasties infiltrated her dreams at night. There, brewing below the surface, was the very real need to tear his clothes off and lick every inch of available bare skin. Lana couldn't recall ever wanting someone so much.

On days like today, she utilized her alternating days off and escaped to draw in the park. While landscapes were her passion, Lana loved to capture people in motion. Hikers, kayakers, children playing ball, the occasional dog, they all eventually found their way onto her sketchpad. On the nice days she'd set up an easel to paint the pictures she'd drawn. All her hidden emotions could be found blatantly displayed in her art.

Currently depressed, she used the charcoal to speak on her behalf. To create the long, graceful lines of Ty's body. To highlight and darken the hills and valleys of his tight abs. Outlining eight distinct muscles along with obliques and a hint of the flat plane that led to the promised land, hidden by the towel gripped in his knuckle-white fist. Wait! What?! Yes, that was the image her mind recalled. Why would his fist have been clenching the material to the extent of cutting off the blood supply to his hand? Lana studied the bottom half of the drawing. Without conscious thought, she had created the beginning of a hard-on. Was that what she had witnessed or was it what she hoped would happen? That he'd take one look at her and whisk her to bed?

She missed their "dates" most of all. He made sure to either eat in his home office under the excuse of working, or invite their families to join them. Breakfast was eaten on the run, as was his lunch. The one time they'd met in the middle of the night to care for a feverish Serena, he'd angrily ordered her to go back to bed. If she were being honest with herself, she longed for the man she'd first met. She couldn't help wondering if he regretted keeping her on. Lana suspected he was too kind to fire her outright.

With a tear for what would never be, she tore the page from the book. She promised herself one last glance and she would throw the likeness of Ty away.

A large hand came from behind her and snatched the drawing. She knew that hand! After all, she'd just sketched it. Lana wasn't fast enough to grab it back. Humiliation stung her cheeks. To be busted lusting over a charcoal rendering of the man himself, made her want to curl in a ball and die. Knowing he didn't feel the same...God!

"What the hell do you think you're doing?" she screeched.

"Me? I'm not the one drawing half-naked men in the

park."

"Give it back," she demanded with an attempt to retrieve it.

"No." He held it up and away. Her reaching it would be impossible. In a huff she threw her supplies willy-nilly back into her art bag and flicked the lid closed. Ten feet away it came to her that he was here alone. Where was the baby?

She whirled and pinned him with a glare. "Where's Serena?"

He nodded to the left of her. She turned to see Jeri Newberry seated on a blanket about forty feet away, glaring in their direction. Ty's daughter slept curled in her arms. A picnic basket lay open with the contents spread in front of her nemesis.

Hurt and anger curled around her heart. Squeezing. Her chest felt a literal ache. Without a word, Lana swung her messenger bag with its supplies over her head and stalked toward the car her brother had dubbed Deathtrap. She prayed the damn thing would start and not make her splendid exit seem ridiculous.

Jesus, she was such an idiot. When, when, when would she ever learn? Never apparently. Blood roared in her ears, making her deaf to her surroundings. She never heard the vehicle roar to life. Never heard the acceleration of the engine or the squeal of the tires. The impact to her side spun her around, causing her forehead to collide with the mirror of Deathtrap before slamming on the ground.

Belatedly, it sank in that someone was shouting her name. Ty.

"Hang in there, Sweetheart. Help's on the way. Don't move. Just hang on." He repeated the phrases over and over like a mantra.

Lana wanted desperately to snort and ask where he thought she would be moving to. As far as she was concerned the warm pavement made a welcoming bed. Though the dark, purply-red substance that was working toward her outstretched hand made her a wee bit nervous. To remove her hand from its meandering path was more than she could manage. She observed the blood's pattern in a detached manner, letting the beauty of the liquid hypnotize her and lull her toward blessed sleep.

Ty wouldn't let that happen. She tried to tell him to leave her alone, but found her mouth refused to form the words. He made it impossible to ignore him as he sprawled next to her and forced her eyes to focus on his.

"You have to stay with me, Sweetheart. The ambulance is almost here," he croaked out. "Lana!"

Lana frowned, trying to decide what colors she should use for the green of his eyes if she ever painted his portrait. Sap green. Yes, with flecks of gold-green highlights. She would paint him this way, with the angst in his eyes. That emotion spoke to her.

Tired. She was too tired to think anymore. As her lids once more drifted downward, butterfly wings caressed her cheeks. The sensation made her smile.

More voices came to disturb her rest.

"Sir. Sir! You have to move so we can do our job. Someone get him out of here."

"What happened?"

"Does she have any allergies?"

"Ma'am, can you tell us where you hurt?"

One question tumbled over another in a seemingly endless cycle. Lana wanted them all to go away. Her head was close to exploding from the agony of it all.

When the blackness finally took her, it was a welcome relief.

***

Ty jerked upright with a start. He glanced around the hospital room, wondering groggily what had disturbed his slumber.

"Ty."

He reached to rub the sleep from his eyes.

"Ty."

Following the sound, he saw the source of the voice. Quinn stood in the doorway of Lana's hospital room. Concern etched his twin's face. Ty tore his gaze away to stare at the lone figure on the bed. Seeing the tube in her throat, breathing for her, caused a hiccup in his own pulmonary function.

"Don't you think it's ironic that she was given the same

room as Hailey?" he asked hoarsely. "I guess we can be grateful she's not pregnant with my child."

"Ty, don't."

"No, I mean really. When they finally take her off those fucking machines, we won't spend another month here waiting for a baby to develop in an incubator. We won't be questioning the paternity. I guess that's a plus."

"Stop!" Quinn ordered. "She's not Hailey, and she's not going to die."

"You don't know that," Ty whispered. Fear closing his throat. "You can't know that."

He felt himself hauled up and arms come around him. His brother's warm hand clasped the back of his neck, bringing them together in their pose of unity.

"It was my fault, Kwee. She sat there under the tree. So beautiful. So intent on what she was working on. I had to see what she was drawing."

He pulled away and stepped to the end of the bed. One hand reached to touch her foot, but he pulled it back, unable to make contact. Because deep in his core, he knew if he touched her, this nightmare would become real.

"It was a picture of me from earlier this morning. She'd come into the kitchen and there I stood like a dumbass in my towel," Ty snorted and turned to his brother. "Normally she would have already been gone by then. On her days off she disappears early. Anyway, I was angry with myself that I hadn't checked before running around the house half-undressed."

"The drawing was of you in your towel?" Quinn asked, confused as to where his brother was heading with all this.

"Yes. She's an incredible artist. I had no idea," Ty said in wonder.

"What makes you think it was your fault?"

"The detail of the drawing surprised me. Enough that I grabbed it from her to get a closer look," Ty explained.

"So she was mad you took her sketch?"

"Yeah, though not as furious as she was when she saw Jeri."

"Jeri? Why was Jeri there?"

"We were going to picnic in the park," Ty mumbled.

"*What?!*" Quinn nearly shouted in his disbelief. "What the fuck were you thinking, Ty?"

"I wasn't, all right?!"

What Quinn would have said, Ty wasn't to know. The strict voice of the ICU nurse interrupted their conversation.

"Mr. Jensen, visiting hours are over. You two are going to need to leave."

"I'm not leaving," he told her.

"Sir, yo-"

"I *said,* I'm not leaving," he ground out. The threatening step he took forward was halted by his brother.

"Ty," Quinn warned.

"I'm not!"

"Give us five more minutes," Quinn commanded in a low

tone.

Ty watched the nurse flounce out in a huff. He knew she'd be back with either security or Lana's doctor, Trace Montgomery. Fuck it. He didn't care because he had no intention of leaving her side.

"Finish the story. Although I can guess what happened from there."

"Yeah, Lana saw Jeri. I'm pretty sure steam came out of her ears. She stormed off toward the road. I assume because her piece of shit car was parked there. I called out when I saw the other car speed up. I-I…She never glanced up." Ty paused to suck in air, bracing himself to continue. "She was so still. I was afraid to touch her anywhere. I've always heard you shouldn't move an accident victim. But I couldn't not touch her. I couldn't not try to comfort her. The fucking ambulance was taking forever. I laid down next to her, trying to get her to see me. To stay awake. I stroked her cheek…

"She was leaving me, Kwee. I could tell. Her eyes…that beautiful sparkle dimmed, and she was leaving."

Ty relived the horror of that moment. The scene played repetitively in his mind. A niggling sensation pushed its way to the forefront of his thoughts. The other vehicle. There had been something familiar about it. If he could just put his finger on what it was… Quinn distracted him.

"Ty, why did you take Jeri to the park?"

"She wanted to spend time as a family. She told me she wanted to talk about Hailey. The picnic was her idea. I didn't see any reason not to go along with it."

"No? How about the wrong damn impression you were giving both women? How about the fact you were screwing *her* on the counter a few short weeks ago?" Quinn pointed to Lana's comatose form.

"Watch your tone! And don't you dare speak of her that way."

"Why is it, you two are always coming to blows in my hospital?" came the wry voice of Dr. Trace Montgomery.

"Trace," Quinn greeted his friend with a handshake.

"I'm sorry to see you under these conditions again," Trace told him, as he walked to the bed to check the monitor.

Ty watched him pull a penlight from his pocket and test Lana's reaction to the stimulus. Next came a checking of the pulse in her wrist. The doctor's carefully blank look told him all he needed to know. No immediate change.

Chapter Nine

Lana's coma lasted precisely eight days, sixteen hours, thirty-nine minutes and eleven seconds. Dr. Montgomery had taken a wait and see approach during that time. Trace's lack of reassurance had Ty living every moment in a hell of his own making.

He worked out an alternating schedule with Liam. It allowed one of them to be on hand at the hospital should Lana wake up. The idea of her being alone bothered him. As Quinn was on hiatus from filming, he took over nanny duty. Ty was relieved to see his brother step up to help. He didn't have the energy to care for an infant and also stand vigilant by Lana's bedside.

In the wee hours of the morning on the ninth day, as Ty strolled in with a black coffee and Liam gathered his things to leave, Lana joined the living. At first, he feared she lay dying due to the horrific choking sound and elevated heart rate. Terror paralyzed Ty's muscles and froze him in place.

Liam's shout brought the medical staff running. Nurses arrived, shoving both him and her brother to the corner of the room.

"Lana, I need you to calm down. Can you hear me? You need to calm down and relax. You were in an accident and brought here to First Memorial Medical Center. You've been out for a few days and we needed to help you breathe. Now that you're awake, we're going to disconnect and remove this tube," the nurse explained.

Ty's own heart raced. He couldn't imagine how disorienting it must be to wake up with a plastic cylinder crammed down one's throat. Her large, panicked eyes found and held his concerned gaze. By small degrees, she calmed down as she stared at him, never breaking their connection.

"Page Dr. Montgomery. Tell him Lana Martell is awake. He's going to want to do an evaluation," an attending resident said to her co-worker.

The staff tried to explain why she was here. Confusion clouded Lana's face. Ty involuntarily stepped forward to the side of the bed abandoned by a nursing assistant who'd rushed to follow orders. The need to ease her mind swamped him. Reaching down, he clasped her delicate hand in his. On the first try, his voice cracked. He swallowed and tried again, "Hey, Sweetheart."

She looked to where their hands met. A frown marred her forehead, or what could be seen of her forehead underneath the bandages. Her mouth parted as if to form words before pressing back together in a thin line. Ty had the impression she experienced frustration.

"It's okay. You're okay," he said, repeating it a few more times while holding her palm to his chest, over his heart. He didn't know who he wanted to convince, her or himself.

"Wa-w...wat..." she worked to expel the word.

He addressed her nurse, "Can she have some water?"

"No. We don't know how her stomach might react. I'll bring back some ice cubes for her to start with. You can give her a few to help with the dry-mouth," she told him. "Gradually, we'll increase her intake and see about liquids, if her throat isn't too sore to swallow."

"Thank you."

"You're welcome, Mr. Jensen. Dr. Montgomery should be here shortly." With a nod, she exited the room.

Liam moved to the left of the bed. "Hey Sis. You had us worried."

"Ha-happened?" she asked with a whisper and a wince.

"You don't remember?" Ty asked sharply.

A slight twitch of her head to the left was her negative reply.

"You were hit by a car, Lana."

Her eyes flared and she fisted her hand, squeezing his. "Ba-by?"

"Baby? You mean Serena? She's fine. She wasn't there."

The frown deepened. "Remember...crying."

Had the baby been crying? He couldn't recall. Lana sprawled and bleeding on the pavement had held all his attention.

"I don't know. But she's fine. I promise."

As her lids headed southbound, anxiety gripped him. He cast an anxious glance in Liam's direction.

"Sis. Try to stay awake."

Lana offered up a tranquil smile before dozing off.

***

The next time Lana woke, Ty was reading a book in a chair in the corner of the room. As if he sensed her coming back to consciousness, he glanced over and smiled.

"Hey, Sleeping Beauty."

"Hey," she croaked around her sore throat.

"We've all been worried about you," he told her. Putting the book down, he stood and walked to the edge of her bed.

"Where's Liam?"

"He went home to get some sleep. He's working tonight. Can I get you anything?"

"Water, please."

"They said you can start with ice cubes first," he said, slipping a few between her dry lips.

After he helped her sit up and the ice had relieved some of the dryness of her cottonmouth, Lana asked, "What are you doing here?"

Ty jerked back, seemingly shocked by her question.

"What do you mean? Do you honestly believe I was going to leave you in ICU with no one to be here for you when you woke up again?" he asked.

Lana ignored his question and raised a hand up to her bandaged head. The memories of the park and everything leading up to it were crystal clear. She had a hazy recollection of his confronting her over the sketch and seeing Jeri seated for a picnic with the baby. As for the accident itself, she drew a blank.

"How long was I out?"

"Initially about eight and a half days. You woke for a bit early this morning. Do you remember me and Liam being here?"

She gave a slight nod.

"Will you get a nurse for me?" she asked.

"What do you need? I can help," he offered kindly.

A brief snort followed by a groan met that comment. "I don't think so."

"Lana, tell me what you need."

"A nurse."

"Whatever you-"

"I have to pee, okay?" she cut him off, impatient with him for not doing as she asked. "Can you get me the damn nurse already before I piss myself?"

"I can-" This time she didn't need words to stop him in his tracks. Her dark look spoke volumes. "Uh, yeah. I'll get a nurse."

Lana almost laughed as he hustled from the room. She probably would have if any movement didn't send a sharp pain through her already throbbing head.

Within mere moments, a nurse named Monica attended her while Ty was ordered out of the room until they were done.

"Standing is out of the question, Hon. You get to use the trusty bedpan," Monica joked with a commiserating smile.

"I don't know if it will hold the entire contents of my bladder. Do they have supersize pans?"

"It's good to know you haven't lost your sense of humor."

"It's quite possible I gained one when I hit the pavement," Lana quipped.

Monica laughed as she helped position Lana. "So what's with the hot guy who's refused to leave your side since you were admitted? Husband? Boyfriend? Inquiring minds want to know."

"Pffft. Yeah, just my boss. I'm honestly not sure why he's here." Lana suspected it might be from pity so she didn't care to examine his reason too closely.

"Hmmm, well, I've never seen a boss that obsessed with an employee's recovery."

"You don't know how difficult it is to find a good nanny in this town," Lana told her. "He's terrified he'll have to replace me."

"If that's all it is I'll eat my scrub top, but your secret is safe with me, Hon," Monica assured her as she finished assisting Lana. "Can I tell him it's safe to come in?"

"Would you mind telling him I fell back to sleep?"

"I don't think that's going to work with that one. I suspect he's just going to park it back in that recliner until you wake up again."

Lana huffed a frustrated sigh.

"There could be worse things than being adored by a man who looks like that," Monica laughed as she made her way to the door. "I'll tell you what, you send him my way if you aren't interested."

The indignant glare Lana cast her, had the nurse laughing again.

"I thought so, Hon. I'll tell him you're ready to see him now."

A giggling nurse waved Ty into Lana's now open door. He shot a questioning glance at Lana, who rolled her eyes and gave a half shake of her head before wincing.

"Fuck," she snarled between gritted teeth.

Three large steps had Ty hovering by Lana's side. "What is it, Sweetheart?"

He thought he heard a snort and the words "just your boss, huh?" from behind him. Lana's bright blush and averted gaze had him deducing what that was about. The nosy nurse must have asked about their relationship and Lana downplayed it.

"Please don't call me that, Mr. Jensen," Lana said.

What the what? Ty cast a glance behind him to find the nurse had already quit the room. Okay, that wasn't for her benefit. Dread created a knot in his stomach. That meant she intended it for him.

"Don't call you what, Lana? Sweetheart? What's wrong with that?" he asked sharply.

"Because I'm not your sweetheart. I'm your employee.

It's not appropriate," she informed him primly.

"Seriously?" He heard the tone of his own voice climb an octave in disbelief.

"I appreciate that you've been visiting, but I know you're busy and must be behind in your work." Lana played with a corner of the sheet and avoided his gaze. Her next words pissed him off. "You don't need to come around anymore. Liam can bring me by to collect my things when I'm released."

"Collect your things?" he repeated, a hard edge entering his tone. "Collect your things. That's rich. So you're quitting on me now?"

"No!" she nearly shouted before grabbing for her head.

Ty mustered every ounce of willpower not to jump forward and try to ease her suffering. A few panting breaths allowed her to gain control over her discomfort again. He noted the sweat beading on her upper lip. Reaching over, he buzzed the nursing station.

"I mean, I thought you'd need to hire a replacement," Lana said softly, holding her head in both hands.

He didn't answer. Instead, he stormed to the door to see why there had been no response to the call button. He leaned out into the hallway and caught the attention of an attendant.

"A little help in here, please. She's in pain," he barked.

"Yes, sir."

"While you're at it, will you check to make sure the intercom is working to her room. No one answered when I pressed the button."

Ty stood with his back resting against the window ledge, arms crossed, and face a blank mask. He hadn't said a word the whole while the staff buzzed around her, rushing to do his bidding. Lana covertly watched him as he practically stared a hole in the floor. The way his hard chest rose and fell, the running of his tongue along the outside of his upper teeth, even the tapping of his fingers in no discernible rhythm on his bicep, all told her he was deep in thought.

The medication that had been inserted in her IV started to take effect. As the room cleared of people, Ty raised his eyes from the spot on the floor which had held him transfixed. For the longest minute, they locked eyes. The intensity in his made it impossible for her to look away. Outside, the sun broke through the clouds. A solitary shaft of light touched on him through the glass. Lana's breath caught and held. He was so very beautiful in that moment. Her hand itched to have a pencil or paintbrush. Anything to capture him in that pose.

"You feeling better?" his rich, deep voice reached in and started her breathing again.

Lana exhaled and nodded.

"Good. Because we need to get a few things straight." He straightened and strode to her side. "Number one, I am not now nor am I *ever* going to hire a replacement. You are who Serena reaches for when she wakes. You are who she loves and trusts. You might not remember it, but the first week in my employ you signed a contract. If you even think about leaving, I'll sue you for breach of that contract. I expect the top notch level of care you've been providing for her to continue."

She opened her mouth, whether in protest or to stop his tirade she would never know because he cut her off with a brisk wave of his hand.

"Let me finish. Number two, you will not call me Mr. Jensen. That's my father's name and I have no intention of answering to it. You can call me Ty, or God forbid, Tyler. And lastly, I intend to be present every day until you are recovered. If it wasn't for me, you wouldn't be lying in that bed right now. I don't take my responsibilities lightly, Lana. Have I made myself clear?"

Lana nodded her head jerkily and closed her eyes against her newest ache. The aching of her heart, which now experienced the sensation of a grape shriveling into a raisin. A secret part of her had wanted him to be here because he cared about her. However, his speech made it quite clear business reigned utmost in his mind. She could do professional. It required digging deep, but she was proficient with delving into those seasoned emotional reserves. She had this under control. Or so she kept telling herself.

"Can I get you anything else before I go?"

"No. Thank you."

"I'll be back in about three hours. Try to get some sleep," he suggested in a kinder, more gentler tone.

She didn't feel the need to answer. Let him think she was about to doze off. The kiss to her forehead had moisture burning behind her lids. Working with him would be torture. She would consult a lawyer if she had to. There was no way she intended to stand on the sidelines while he carried on a romance with Satan's Spawn Jeri.

**

True to his word, Ty spent a part of each of the next four days at the hospital with Lana. He refrained from calling her sweetheart, and for that, Lana was thrilled. When he called her by the pet name with that sexy, light accent, Lana found it difficult to remain aloof.

Today he rested against the wall by the door chatting up Monica, while Lana silently stewed.

"Jerk," she muttered, burying her head in her cell phone screen.

"What was that, Lana?" he asked.

She thought his tone a little too cheerful, and so she pretended she hadn't heard him, continuing to surf the web from her smartphone.

"Sweetheart."

Her head whipped up in anger, which she immediately tamped down upon seeing his smirk.

"I thought you might be ignoring me on purpose."

The glare she shot him confirmed this. "What do you

want? I'm busy," she snapped.

Ty burst out laughing at her blatant lie. Lana fought the full-body blush struggling to make itself known. If he'd been within range, she would have struck him.

"I'm making a DQ run. Can I talk you into a hot dog and Strawberry Cheesequake Blizzard?" he offered up two of her favorite junk food items.

Knowing he didn't eat Dairy Queen and his driving there for food was out of character, Lana questioned his actions.

"Why are you going there? I highly doubt you are craving ice cream," she snarked.

Amusement lit his eyes. She had made a study of him during the time she'd known him and was familiar enough with his emotions.

"Monica is craving a treat. I thought I'd spring for something special for the staff. They deserve a reward for dealing with your cranky ass these last few days," he taunted.

"Bite me," she snarled.

"Exhibit A, your honor," he quipped.

"Whatever. I'm not hungry." Her stomach made a quick lie of her words with a loud rumble.

Monica giggled as Ty outright laughed.

"Look, if you two want to carry on your little tête-à-tête, by all means don't let me stop you, however could you do it somewhere else? I'm trying to read this article," Lana moderated her tone to bored. She couldn't manage polite.

"Monica, if you would gather a list of what the staff would

like and call it in, then I'll leave here in a few minutes to get it. Be sure to add a hot dog, ketchup and mustard only, and a Strawberry Cheesequake with extra stuff to the order, please."

Lana addressed Monica directly. "Cancel that last bit. I said I didn't want anything."

"Thank you," Ty told the nurse, acting as if Lana hadn't spoken. "Do you mind closing the door on your way out?"

The nurse looked warily between the two of them and left with a nod in Ty's direction.

"Dude, what the fuck?" Lana burst out. "Do you think you could flirt up the nurse somewhere other than my room? Even for you that's a bit cold-hearted, don't you think?"

Ty shoved off the wall and sauntered in her direction.

"Jealous?"

"Pffft. Not hardly."

His knowing grin had her grinding her teeth. "Hmmm. 'The lady doth protest too much, methinks,'" he quoted Shakespeare in an effort to annoy.

Lana refused to dignify his taunt with a comment of her own. Opening an app on her phone, she started a game of Angry Birds. The idea of blowing things up appealed to her right then.

Ty snatched the cell from her hand. "Interesting article you have here."

"I'm not talking to you."

"Sure you're not. You'll be in a better mood when you get some sugar in you," he said with chuckle. A hopeful note entered his voice as he offered, "Of course, if you want some immediate sugar, I could always help you with that."

Left in little doubt which type of sweet he referred to, Lana made a grab for her phone so she could concentrate on ignoring him again. He held it out of her reach.

"You can have it back on one condition."

"What's that?"

The sensual smile blooming on his face alerted her lady bits to danger. Her nipples tightened and dampness started down below. How the hell did he manage to do that?

"A kiss."

"I'm not playing your stupid games, Ty," she warned.

"Who said it was a game, Sweetheart?"

Ah fuck. There he went with the nickname.

"One kiss," she said sternly, reaching for him as he came for her.

He surprised her when he didn't immediately go for the gold. Instead, he licked the seam of her lips. Her mouth parted on a gasp. Next, he bit down and tugged gently at the flesh there. White hot need took hold of Lana. She curled her fingers in the thick strands of his hair and pulled him close, moaning his name. His kiss seared her very soul.

"Sweethe-"

A clearing of a man's throat interrupted whatever he planned to say.

"Goddammit," Ty muttered. "What is it with people always barging in on us?"

A giggle escaped. Lana was helpless to subdue it. Ty's happy green eyes bore into hers.

The second time the man cleared his throat laughter erupted between the two of them. Ty kissed her on the nose and straightened up.

"I'll be back with your food in a bit. Anything else you need while I'm out?" At her negative gesture, Ty turned and nodded to the male figure lurking at the end of the bed. "Hey, Doc."

Chapter Ten

Two more days had passed since Ty's kiss re-ignited Lana's hope that maybe they still had a chance at a relationship. He'd stayed longer each day, playing cards or platonically snuggling on the bed to watch tv with her. The reason for the latter had been because Dr. Montgomery had given them a stern tongue-lashing on hospital etiquette. The twinkle in his eye had undermined the point he was trying to make, but Ty didn't want to be caught in another compromising situation.

Trace also told her she could go home by the weekend as long as the next set of scheduled CT scans showed clean. He'd told Lana and Ty he had little doubt they wouldn't. The major concern had been the continued migraines. Other than that, there was nothing to indicate she hadn't satisfactorily recovered from being struck down by the hit and run.

A movement in the corner of the hospital room startled Lana fully awake from her mid-day nap. At first, because she'd been expecting him, she thought it was Ty. Upon closer inspection, she realized it was his brother.

"Why are you here, Quinn? Planning on trying to buy me off again?" Lana asked the man hovering by the window.

Quinn wasn't immune to her snide tone or the truth behind

her words. Still, he wanted to smooth things over for Ty's sake. He recognized that she held a special place in his brother's heart, and she was beginning to matter to him too.

"It wasn't like that, Lana."

"Really? Maybe I hit my head harder than I thought, because I'm pretty sure I remember *exactly* how it went."

She closed her eyes and rubbed the place between her brows.

"Headache?" Quinn shifted forward, as if he wished to relieve her pain.

"I repeat, why are you here?"

He threw up his hands in the symbolic gesture of giving up. "Ty needed rest, and your brother is caring for your mother and Serena."

The stern, questioning look still graced her features.

"My brother can't stand the idea of you being alone."

"So he leaves me with the guy who was probably driving the car that ran me down?"

"Careful," he warned. "The walls have ears in this hospital. I've learned that the hard way. Your ridiculous accusation will be headlining the news tomorrow morning."

"Good. Maybe they'll investigate your sorry ass," she huffed.

Quinn took the few steps to the bed's edge. Leaning over, he placed a hand on either side of her head.

"Lana, I need you to listen to me and listen good." When he had her complete attention, he told her his reasons as to why he wanted her gone. He explained Jeri's poisonous tirade and Hailey's toxic influence in both his and Ty's lives.

"I thought I was protecting him. Can you understand that?"

She gave a thoughtful nod and his shoulders sagged in relief.

"Good," he said, placing a friendly peck on her lips. He stayed leaning over her for a few extra seconds thinking how much she reminded him of Annie.

"Sure you don't want to take me up on that offer to sleep with me," he teased.

"Pretty sure. Thanks. It's a nice offer though," she laughed.

As he stood and turned, they both noticed Ty in the doorway, coffee in hand. Anger radiated off him in waves. The rigid stance said Quinn was in for a shitstorm.

"Get out!" Ty growled through clenched teeth.

"Ty."

"Get. The. Fuck. Out."

Lana could tell Quinn was torn. She feared if he walked out that door now, there would be a permanent fracture in the brothers' relationship. Although, truthfully, he'd set himself up for that the moment he first approached her behind his brother's back. She'd never told Ty for that sole reason that she didn't want any conflict between the men. They were finally getting back to being a family after the Hailey incident.

"No."

Three sets of eyes swiveled to the fourth person entering the room.

Lana surveyed the petite woman from head to toe.

"Annie."

The raw emotion in Quinn's voice startled Lana. That rawness had her taking a closer peek at the most recent member of their quartet. First impression said fragile based on the cane she used to rest against, and yet there had been a hint of steel in her "no." Lana couldn't wait for this to play out. She was petty enough to enjoy Quinn's discomfort after what he'd put her through.

Annie tilted her head and regarded Lana with an expression akin to curiosity.

"Do I know you?"

Lana shot Quinn an odd glance. He'd asked her the same question.

"I don't think so. Not unless you're into nannies who used to be strippers." She winced as the words left her mouth. For once a woman was treating her without hostility. She should be grateful, not snarky and rude.

Annie's delighted laughter burst forth. The honest reaction would have floored Lana had she been standing.

"You and Sammy are going to get along famously. She doesn't have a filter either," Annie told her, a huge grin playing about her lips.

She maneuvered around Ty, who seemed rooted in the entrance, and came to rest on the opposite side of the bed from Quinn.

"Who's Sammy and why should we get along at all?"

"My youngest sister. And since you and I are going to be the best of friends, I expect you'll meet her soon enough."

Recognition came and before she could stop the words pouring forth from her mouth, Lana blurted, "You're the crazy stalker from the funeral!"

Lana referred to the media storm Annie had created when she showed up with her sister at the service for Hailey Newberry. Quinn had created a scene by forcing them to leave. The press spun it to appear like Annie was a psycho.

"She's *not* crazy," Quinn snapped. "And she's not a stalker."

"You can't help that people believe it, Quinn. You're the one who gave everyone that impression," Annie's quiet voice scolded. She twisted to view his brother. "Ty, are you planning on standing there all day? I'd really like that coffee you bought me."

Annie's skillful manipulation of the twins impressed Lana. She thought she could benefit from lessons with this woman. Especially as Ty leaped to comply.

"Coffee? You don't drink coffee. It makes you jittery," Quinn inserted inanely, earning him a frown from everyone in the room, except Annie.

Lana's questioning gaze ping-ponged back and forth

between the two.

"You're in love with her!" she exclaimed. For whatever reason, this thrilled her beyond reason. Oh, how the mighty have fallen.

"No!" Two voiced nearly shouted in unison.

"You totally are!" Lana crowed, grinning up at Quinn.

"Drop it," Ty barked. "You're making Annie uncomfortable."

"Oh. I'm sorry." Lana reached and grabbed the hand of her new friend.

"No problem, however you're mistaken."

Annie schooled her features into a smooth mask. Lana suspected she did it to cover a deeper hurt. The blank expression was one she mastered herself many years ago.

"Why are you here, Annie?" Quinn asked in a more moderate, even tone.

"I saw her in the lobby and thought she and Lana might hit it off. Nothing sinister. Unlike your volunteering to sit here while I ran out," Ty said in the midst of handing off the drinks. He gestured toward the door with a shove of his brother's shoulder. "You can go. You're not wanted here."

Again, Annie spoke up. "No. You two need to resolve this. Shut the door, Quinn. There could be another Nurse Hatchet Face lurking around."

As Lana would have questioned the identity of the nurse, Annie anticipated her and explained, "When I was here earlier this year, she was a sour-faced bitch, who spent her days spying on everyone. Quinn was the favored target for her particular brand of evil. I haven't seen her in recent visits, but I'm sure she's lurking around somewhere."

"Actually, she's not," Quinn spoke up. "Nurse Hatchet Face was dismissed not long after you were discharged."

Staring down at the tip of her cane, Annie nodded to acknowledge his words. The tension between her and Quinn was palpable. Lana's gaze sought out Ty, a silent inquiry in her eyes. His hard-as-glass stare greeted her in return. Apparently, it wasn't only his brother he was mad at. Good to know.

"Okay since I'm suffocating under the weight of the emotions in this room, it's time to have a come-to-Jesus meeting."

Lana laughed at Annie's direct approach.

"Ty and I heard a very damning statement as we came in. Quinn," she spoke his name and cast a glance in his general direction without making eye contact. "You should clarify your actions. And try not to be an asshole about it."

Once again, Lana had to fight the urge to giggle. She bit her lip...hard. Her sparkling amber eyes flew to Annie's bright blue. The wink almost undid her. Yes, they were going to be the best of friends.

In great detail, without the slightest hint of the embarrassment or impatience he must be feeling, Quinn laid it all out on the line, from the proposition in the nursery, to planting doubts in Ty's head, to coming in here to apologize to Lana. She almost felt sorry for him. Incurring Ty's wrath was no small thing.

"What the fuck were you thinking?"

"That you were lonely and overwhelmed with a newborn. You were an easy target, Ty."

The women were smart enough to stay quiet as the battle raged.

"Really? What makes you the resident authority on anyone's feelings? You can't even acknowledge your own," Ty snarled.

"Right. Let's throw this back on me. You can't even see how tangled up she has you! When was the last time you spared a thought for your daughter? Hmmm?"

Annie jumped between the two men at the precise moment Ty drew his arm back to strike. She staggered against Quinn as she lost her balance. And just as quickly, she shoved off him so as not to be touching him.

"What the hell is wrong with you? Did I not just say be nice?" she hissed. "Of course, he thinks of Serena. Her welfare is always utmost in his mind. Although that's not the issue here, or at least not the real one. You're pissed because your own emotions are a hot mess. You are projecting onto your brother. And why not? He's your mirror image. The perfect person to take things out on."

"We've had this discussion, Annie. Stop with the fucking empath bullshit. I don't need you trying to counsel me." Although his words were harsh, his movements were courteous and tender in nature as he picked her up and set her in the nearest chair. "I'm done here."

"*No,* you are not! As usual, you still haven't apologized."

Lana got the distinct impression Annie no longer referred to his argument with Ty.

"I don't need this shit."

"Then by all means leave. It's what you're best at."

"You're playing with fire, little girl," he growled his frustration.

Finally, with great deliberation, Annie's rage filled eyes lifted to glare at Quinn. Lana heard his sharp inhale.

"I'm not *playing* at all. Your games are tiresome and boring." The tone she used, while soft, had the hairs on the back of Lana's neck lifting. "If I never saw you again, it would be too soon."

She reached to shove his chest, and he jumped back as if to avoid getting burned himself. Annie's lips lifted in a smirk of satisfaction. Lana wondered why he would be afraid of Annie's touch.

Quinn stalked out without another word.

"Well, *that* was fun," Annie said to no-one in particular.

Shortly thereafter, Ty left to make phone calls and allow the two women to get acquainted.

"Care to tell me what that was all about," Lana asked her gently.

"It's not worth talking about."

"Oh, I don't know. I'd say it is, but I understand. You

don't really know me."

A snort escaped Annie. "I know you better than you think."

In an effort to disperse the leftover tension, Lana asked questions about Annie's family and previous hospital stay to distract from the drama they'd been party to. The visit flew by. Eventually, Lana could see her new friend getting tired.

"Are you going to be okay to drive home?"

"I've got to bust my ass in physical therapy first. I have a ride set up for afterwards."

"Are you sure? I'm positive Ty wouldn't mind taking you."

"You're sweet. Seriously, I'm good. I do have to get going. My PT is in ten. It was such a pleasure meeting you."

"Ditto."

The word made Annie smile. "My sister and brother-in-law use that term all the time. You really do remind me of her."

"I think they plan to keep me a few more days. If you have another appointment in the meantime, I'd love for you to stop by," Lana offered.

"I'd like that."

They exchanged numbers and promised to keep in touch.

After she left, Lana couldn't wipe the smile from her face. Annie's non-judgmental friendship was refreshing after a lifetime of dealing with prejudice.

***

When Ty returned to her hospital room, there was an arctic quality still lingering in his previously warm and caring green eyes. Lana was struck by the thought that in all the time she'd known him, he'd never resembled his brother as much as he did in the moment. The way in which he viewed her made him truly identical to Quinn. As if she were an insect he detested and wished to squish under his foot.

The urge to speak up, to ask why he now held her in contempt overwhelmed her. She searched her memory to find what might have him so upset with her. Finding nothing, she centered herself, working to dispel her nerves, and went for the question of the hour. Better to have it out in the open.

"What is it, Ty? You seem pissed with me. What have I done?" she asked.

"Why were you kissing my brother?"

Her brows drew together in confusion. His cold attitude reached out to her, sending a chill skittering down her spine.

"What the hell are you talking about? I didn't kiss Quinn!"

"Are you going to sit there and tell me you weren't kissing him when Annie and I walked in earlier?" he demanded.

His aggressive stance set her heart beating faster. Not in a good way. Lana knew she could offer up no answer in which to satisfy him. She'd been honest with him about all things from the moment they'd met, with the exception of Quinn's proposition. The only reason she kept it to herself had been to avoid a situation like this. Why was he treating her as if she'd been keeping secrets or lying to him? There was something deeper at play here. She only wished she had time to figure out what it was.

"He kissed *me*. And it wasn't like there was even any tongue involved. It was a friendly peck," she said with an attempt at a soothing smile. "Ty, you were right there. Nothing happened."

"I was right there. And I saw him leaning over, kissing you. From my vantage point, you were doing nothing to stop him or shove him away." He paused for effect. His cold tone dropped a few more degrees. "It makes me wonder if you didn't want to take him up on his offer to fuck you."

The accusatory attitude and ugly words bothered Lana, but his next words broke her heart.

"I don't suppose prostitution is a stretch for someone who used to provide lap dances for skeevy, drunk men in a strip club."

The shock hit her square in the chest, freezing her. Lana couldn't catch her breath. Falling through ice and plunging into frigid water couldn't have frozen her more thoroughly. Cold seeped from the uselessly beating organ in her sternum to inch its way to her extremities, and finally, into her mind.

She couldn't look at him any longer. Couldn't bear to see the distrust and hate, the loss of what she held dear.

Whatever demon possessed Ty left as quickly as it had

arrived. The devastation that had passed across Lana's face after he uttered those asinine words left him longing to build a time machine to go back and slap duct tape over his mouth. Watching those bright, incredible eyes dimming by degrees until they were more lifeless than when she'd lay bleeding on the pavement only thirteen days before had Ty wanting to vomit.

What had he done?

He stared at her as her gaze locked on a point beyond and to the right of his hip. Ty longed for the words to call her back to him. To make their relationship whole and to resurrect what he'd so carelessly destroyed.

"Lana. Sweetheart."

Her head jerked as if she'd been struck. She focused back on the spot she'd briefly lost when she reacted to his addressing her.

Finally, as the silence screamed "Idiot! Idiot! Idiot!" over and over at him in its constant refrain, she lifted her head and regarded him as if he were a stranger. Uncaring. Distant. The calmness in her voice when it came squeezed his heart.

"I thought you, of all people, wouldn't use my past against me," Lana said as she shifted her empty gaze to stare out the window. Her chin inched up as she formed her next words. "I refuse to be embarrassed or defend what I did to survive."

"Sweeth-"

"I'm glad we had those few weeks of fun, but now I know that's all they were."

"No! They-"

Once again, Lana cut him off. "Your judgement surprises me. I mean, what if I measured you by the scale of your past actions? If we ever had developed into more than a casual fuck, I guess, based on your yard stick, I should worry about you fucking my friends or Quinn's future girlfriends."

Ty felt the blow like a physical fist to his stomach. The air was sucked out of him, and he struggled not to bend double.

"It doesn't feel good, does it? Having your past thrown in your face every time you turn around? For the record, in spite of what an asshole you've been recently, I don't think that of you. I never could." Her voice dipped to almost inaudible, and Ty watched as her lips trembled. "Maybe I'm an idiot because I really don't know you deep down, do I?"

He remained silent, hand over his heart, still reeling from her harsh words. For a brief moment, he forgot what a fierce little scrapper she was. Lana had the ability to get down and dirty with the best of them.

"I learned how to be vicious a long time ago. I also learned words have consequences, Ty. Some things cannot be unspoken." Those words confirmed his exact thoughts. "Please leave."

"No!" he practically shouted. "Lana, I-"

Lana's body flopped against the pillows. At the same time, her arms dropped to her sides.

At first, he thought she'd passed out and surged forward to assist her. His pulse beating triple time. A half foot from the bed, Ty came to the realization she'd done this in dismissal.

"Sweetheart. Please," he begged, reaching for her. "Please, listen to me."

He gripped her chilled left hand in his clammy one. And as her right hand came up in return, hope flared. That little flame of hope was extinguished as she clasped his wrist and flung it from her person.

"Don't you *ever* touch me again. Get. The. Fuck. Out!"

"I'm sorry, Lana," he whispered hoarsely. Devastated. "So very, very sorry."

"I don't care," replied her lifeless voice.

Chapter Eleven

Within the hour, the first of Ty's apology gifts arrived; three dozen long-stemmed roses. The note read, "Please forgive me." Lana buzzed the nurses' station and requested they be removed and given to a patient who might not receive many visitors. Maybe those beautiful flowers could brighten somebody else's day. They only depressed her.

An hour later, enough balloons to lift a house like the animated movie *Up* were delivered. Tied to the ribbons were construction hearts stating "Forgive me." Once again, Lana buzzed the desk to have them taken away. This time she instructed they be taken to the children's ward to be handed out.

Already Lana could hear the buzz starting through the corridors. People loitered outside her door to catch a glimpse of the next present to be delivered, and to see if it would be the one to soften her heart. To forgive the mysterious sender.

Ty didn't disappoint the masses.

This time it only took forty-five minutes for the next present to show up. A ginormous teddy bear was hauled in to monopolize all the space in the room not already taken up by her bed. Dangling from his neck was a plaque with the words "Forgive me, Lana."

None of the objects moved Lana. Gone was the cold from

her veins. In its place, white-hot rage flowed. Who the hell did Ty think he was to attempt to buy his way back into her affections? She lay stuck in bed while people started to gossip about her. The humiliation of the situation made her long to be anywhere but here.

An idea struck as she watched a child being wheeled by her door.

"Wait!" she called out.

The orderly spun around and wheeled a little girl into her room. Lana noted the shaved head and the gray, sickly pallor of her skin. If she had to guess, she'd say the child was around five or six years old. Guessing an exact age was difficult due to the large surgical mask covering her nose and mouth. The battered look in her large, blue eyes lent to the ageless quality of the girl.

Those same eyes lit from within when she spotted the beast of a bear in the corner. For the first time in hours, Lana smiled.

"What's your name?"

"Nicki."

"Nicki. What a pretty name. My name is Lana. How old are you, darling?"

Lana watched as the little girl lifted her hands to show six fingers.

"As old as that, huh?" she asked with a grin. While Lana couldn't see her mouth to determine if she smiled in return, she did notice Nicki's eyes lower and crinkle as if she was.

"Nicki, do you like that big beastie in the corner?"

A slight nod indicated the affirmative.

"Would you like to have it for your own? You would be doing me a huge favor if you would keep him for me. Do you think you could care for him if he found his way back to your room?"

A vigorous nodding came this time.

"Excellent," Lana laughed. She then addressed the orderly who stood grinning behind Nicki. "Chris, right? Chris, do you think you could make sure our friend gets settled in Nicki's room all right?"

"I'll see to it, Ms. Lana."

"Thank you," she said, gracing him with a smile. Lana turned her attention back to the happy girl in front of her. "It was a pleasure meeting you, Nicki. Thanks for taking care of my bear dilemma."

Muffled giggles could be heard from behind the mask.

Immediately after Chris removed the bear, another gift arrived. Frustration mounted. Lana wanted to scream her rage at the top of her lungs.

***

Lana thought long and hard about the situation. The plans she had formulated over the day and a half since she evicted Ty from her room became clearer with every object he sent in his attempt to soothe her hurt. The only viable solution to the problem she could find was to resign her job and move out.

She shot off a text to Liam, and scanned the web from her smartphone for the classifieds as well as for potential apartments.

A soft knock against wood brought her head up in search of the identity of her visitor.

Ty. Jesus, he was a stubborn fucker.

The daggers shooting from her eyes should have given him a clue as to her feelings. He refused to take the hint and sauntered further into her room.

"Are you ready to listen to me?" he asked.

He came across as subdued yet hopeful. Lana wanted to obliterate his hope.

"No. You made your feelings for me quite clear over the last weeks. The other day was the icing on the cake. Stop sending me stupid shit and leave me alone. I'm done," she told him in a tone as cold as she could muster.

Frustration flashed across his features. "Lana, I don't know how to make this right if you don't give me a chance."

"You can't make anything right, Ty. Stop trying."

"I can't stop," he said achingly.

"What part of 'leave me alone' and 'I'm done' don't you get?" she asked in stunned disbelief, the level of her voice raising two octaves.

"Keep your voice down. We're going to discuss this like adults."

"The fuck we will," she growled.

Ty's charge to her bedside made Lana scramble for the call button. He snatched the cord away before she could press it or ask the nurse to send security.

"Goddammit! Knock it off," he growled.

"You have to the count of three to get out of my room or I will scream."

His stony countenance met her challenge.

"Fine! One…Two…"

She never made it to three. He swept in as the end of word two departed her lips and closed his mouth over hers, effectively cutting off her speech.

Oh no he didn't, screamed inside her head. Of all the damn nerve…the remainder of the thought scattered in every direction. His kiss consumed her. His tongue swept in and tangled with her own. Breathing became impossible. Lana tangled her hands in his thick hair and drew him toward her. He responded by wrapping an arm behind her arching back and cupping her head with the palm of his other hand in an effort to keep her close. They broke apart, dragged in much needed oxygen, and got back to business.

Ty pulled back first, leaving a dazed Lana in the wake of his passion.

Clapping had the two of them whipping around to see the hospital staff and a few stray patients standing in the opening of the door, grinning like a group of lunatics. Shouts of "we knew she'd forgive you" and "well done, man" greeted them.

"For fuck's sake," Lana muttered. She shoved Ty off the

bed and onto his ass before turning to the crowd in the doorway. "Nobody has forgiven anyone, and I'm not here for your personal entertainment."

They scrambled like cartoon roaches in a bug spray commercial. She would have turned her rage on Ty, only there he sat, back against the wall, hands draped over his knees, and desire stamped on his features. The heat of his stare had her lady parts pleading with her to accept his apology.

She clenched her hands and worked to steady the live wires that were her nerves.

"Say what you have to say, Ty. But please understand, it isn't going to change my mind."

"I love you."

Okay, that might - No! Lana shut that internal voice down. She lifted a brow and remained silent.

"I thought I loved Hailey. I didn't. I didn't know what love was before you walked through my front door." Ty scrutinized his hands, now upturned as if they might contain the words he needed to sway her. "I realized I was crazy about you the day I heard you confess to your crush on me. I couldn't wipe the stupid grin off my face. Then the sex…it blew my mind. I've never in my life experienced that with anyone else.

"By week three of you being in our lives, I knew I loved you. The way you cared for Serena, for me, hell even for my dumbass brother, made me understand you were one in a million."

"Why did you pull back after that second week?" she had to know.

"Quinn got in my head. While my heart said you were nothing like Hailey, Quinn had me believing you were. He went on, ad nauseam, about how you were only after me for my money. He said a prime example of how tangled up you made me was your family moving into the guesthouse. He wasn't wrong. You do tangle up my mind," he confessed. "Sex with you added to that, Lana. I wished the days away so I could cuddle with you in bed at night. Each time you brushed up against me or I touched you, I was drawn further under your spell. I won't lie. I got scared."

Lana cleared her throat to dispel the lump forming there.

"Is that why you stopped coming to my room? Is that why you started dating Jeri?"

"Yes and no. Yes, it was the reason I stopped seeking you out. And no, I never dated Jeri."

"You did! I saw you in the park together," she insisted.

"You remembered?"

"I never forgot. Not that. What I said was I didn't recall the accident."

"It wasn't a date. Not really. She wanted to spend more time with Serena. Or at least that's what she told me. She wanted it to be when you weren't around because you two didn't get along," he explained.

"And you were stupid enough to believe that?" she asked, skepticism coating every word.

"Apparently," he answered wryly.

"Whatever."

Ty surged to his feet and moved to sit on the edge of the bed. Lana pressed back into the pillows in an effort to maintain some semblance of distance.

"Sweetheart, when you were struck by that car...as you... you lay there, I knew. I knew I loved you. I thought if you didn't make it, I didn't know what I'd do. I certainly didn't want to face a life without you in it."

"All pretty words, Ty. But you don't do the things you've done. You don't make horrible accusations. You don't say unforgivable things. And you certainly don't date other women. Not if you love someone. Not the way you confess to." Her words were harsh, punctuated with a fist to his chest with every sentence.

"I went insane with jealousy, Lana. You can't know what it's like to have someone you love throw you over for your sibling. You can't know the hell of watching them together."

"She didn't throw you over, Ty," she stressed. "Think about it. By your own admission, she was never *yours*. She met you, then met Quinn a short while later. You became obsessed with a relationship you built in your own mind."

"None of that matters now," Ty ground out. "None of it except as a reason for my behavior in accusing you of kissing my brother."

"Oh, not just kissing him according to you. Again, in your own mind, you built up a relationship between two people that never actually happened. You know what that says about you? Do you?" Lana taunted, ready to label him.

"Don't say something you can't take back," he warned.

"Why not? You did," she taunted.

Crossing her arms over her chest, she turned to stare into the dark night outside her window. Instead of the world outside, Ty's reflection dominated the glass. His tortured expression convinced her of his remorse. Nevertheless, she wasn't prepared to forgive. Not now. Maybe not ever.

"You don't love me, Ty. You don't know what love is. You only know obsession and suspicion." Lana heard the catch in her own voice and worked her throat to shove back the emotion suffocating her. "You've said what you came to say. Please go."

"I need you to forgive me. Please."

She met his eyes. Saw for herself the sincerity and anguish there. Lana understood he believed he truly loved her. However, she wasn't so sure.

"Okay." The word was out before she could halt it.

"Okay?"

She saw the hope flare to life. Saw him react to what he thought was allowing him to be part of her life. This time crushing that hope was more painful.

"Okay, I forgive you. Unfortunately, I can't be in a relationship with you, Ty."

"Why? Why would you throw away what we have?" he demanded, his anger a palpable thing.

"We don't have anything. We had some great sex. Nothing more, nothing less."

"Bullshit!" he spat. "Are you honestly going to sit there and tell me you don't love me?"

"Yes."

"For Christ's sake, Lana," Ty surged off the bed and paced the room. She saw the exact second it sunk in that not one of his gifts remained in the room. He spun around and pinned her with a look. "You got rid of everything?"

"Yes."

He nodded absently, looking inward at something only he could see. Lana let him have the time to come to terms with her decision.

"Say it."

"What?"

"Tell me you don't love me. Make me believe you really don't care and I'll go."

She made a sweeping motion with her arm to encompass the room. "I thought I had. However, if you need me to say it again, I will. I. Don't. Love. You."

"You're a liar."

"And you're in denial."

"We'll see."

"You said you'd go if I said the words."

"No, Sweetheart. I said 'make me believe.' You didn't. By getting rid of the gifts, you showed just how much you *do* care," he said with a smug smile.

She screamed her frustration and threw the cup of water from the nightstand at his head.

"I hate you!"

His grin widened, nearly splitting his face in two. "No. I don't think you do. Not even a little bit."

Lana sent him the old Italian salute.

Ty threw back his head and laughed. The light of determination had come back to his eyes.

"Yep. I'm more convinced than ever that you love me too," he said as he exited.

Lana thought perhaps he seemed a bit too smug.

Chapter Twelve

The gifts resumed the next day, although, they arrived in an altogether different manner. Every hour a photo would appear in a text message from either Liam or Ty. The picture would show an individual wearing a huge smile, holding a check in one hand, propping up a sign in the other with the words "Thank you, Lana. Forgive him." Lana could only assume, between the two men, they'd found all the charity cases she had been forwarding the previous two days worth of gifts to and started on a journey to ease their plights.

When Ty arrived in her room around the time dinner was expected to be served, she had thawed toward him considerably. He'd brought her a visitor. Serena. Tears welled as Lana observed him unbuckling the baby from her carrier and bringing her forward.

"She misses you. Maybe as much as I do," he said softly.

His hair was once again rumpled, and perhaps those devastating green eyes were a little less frantic than their first meeting, but the desperate quality to his features was back. He wore three days worth of stubble, and Lana thought he wore it well. Made him more approachable. Oddly, the beard growth drew attention to his full lips. The same lips now spreading in slow increments with slight twitches, as if he was amused.

Lana almost smacked herself in the damn head. Why wouldn't he think it's funny she couldn't seem to stop lusting over his body parts, even when she swore they were over. Idiot woman.

Her gaze shot to his. Love shone there. Bright and bold. He did nothing to hide his feelings.

"I love you, Lana. You cannot possibly know how much."

The waterworks started. Lana couldn't hold back. She folded her arms over her knees and buried her head there, hiding, as sobs wracked her body. She felt the bed dip as Ty joined her. His large hand rubbed light circles on her back as she let loose all the pent-up emotions she'd been dealing with from the time she woke up.

"If I could take back those shitty things I said, I would. I *will* promise you, nothing like that will *ever* pass my lips again," he stressed. He cleared his throat and continued, "Our whole lives Quinn was the outgoing twin. People loved him. They couldn't help it. His charm, his spark. It was only natural Hailey would be attracted to him over me. And yet, at the thought that you might prefer him — I went nuts. I had never been so jealous in my life, Lana. *Never.*"

"I told you nothing had happened!" she cried. "I'm not her, Ty. I didn't deserve your ugliness."

"I know that, now. I think I even knew it then. It didn't matter, Lana. The old insecurities took hold. The weeks leading up to the accident, Quinn played on those. Trying to convince me you were up to no good." A hitch in his voice had Lana's head popping up to survey him. "If you give me a second chance, I promise I will invest in us. I will always believe you."

Nerves clawed Ty's insides. He realized there hadn't been anything he had ever wanted as badly as he wanted Lana's love and trust. Her insecurity was his fault. He'd made her feel less than. A burning started behind his lids, and her image became blurred from the tears forming. He cast his eyes heavenward and blinked while offering up a silent prayer to whatever entity might be listening.

Ty silently called himself seven kinds of fool over the last few days. He missed Lana and wanted her sparkling soul back in his life.

He wasn't beyond begging. "Please, Sweetheart. One more chance."

Her response, when it came, had him doubting his hearing. "Okay."

"Okay?"

Lana nodded, and Ty almost wept in gratitude. He pulled her close with his free arm, careful not to crush Serena.

"Thank you," he said, humbled.

"You should know, I'm not embarrassed by my past, Ty. It happened because it was a necessity at the time," she said. "But I'm damn tired of everyone trying to make me feel bad about it. If you ever mention anything about my stripping again, we're done. No amount of gifts, however charitable, will buy your way back into my good graces. Do you understand?

"Does that mean a stripper pole in the bedroom is out of the question?" he half-joked.

Her snort told him she wasn't offended. "I didn't say that," she said, grin wicked, dimple flashing. "I've still got those little pink pasties with the matching thong."

The reaction those words had on his dick was immediate. It slayed him because there was nothing he could do with a baby in his arms, in the not-so-priviate hospital room.

"You've got a mean streak. You know that?"

"So I've been told."

***

On the day Lana was scheduled to come home, Ty enlisted Liam's help for the finishing touches on the surprise he'd planned. He put down the paint roller and surveyed their handiwork.

"Do you think she will like it?"

"Pffft. Dude, she is going to flip the fuck out," Liam said on a laugh. "She's always wanted an art studio. That you've managed to make it light and airy *and* add her favorite colors? Yeah, she's yours for life if you'll have her. Please say you'll have her. I need someone to take her off my hands."

Ty shoved Lana's brother with a hand to the shoulder. "Okay, I'm off to get a shower and change. Can you get this cleaned up and bring in the furniture or do you need help?"

"Nah, man. I've got it. Go on."

He paused in the doorway to give the room one last inspection. Satisfaction filled him. Yeah, she was going to love it. Ty shot Liam a half smile.

"Thank you."

"Yeah, just treat her right, or I'll have to hurt you," Liam said with a serious note.

"I promise."

***

The woman watched from behind the wheel of her vehicle as Tyler Jensen pulled out of his garage and turned left at the end of the driveway. Today was the day he was bringing Lana home from the hospital, or so her friend Monica at the First Memorial Medical Center had told her. Just thinking of that little home-wrecking bitch Lana enraged Ashley Nichols. She thought about the strife in her own marriage. After Ty left the night he'd come by demanding back pay for his new slut, a drunk Carter had confessed to lusting after their ex-nanny from the time he'd seen her ten years ago in some stupid club. He further admitted to hiring her so that he could get her in his bed. He raged that Ashley was a frigid bore and could never excite him the way Lana did.

Too bad the tramp had survived being hit by the car. Ashley started the engine of her new Lexus and swore this time she would take out Lana Martell for good.

***

"You take it easy, Lana. I expect to see you back for a check-up in about a week to ten days. If the migraines continue, I may want to rerun some tests," Dr. Trace Montgomery told Lana as he wrote her a prescription for additional medication. "I mean it. Ty, I want her on light duty until she returns to see me. If everything's all good, I'll give her the all clear to return to full time."

"We've got it covered, Doc," Ty said, relieved to be finally able to take Lana home.

Trace opened his mouth to reply but his attention was captured by a point behind Ty's shoulder. As one, Ty and Lana spun to see who, or what, had him so fascinated.

"Annie!" Lana called in delight.

Ty watched as Annie limped in their direction. The frown taking up residence on her face had the hairs on the back of his neck standing on end. Only once before had Ty ever noticed Annie this distracted. The news hadn't been good that time. Hailey's death happened within hours after Annie informed Trace, Quinn, and himself of her premonition.

"What is it, Annie?" he asked, attempting not to overreact. Worry creased his brow. Annie had yet to take her eyes off Lana. Her pupils were overly large, the black practically taking over the blue of her irises.

Upon hearing the sound of his voice, Annie glanced between him and Trace, then back to Lana. "Her aura is darkening. I'm afraid for her."

She shifted to grab Lana's hands, lost her balance, and slammed into the wall. Ty reached to steady her and return the cane she'd dropped. He saw Lana jump back as if burned.

"What the hell was *that?*" she asked. "Did you—how—where did that image come from?"

"You need to listen to me very carefully, Lana," Annie said, her voice laced with urgency. "The hit and run wasn't a random accident. That woman I showed you? She's coming for you again. Today, unless I miss my guess."

Placing her hands behind her back, Lana shook her head and backed up. Ty rushed to her side and wrapped her in his arms. The embrace was awkward due to her inability to disconnect her gaze from Annie's. Lana still held her hands behind her as if she feared Annie touching her again.

"What the hell is going on, Annie?" Ty demanded.

Both women ignored him. Annie was frantic to convey the warning to Lana. "I'm serious, Lana. She's gone off the deep end. Do you know who she is?"

"Y-Yes. Her name is Ashley Nichols. But how—"

"It doesn't matter. You need to contact the police, like right now! I think she may have already done something... hurt someone..." Annie's gaze shifted to the floor, her eyes losing their focus the longer she stared. "Yes, today. She's furious and blames you...for something she felt compelled to do…"

Annie sagged against the wall and Trace rushed to help her.

"The trunk," she whispered. "Lana, don't get in the trunk."

"What? What the hell?" Terror unlike any Ty had ever known clawed at his insides. He'd seen Annie predict some seriously crazy and unexplainable shit in the short time since he'd met her.

"I'm sorry. I don't have any more details," she cried softly. "Don't get in the trunk, Lana."

Trace caught Annie as her eyes rolled back in her head and she collapsed.

"She's fainted," he said unnecessarily, before whisking her up and away in search of an empty room. He barked orders along the way to the staff trotting beside him.

"What the fuck was that about?" Lana asked, appearing shaken to her very core.

Ty didn't answer. Instead, he whipped out his cell and dialed Quinn.

"Ty. What's going on? You wouldn't be calling me—"

"Kwee, listen to me. I need you to see if Liam can watch Serena. Make sure the house is secure and the alarm is on, then get your ass here to the hospital STAT!" Ty ordered.

Thankfully, Quinn didn't question him. The intensity in his tone must have convinced his brother to do his bidding. "I'm on it. Who are we worried about?"

"Ashley Nichols."

"I'll inform Liam."

When Quinn would have clicked off, Ty gave him the additional news. "Kwee, Annie's the one who—"

"Is she there now? Is she okay?" The worry was evident in Quinn's words.

"Yes and yes. Just get here as soon as you safely can." After Ty hung up, he noticed how pale Lana had become. "Come here, Sweetheart. It's all going to be okay. I promise."

Instead of walking into his arms as he expected, she spun and headed for the exit.

"Lana, wait!"

"I can't, Ty. I need air. I can't breathe in here," she said in a panic.

"You are *not* going outside without me. You need to hold up until Quinn gets here."

"You don't understand. I'm going to yak. I need fresh air."

"Okay. Okay. Just let me check it out first," he gestured to the outside.

Lana bit the corner of her lip and nodded. Sweat broke out on her forehead.

Hand in hand they headed out the door, never expecting the attack to happen so quickly.

As they cleared the entrance and moved toward a set of benches by a shade tree, Ty noticed the Lexus slightly to their left. He was distracted by the open trunk and failed to notice the woman charging up to them. The current from the taser prongs Ashley shot into Ty's left bicep carried through to Lana through their clasped fingers, taking them both down to their knees.

Even though the electricity highjacked his nervous system, Ty had enough presence of mind to release Lana's hand and take the brunt of the jolt. He writhed on the ground in agony, seeing the satisfaction in Ashley's face. Sick bitch.

"No! Stop, you're hurting him!" Lana screamed, struggling to her feet and launching herself at the crazy woman wielding the weapon.

In the back of his fried mind, Ty felt pride in Lana's tackle. His woman was a badass. Although, his main worry was her having just been released from the hospital, and that she wasn't strong enough to fight. As for himself, he was useless at this point, unable to even cry out for help. Knowing what he did of taser units, it might take him valuable time to recover and help Lana.

Shouts could be heard from across the parking lot. Upon seeing Ashley's fist slam into Lana's head, Ty feared it was too late. Lana dropped like a stone. Their psycho attacker reached to haul her up, working her way to the open trunk. Panic assailed him as he recalled Annie's words, "Don't get in the trunk." Trying to override the effects of the taser, Ty worked to get control of his body, to no avail. The best he could do was roll to his side and lift his head to look around for help. He refused to acknowledge the puddle of drool he'd created.

"A-Ashley, stop…" he croaked. The words never reached her ears, or if they did, she ignored him.

Footsteps could be heard pounding the pavement, coming closer. Helplessly, Ty watched Ashley shove Lana's upper body in the trunk and bend to grab her feet. Fear permeated every cell of his battered body.

A concerned Quinn ducked into his visual field. Ty tried frantically to shake his head and motion for him to help Lana whose body was quickly disappearing into the back of the Lexus.

"Lana…Annie…no trunk…" he panted.

His brother realized the direness of the situation as he leaped to his feet and charged Ashley as she started to close the lid.

More people gathered to help. Trace Montgomery rushed for the car. Ty saw him halt abruptly in shock.

"W-what?" he attempted to ask.

When Trace pulled Lana out, her body was covered in blood. In the next moment, his vision was blocked by another person kneeling in front of him.

"Annie, m-move!" he commanded, terrified and struggling to regain control of his muscles.

"She's okay, Ty. She's okay," Annie said as she stroked his face and forced his jaw up so he could meet her eyes.

Chapter Thirteen

When Lana woke, Ty was reading a book in a chair in the corner of the room. As if he sensed her coming back to consciousness, he glanced over and smiled.

"Hey, Sleeping Beauty."

"Am I having serious déjà vu or have we done this before?" she asked half jokingly.

Ty rose and moved to sit on the edge of her bed. "Well, hopefully this is the last time we're going to do this. Otherwise I'm going to need to hire you an armed guard."

"I don't remember anything after that crazy-ass bitch hit me in the head. Care to fill me in?"

"I'd rather touch you to make sure you're real and unharmed," he said with a half smile, while stroking her hair back from the newest bandage.

Lana felt up the gauze attached to her head. "Ugh! Again?"

"You cracked your head against something in the trunk. Cut it pretty bad too. When they pulled you out, I almost had a damn heart attack. All that blood..."

She watched him shudder in remembrance, a haunted look in his eye. Reaching out, she grasped his hand and brought his palm to her cheek. "I'm fine. A slight headache because even I can only take so many hits to this hard head," she informed him with a slight smile.

"Jesus, Lana. I don't think I've ever been so scared in my life," he told her feelingly. The tightness around his mouth told her more than his words ever could.

"Ty." He glanced from his hand against her skin to her warm amber gaze. "I'm okay. Really."

"If it wasn't for Quinn…"

"I'd like to think I had something to do with rescuing the fair maiden," came a deep voice from the doorway.

Lana and Ty shifted to see Trace resting against the frame of the door, arms crossed over his chest and a grin on his face.

"My hero," laughed Lana. "Did you slay the dragon while you were at it, Doc?"

"I'm assuming by dragon you meant Ashley Nichols," piped in another voice from behind Trace. Annie ducked around him to limp into the room, followed closely by Quinn.

"Sweetheart, may I present to you the newest members of the Justice League," Ty joked. "All superheroes in their own right."

"So did someone tie her up and throw her into a volcano somewhere? Please tell me you did."

"Does jail work?" Quinn asked.

"I suppose it will have to do. A volcano would have made me happier though," Lana groused, making everyone laugh.

"Me too, all things considered," Ty sighed.

"What aren't you telling me?" Lana questioned, reading his body language. The others had grown quiet.

"They found Carter's body in that trunk, Lana," Annie said quietly.

"His body? Like in *dead?*" Lana couldn't hold back the screech in her tone if she tried. The ewww factor of being in the trunk with a dead body was high. "She killed Carter?"

"She did," Ty confirmed.

"How? I mean...I don't know what I mean." Vertigo swamped her, forcing her to close her eyes against the dizziness. Fingers touched her jaw. Lana opened her eyes to see a worried Ty leaning over her.

"I'm okay." Maybe if she kept telling herself that, it would be true.

Trace answered her original intended question. "She poisoned him, wrapped him in plastic and threw him in the trunk. The police believe she intended to do away with you both and hide the bodies at the same location."

She nodded in understanding, stunned someone hated her so much as to try to kill her.

"How did she know to attack me here, today?"

"That's the question of the hour. Only hospital staff, Ty, and your brother knew you were scheduled to be released today." Trace sighed his frustration. "The police are questioning Mrs. Nichols at the station. I hate to think we had a second leak in less than six months here."

Trace directed the last sentence at Annie and Quinn. They'd been subject to the nursing staff releasing information to the press a few months earlier.

"It would stand to reason, whoever volunteered the information had to be someone she was close to. I can't see the hospital staff giving info to random strangers. Not with everyone cracking down on privacy policies," Annie offered up.

"I was thinking the same," Quinn stated grimly.

"I owe you all a huge thank you. I don't doubt you saved my life," Lana said softly, stunned by the possibility of what would have happened without the warning from Annie, Quinn's assistance, and Trace's medical attention. They really were her own personal superheroes. "How soon before I can go home, Doc?"

"Tomorrow at the earliest. We are keeping you overnight for observation. You were out cold there for a while. It made this crowd nervous."

Ty smiled at her and told her it gave him another day to finish up the surprise he'd planned.

"Surprise? What surprise?" Lana demanded.

"You'll see." His grin widened upon seeing her displeasure.

"I can't stand surprises."

"You have an adorable pout," he teased with a quick kiss.

As she rolled her eyes, Lana noticed Annie's white face. "Annie? What is it?"

The other woman opened her mouth and closed it with a shake of her head. With a frown, she looked to Quinn who had been silently observing her.

"What is it, Annie?" he asked.

"Do you all mind if Lana and I have a moment alone?"

Lana could tell Quinn wasn't happy with Annie shutting him out. Ty didn't care for it for that matter either.

"What can't be said in front of all of us?" Ty wanted to know.

"I've had enough of wrecking people's lives with a gut feeling," Annie snapped.

"Are you planning on wrecking my life again?" Quinn asked softly. Lana had the feeling there was a double entendre in there somewhere.

"Annie, whatever you have to say, I have no secrets," Lana said.

"Fine. I'd like you to have a DNA test done."

If Annie had hit her over the head with a bat, Lana couldn't have been more stunned. Neither could the other occupants of the room if their slack-jaws meant anything.

"You are so similar in looks and personality to my sister, Sammy. I…well, I can't help thinking we must be related," she explained.

"I don't understand. Aren't your mother and father hers? You told me during a visit last week that your parents were celebrating thirty-eight years together. Did your mom have an affair?" Lana was trying to make sense of the request for proof of her DNA. Maybe somehow her father had slept with Annie's mother?

"My father was the one who had an affair on my mother.

It was about thirty years ago, when she was pregnant with Samantha."

"My mother adored my father, loser that he was. I can't imagine her sleeping around on him," Lana hedged, uncomfortable with the thought of her father not being her biological parent.

"I'm sorry. I didn't mean to…it's just I have this feeling," Annie said, helpless to explain. "Ever since I met you, it's been nagging me. I know I have a sibling out there who I've never met. I guess I was hoping it was you."

Lana found herself nodding, slowly at first and gaining momentum with her decision. "Sure. Okay. If it will make you feel better, I don't mind having my blood drawn or whatever they need to do."

"It's usually a saliva sample," Trace piped up. "We can do it here if you're serious. The lab connected to the hospital is one of the best in the state."

Nerves gripped Lana. She bit her lip and threw one last questioning glance at Annie. A smile was blooming on the other woman's face. For whatever reason, it soothed her own anxiety about the test. Lana answered Annie's smile with one of her own. "Let's do this."

"It may take a few days to get back, even with a rush on it," Trace warned.

"I don't think either of us is going anywhere, Doc," Lana laughed.

"Now that that's settled, everyone out. Time for my

patient to get some rest."

"I'm not leaving," Ty warned.

"Why doesn't that surprise me?" Trace asked no one in particular. With a shake of his head, he sailed out the door, followed closely by Annie and Quinn after they said their goodbyes.

"You should go get some rest, Ty. You've had a rough day yourself. Not to mention Serena is probably driving my brother crazy. I assume you have Liam watching her?"

"Your brother has fallen in love with her, and she with him. It's ridiculous. I can't separate the two. What is it about you Martells that has my daughter so enthralled?"

"Family secret. I could tell you but..." Lana made a gesture of slicing her throat to indicate she'd have to kill him.

"Right. Scoot over, I want to cuddle my girlfriend."

Because it was what she wanted too, Lana moved to make room in the bed. Wrapped in his warm embrace, she started to doze off.

"I love you, Sweetheart," he whispered into her curls.

"I love you, too."

***

"Close your eyes," Ty ordered. "Close them!"

"No. Why won't you just let me walk on my own?"

"Okay, that's it." He scooped her up in a fireman's hold and carted her down the hall.

"Ty, I'm going to be sick! Your boney shoulder is digging into my stomach!"

Reaching up, Ty swatted her ass. "My shoulder isn't in the least bit boney. However, if you really want something along those lines, I can show you what I got later."

Her snorted laughter pleased him. He loved that Lana got his humor.

"I've seen what you've got. I don't quite remember it being boney, though it has been a while."

"Hmmm, yeah, keep talking along those lines and we're going to need to make a detour to my bedroom," he warned.

"You started it!"

Another swat on her ass was his answer.

"Keep spanking me and I'll *demand* you take me to bed," Lana sassed.

Ty did an abrupt about face to head to the master suite. A clearing of a voice at the end of the hall had him halting in his tracks and muttering, "Dammit."

"You have people waiting, Ty," Quinn reminded him from the doorway of Lana's new studio, amusement heavy in his voice.

Debating whether to continue his current trajectory or let them all wait, Ty decided the surprise took precedence over his lust. "Fine!"

Lana's giggle earned her another swat.

"Shut it, wench."

Lana arched up and stuck her tongue out at Quinn as they

went by. His deep laughter followed them into the room.

Before she could glance around, Ty had her in front of him with his hands covering her eyes.

"How many people are here? What if I have spinach in my teeth?" she asked.

"You didn't even have spinach for lunch. Be still and accept someone is trying to do something nice for you," Ty ordered.

"Fine," she grumbled.

With that, he lifted his hands away and allowed her to absorb the impact of the studio he and Liam had worked so hard to create. Her frozen face and silence caused nerves to flit along his system. Real worry that she hated it was taking form. Ty tried to see it from her mind. He took in the cream walls, the pale pink and white striped curtains, and the red and purple throw pillows on a pink and white striped chaise in one corner. Next, he took in the easel, the tables with expensive art supplies, the French style decor and the crystal chandelier casting light around the room. Had he gone overboard? They'd hope to capture a European motif.

"Sweetheart?" he asked, tentative.

She spun and flung her arms around his neck, standing on tiptoe to rain kisses on his face. Tears flowed down her face and her silent sobs shook her slight frame.

After she calmed somewhat, she exclaimed, "I'm such a mess."

"I think you're beautiful. Minus the Alice Cooper eyes,"

Ty joked.

Lana used the edge of his t-shirt to wipe off the worst of her smudges.

"So you like it?" he asked with a grin and a tight hug.

"I love it, and I love you more for creating it. How did you know?"

"That would be my doing," her brother said, stepping forward. "All those endless hours of listening to you rattle on about what your dream studio would be like gave me a picture of what you wanted, when I didn't want to puke at the girly-ness of it all."

"Don't be an asshole," she said with a last sniff and a punch to Liam's shoulder. She followed it up with a hug. "And thank you."

"My pleasure, sis."

Ty saw the moment Lana noticed Jeri holding the baby by the door. Her whole body stiffened, and she shot him an accusatory look. Although he hated to see her upset, and hoped he hadn't spoiled the reveal for her by inviting her old nemesis, he knew they needed to settle their differences. The idea had come directly from Jeri. She claimed to feel bad for her part in sending Ashley over the emotional edge.

"Don't blame him, Lana. I wanted to be here," Jeri started her apology. "I want to be a part of Serena's life, and I know you aren't going anywhere. Anyone can see Ty is crazy about you. I'd hoped we could call a truce of sorts, or maybe even start over. I know you hate me, but can you try to forgive me for being so horrible to you? I can't say how sorry I am for-"

Lana held up a hand to cut off Jeri's speech.

"Lana." Liam caught her attention, a warning note in his voice. Ty watched as Lana's eyes widened and flew between Jeri and Liam. Upon closer inspection, he noted the blush starting on Jeri's cheeks. Of its own violation a laugh bubbled up, causing him to be the recipient of three glares.

Holding his hands up in supplication, Ty backed to where Quinn stood by the door. "Forgive me. Carry on."

His brother's soft chuckle had Ty elbowing Quinn lightly in the ribs.

"You should have taken her in for the sexcapades before showing her the room," Quinn murmured. "You're on her shit list now."

"Fuck off," Ty whispered back without heat.

The twins turned their attention back to the scene unfolding before them.

"We should have made popcorn," they muttered in unison.

Lana cast the brothers a dirty look before turning her attention back to her brother and Jeri.

"Okay, a) I don't even *want* to know what is going on between you two. Ewwww! And b) before you so rudely interrupted me, Liam, I was going to tell Jeri I am willing to start over if she is. On one condition," Lana paused for effect.

"Name it," Jeri said firmly, more than willing to meet half way.

Ty watched Lana work to suppress a grin in an attempt at

stern. She had a forgiving heart, his Lana. Catching his eye, she winked before naming her condition.

"I want you to pose for a portrait. You holding Serena in the park, like at the picnic."

"Oh!" Jeri squeaked her surprise. Then she shoved the baby into Liam's arms so she could wrap Lana in a tight hug. "Ohmygod, thank you!"

"I hate to interrupt such a touching moment, but I think there's one other thing Ty had planned," Quinn said dryly.

Lana noticed all the grinning faces. "Another surprise? I hate surprises."

"Park it," Ty ordered her with a gesture to the chaise.

Her "pfffft" had him laughing outright as he kneeled at her feet. He watched as her bright amber eyes flew wide at the implication.

Clasping her hand with his, Ty kissed her knuckles before digging in his pocket for the amber and diamond engagement ring he'd so painstakingly picked out.

"Lana, you came into my life and upset my world, in the best possible way. I think I've loved you from the moment you sat huddled on that bus stop bench, cold and alone but still pissed at the world. Every day since, I have fallen in love a little bit more. I cannot imagine my life without you in it. Will you, Lana Martell, do me the honor of becoming my wife?"

For the second time, Lana flung herself at him and wrapped her arms around his neck. "Yes! Yes! A thousand times, yes!" she laughed and cried.

Ty captured her lips with his, forgetting anyone else in the room existed. He heard the faint click of a door closing and lifted his head to glance around. Delighted to see everyone had vacated, he turned back to his new fiancée.

"Sweet," he murmured against her lips. "I wanted to break in that chaise."

"We are *not* doing it on that beautiful chaise without a blanket down," Lana scolded, unbuttoning his shirt. "This fuzzy rug on the other hand..."

"You realize this rug cost as much as that piece of furniture right?"

Her giggle was his answer. Ty had their clothes off in record time and then lifted her to place her in the exact position of the fantasy he created when he'd first seen it. Reverse cowgirl.

"I thought we agreed you were to leave your socks on," Lana quipped.

Ty smacked her ass in response. The wicked grin she shot over her shoulder shot straight to his groin. Damn, he loved this woman.

Epilogue

One week later...

"Is he gone?" Lana asked from her position on the living room sectional.

Ty waited a heartbeat until he heard the garage door close. He ran and leaped over the edge of the sofa, directly on to a waiting Lana. "Yep. Now let's help you lose some of these clothes."

Her tinkling laughter warmed him inside. To think he'd almost lost this, not once, but twice, made him appreciate her joy all the more. Without waiting for her to remove her shirt, he tore the tee down the center from the v-neck. Her startled gasp had him chuckling.

"That's hot as hell!"

"Mmmhmm," he murmured against her throat as he reached up to help dispose of her bra. "Another fantasy."

"I must say, I do like the way your mind works," she panted, drawing his shirt up and over his head.

Finesse flew out the window as their mouths melded into one long, searing kiss.

Reaching up, Ty cupped her luscious breasts in each hand. He pulled a pebbled nipple into his mouth and sucked.

"Good christ! Again? I didn't even get out of the

driveway."

"Fuck off!" Ty and Lana yelled in unison, as they both slapped their hands over her chest.

"I think I've got them covered, Sweetheart," Ty joked as she clamped her hands over top of his.

"Pfffft. Cupping is not covering. And stop massaging them in front of your brother!"

Quinn's wicked chuckle greeted them. "Okay, as much as I'm enjoying the display, you might want to put on some clothes for your company."

A strangled cry escaped Lana. She had no shirt to cover up with this time. Ty dropped his head to her chest and let loose a deep belly laugh at the horror written all over her face.

"You're embarrassing my sister, fellas," Annie scolded, coming all the way into the room. She reached to scoop Ty's shirt off the floor and dump it next to them on the couch.

"What?" Lana upper body came straight up off the couch like a vampire rising from a coffin, Ty's shirt her only concession to modesty. "What did you say?"

Annie's wide smile said what words could not. Not only did the DNA come back positive, it appeared she was thrilled to have Lana as her sibling.

Ty stood, buttoned his jeans, and snapped at his brother, "Kitchen!"

It was time to leave the two women to get better acquainted. Ty had the rest of his life to make love to his soon-to-be wife on their sofa. He paused to use the edge of his shirt to wipe away her happy tears, before unfurling the shirt and sliding it over her head.

"This calls for a celebration. I'll grab Quinn and we'll run pick up some champagne." As Annie would have side-stepped to let him pass, he hauled her into his embrace and placed a peck on her lips. "I'm glad you are going to be my sister. I know we started out on the wrong foot, but I love the hell out of you now."

"Oh!" Annie's own tears started in earnest. Ty bussed one last kiss on her forehead, winked at his intended, and started to leave the room.

"Ty!" Lana's amused voice checked his exit. "You might want to grab another shirt before you go. We can't have the women at the liquor store catching a glimpse of your scrawny chest and being overcome with lust."

"Already it starts. Nag, nag, nag," he sighed with mock disgust. "It's a good thing I love you, woman."

Her giggle had him whistling a happy tune as he changed direction to do her bidding.

Annie's eyes followed the movement of Ty's ass out of the room. She turned to her new sister with a raised brow. "Scrawny? What about that boy is scrawny? Woman, are you blind?"

"Nah, I know his body is impressive as hell. I say those things to keep him humble."

"Does it work?"

"Pfffttt. No. I doubt anything would with either of those

two brothers."

Annie nodded her head in understanding before settling next to Lana on the couch.

"Our siblings want to know if you are up for a road trip. They can't wait to meet you."

"Seriously?"

Annie's happy nod had Lana squealing and hugging her close. She'd always wanted a large, loving family and now it appeared as if she'd gotten her wish.

A NOTE FROM THE AUTHOR

Thank you for taking the time to read THE NANNY CRISIS. I appreciate that you took a chance on a new author. Be sure to keep an eye out for Annie's & Quinn's Story, AFTER THE WRECK (due Fall 2016). Turn the page to find an excerpt for FINDING YOU, Sammy's Story, available for purchase now.

Please sign up for my newsletter for future updates, contests and book release dates: www.tmcromer.com

You can find me on social media sites at:

Facebook: www.facebook.com/tmcromer
Street Team: www.facebook.com/groups/themagnificentminions
Twitter: www.twitter.com/tmcromer
Instagram: www.instagram.com/tmcromer
Goodreads: www.goodreads.com/tmcromer
Pinterest: www.pinterest.com/tmcromer

Finding You

Lightning, like long, skeletal fingers, streaked down from the heavens. Thunder boomed so close and loud, the panels of the window rattled. An involuntary shudder found its way down Samantha Holt's spine. Was it an omen? Perhaps. At one time, she would have believed so. At one time, she believed a lot of things. But not anymore. That was the past.

The doors of the clinic mocked her unwillingness to open them. Once she walked out that door, she would have to leave the past behind and start over. She wasn't so sure she wanted to do that. How was she supposed to forget and go on as if nothing had ever happened? As if there had never been a Michael in her life?

The sting of ever-present tears pricked her lids. Oh God, why? *Why?!* Her brain screamed for what seemed the millionth time. There never was an answer. There never would be.

"Just a few short steps and you're free. Free to be whoever, whatever you choose to be from this moment forward."

Dr. Stephen Montgomery stood a few feet away, but his words still startled her. His deep voice, always so welcoming and kind, drew her close. He had been with her from the beginning when she had been admitted to the hospital eight months before. He had been her confidant, mentor, and therapist. More recently, since removing himself as her doctor for reasons he refused to divulge to her, he'd become her closest friend. Had it really been that long since Michael's accident? Eight months? Michael. Would she ever hear his name and not feel the sting of his loss?

"I can't do it, Stephen. I can't walk out that door today," she said in a panicked whisper.

"Why?" he asked, though she suspected he might already know the answer.

Indignation surged through her. The feeling of being misunderstood, mocked, and helpless all rolled about in her chest nearly suffocating her. He only meant to help. She realized that. Still, it didn't make her any less angry.

"You damn well know why. Number one: it's exactly eight months and five days to the day that Michael was in that accident. *I'm not ready!* Number two: I have to go out into a world of people who saw, and will still see, me as a lunatic. They will watch me, waiting for me to do something crazy again. How am I supposed to live under that kind of pressure? People judging me all the time? And number three: I hate storms. I freaking hate lightning and thunder and the fear of being struck down."

Raging was her release when she was frightened, as Stephen was well aware. There wasn't much he didn't know about her. Sometimes, it frustrated the hell out of both of them. He gripped her arms, giving her a gentle shake.

"Stop it, Samantha. You have come too far. Do you re-member what it was like when you first arrived here? What *you* were like? You were practically catatonic. You had no will to live. Now that's changed. You are a living, feeling hu-man being again. You are experiencing fears and misgivings. That's normal. That's progress. You aren't the empty shell you were."

"I'm scared." Samantha was loath to admit it, but she felt paralyzed with fear.

"I wish you could see yourself the way I see you. I've seen your passion for living spark back to life. You're intelligent. Funny. I've caught glimpses of the person you want to be-come. The person I know you can become. You just have to learn to believe in yourself again. No one can force you to do that in here. You have to pull that from deep within you."

"What if I can't?"

"Don't sell yourself short. You *can*. You're ready. Once you step out that door and taste freedom, the desire to live life again will hit you. Then you'll understand the point I'm try-ing to make." Something flashed in his eyes, but it flitted away before she could interpret it. Something fierce. Intense. He dropped his arms and shifted his gaze to the window, watching nature's light show. His voice was much softer when he said, "I believe in you, Samantha. Believe in your-self."

The realization he was right didn't make it any easier to walk out that door and leave the only sanctuary she had known for the better part of a year. As she glanced around her, she saw none of the bustle of the hospital or the staff. She remembered another time, another place, another life…

Made in the USA
Charleston, SC
22 January 2016